VISIONS FROM A
FOXHOLE

Author during basic training, Camp Blanding, Florida, 1944.

VISIONS FROM A FOXHOLE

A Rifleman in Patton's Ghost Corps

William A. Foley Jr.

PRESIDIO
PRESS

BALLANTINE BOOKS • NEW YORK

A Presidio Press Book
Published by The Random House Publishing Group
Copyright © 2003 by William A. Foley, Jr.

Published in the United States by Presidio Press, an imprint of The Random House Publishing Group, a division of Random House, Inc., New York, and simultaneously in Canada by Random House of Canada Limited, Toronto.

Presidio Press and colophon are trademarks of Random House, Inc.

www.presidiopress.com

ISBN 0-89141-850-4

Manufactured in the United States of America

First Hardcover Edition: June 2003
First Mass Market Edition: August 2004

OPM 9 8 7 6 5 4 3 2

Books published by The Random House Publishing Group are available at quantity discounts on bulk purchases for premium, educational, fund-raising, and special sales use. For details, please call 1-800-733-3000.

This work is dedicated to all American infantrymen who, through the toughest of times, stood tall and did what had to be done.

Contents

Acknowledgments

Without the devotion and love of my wife, Nadia, this book would still be locked and lost in the hard drive of my mind. Much inspiration came through observing the sustained courage of my son, Bill, who is always there to back me up. My daughter, Irene, and my nephew Bill Russo put their heads together and eventually turned up the moldy portfolio of war art—almost lost forever.

Kathy Wood, a friend indeed, always made herself, her typing, and her organizational ability available when needed, and she was always needed (this book was written in longhand). My art agents, Gene Amend and Nancy Bohlander, somehow convinced me that designing a painting was little different from designing a paragraph. I gratefully acknowledge their friendship and assistance in all phases of my work. Bill and Cheryl Rogers were as generous with their knowledge of the publishing world as they were with their friendship and flow of ideas.

My thanks go to an anonymous soldier who, after half a century, returned six of my best drawings. They were, without my knowledge, taken from the 81mm mortar tube in July of 1945. The envelope had no return address but was postmarked "New York City."

The dates and chronology of events recorded here leaned heavily on our excellent *History of the 94th Infantry Division in World War II*, edited by Lt. Laurence G. Byrnes

(Nashville: Battery Press, 1948). I borrowed its maps, although I altered some to point up my end of things. Also of major help was our *Commemorative History of the 94th Infantry Division Association, Volumes I and II,* edited by Robert U. Cassel, Donald E. Mulry, et al. (Dallas: Taylor Publishing, 1989 and 1996). Dr. Nathan N. Prefer, author of *Patton's Ghost Corps* (Novato, Calif.: Presidio Press, 1998), always was available to answer questions from a nonprofessional writer. His patience and historical expertise proved to be invaluable. Thanks to the suggestion of Bob Cassel of the 301st Regiment, I designed a mural of our division. The idea was passed into law and will come to fruition in the state capitol of Boston, Massachusetts. Much credit must go to Rep. Mary Jane Simmons and her staff for guiding the legislation so skillfully. The 94th Division Association, as always, gave their best efforts. Division historian Don Mulry, Harry Helms Jr., Marion Jereb, and the Mural Committee never relaxed their efforts in seeing this through. Finally, Netty Kahan, Presidio's freelance copy editor, devoted a month force-feeding the English grammar into my head that I had so carefully avoided in high school. Netty, along with E. J. McCarthy, Presidio's executive editor, were instrumental in getting this book into its present form. The by-product of growing friendship between us made the entire process a most pleasant one.

Note from the Author

During a long stint of guarding one August night in Czechoslovakia in 1945, a recently arrived replacement shared the duty with me. We stood together on an isolated dirt road one mile or so from the Russian sector and faced a boring passage of time speaking briefly of this and that. After a long silence, he made a request that I was inclined to turn down, but after turning it over in my mind, I agreed to relate my experiences of combat. For the next several hours, I narrated those events that had resulted in an imprint chiseled deeply in my consciousness.

One important attribute of being talented in graphic arts is an eagle-eyed ability to see and record events more accurately than most laymen would. We make better-than-average witnesses. As a rifleman of the 94th Infantry Division in World War II, I had this ability materialize in my undeniable need to record events with a drawing pencil. Half a century later, I decided to back up the artwork with my written words. What follows is my attempt to augment the account told to my fellow guard and to commemorate our 2d Platoon, G Company, 302d Regiment, of one of Patton's best divisions. For the most part, each day and night of combat had a logical flow that easily took my memory from one action to the next. But in those instances where I doubted my recall or was confused due to the intensity of the battle, I did not hesitate to fill in the best I could to keep up the flow of the narrative.

During the three years of piecing this account together, I have had to relive and finally resolve those combat events that were, by turn, dreamlike and nightmarish. But the writing of it, tough as it was, has brought a release in me deeper than I would have expected at the beginning of my recount. I often forget the names of people seconds after being introduced to them. My father was like that, too. In this book—for the most part—I have had to invent the names of men I knew well. Aside from having forgotten their names, I admit another reason: Two or three of the men would just as well not have their names mentioned due to behavior they would not be proud to identify as theirs. I did include the names of officers correctly and that includes Lt. Davis F. Nations. Although, like so many second lieutenants, he only lived a few days as one, I was moved to include his correct name because I have lived a half century with the clear memory of his wife and children's likenesses on the photo carried in his wallet. Perhaps one of those children, now growing old, may wish to be in touch with me. He was killed a few feet from me, and our growing friendship was abruptly cut off.

In April of 1997, Nadia and I rented a car in Frankfurt and crossed the Rhine north of Manheim. Traveling the autobahn west, we arrived at the Saar–Moselle Triangle in a shockingly short time. During 1945, the same trip going east took months. We stopped in the small town of Eft-Hellendorf and ate in a restaurant called the Sonnenhof. The room was packed that Sunday afternoon with local German folk; we were paired at a table with a middle-aged couple. The gentleman sitting across from me attempted conversation, with a severely limited English vocabulary. He wondered what we were doing in such an out-of-the-way place. I was hesitant to admit that I was here to look over old battlefields, so I managed to convey to him another motive for being in the area, to locate a young Luxembourg man named Alex Arendt. At the mention of Alex Arendt's name, the gentleman's face turned red, and he exclaimed, "He's my son." And then he roared, "You are a 94ther. I, too, am a 94ther."

While I was gratified at this highly unusual coincidence, I realized that most of the Germans in the dining room were paying close attention to this outburst from the gentleman from Luxembourg. I really did not want them to know that a former soldier who had done his part in blowing away their homes fifty years earlier was in their midst. In fact, this very town, which had been used as a rest area several times by our rifle companies, had been shot up pretty badly.

Our fellow diners returned to their own conversations, however, and after finishing our meal, Nadia and I were invited to follow the Arendts' car on a tour of Munzingen Ridge. This had been the backbone of the Siegfried Switch line of fortifications. At the top of the ridge, we pulled into a treeless, windswept parking area to walk around the only monument in Germany dedicated to an American division. Named the Peace Monument, it has two sides—one dedicated to our 94th, and the other to the German 11th Panzer Division. We drove past Sinz—my first combat site—to Nennig where the Arendts arranged a room for Nadia and me in a bed-and-breakfast. Later, their son Alex joined us.

Then in his twenties, Alex had been fascinated since his earliest years with the 94th Division battles there, and he compiled a large collection of the weapons and equipment of both armies. Armed with shovel and metal detector, he roamed the battlefields for years—somehow avoiding mines and booby traps. The items he gathered were displayed in attractive cases filling a room in his parents' home in Remich, Luxembourg, and the overflow was at his grandmother's home in Nennig, Germany, just across the Moselle River. Alex has become well known by many men of our 94th Division Association for consistently being there to guide them to old foxholes still evident in the fields and forests. More than once I had the feeling he is a composite reincarnation of our men killed there—a protector of our legacy.

Preface

No-man's-land on the 14th of January 1945—that vacillating strip of mud and snow that stretched four hundred miles from the North Sea to Switzerland. The deflation of the Ardennes Bulge was to once again place U.S. divisions in front of Hitler's legendary West Wall, the Siegfried line. Most divisions, infantry and armored, at some point along that wall would have to fight their way into and through those reinforced concrete forts and the belts of minefields, dragon's teeth, and trenches. The southern anchor of the December breakthrough was the ancient city of Trier, where the Moselle and Saar Rivers meet. Immediately to the south, the Saar–Moselle Triangle became the battleground of the 94th Infantry Division, which was responsible for a ten-mile stretch of that front.

Few historians have noted the unique combat situation facing this division. Of the thousands of pillboxes and bunkers that faced the Allied armies, 25 percent were in the ten-mile-long triangle. There, the Siegfried line was actually composed of two walls, each several miles deep. The 94th, with little or no help from armored divisions, would continually attack during January and February against first-line panzer and infantry divisions. Much to Adolf Hitler's and Hermann Goering's anger, these GIs eventually broke through what Berlin considered impregnable defenses. This rupture of the strongest section of Hitler's vaunted West Wall and the capture of the Remagen Bridge by the 9th Armored Division, according to Goering, were the two most catastrophic disappointments for the dictator at that juncture of the war.

It proved to be especially bad news for the Nazi hierarchy that the famous 11th Panzer Division and two other infantry divisions were mauled close to extinction by the 94th and had to be withdrawn. The 90th Division had held this line since November of 1944. For most of that time it had remained static. But, two units—90th Division and 3d Calvary—had penetrated the Siegfried and taken the village of Tettingen. Typically, the German reaction was strong and casualties so high that the American unit was withdrawn a mile to the original main line of resistance (MLR).

When Patton swung north to attack the south shoulder of the Bulge, he took the 90th Division with him. He was given the 94th Division to replace the 90th in the triangle. Then the 94th was shifted east to the Third Army, after containing the pockets of St. Nazaire and Lorient on the west coast of France. As they were so urgently needed to contain the Bulge, all divisions of the western front had to spread out and dig in. With replacements hard to come by, most divisions were on the defensive. Some replacements were trucked in, and I was one of them. I joined the 94th a few weeks after they had replaced the 90th Division. All three regiments—the 301st, 302d, and the 376th—had already begun heavy and bloody combat there.

Little armor was available to support the dogfaces of the 94th as they squared off with the superior tanks and equipment of the 11th Panzer. Nevertheless, we were ordered to attack and take ground, but it was stipulated that all attacks be limited to company or battalion size. We soon learned that Gen. George Patton was neither a patient nor defensive-minded commander.

When finally in late February we had broken through enough fortified areas to impress higher authorities, we were given permission for a full-size divisional attack, up and over Munzingen Ridge. After breaking through the first wall, we began moving east to the Saar itself. There, in the gloom and fog, we saw the pillboxes and bunkers lining the other side of that fast-moving and icy river. This would be the second Siegfried line we faced. The Germans were on the hills and cliff tops more than four hundred feet up, and they lay waiting just beyond the water's edge at the base of the cliffs. General Patton placed heavy hands on this operation. It will remain for the archivists and historians to assess whether he was justified in pushing the 376th and 301st Regiments across the way he did: in broad daylight, to suffer terrible casualties. My regiment successfully crossed on a foggy night and surprised the Germans.

At eighteen years of age, I joined G Company, 302d Regiment of the 94th. The wrenching experiences that I shared with the men of my outfit became the basis of a fraternity of brothers whose depth of commitment to each other remains today as strong as ever. Ample proof of this bond has been evident more than a half century later at our annual reunions.

Within days of my first combat experiences, I spontaneously began drawing on V-mail paper or anything that would take a pencil mark. If it is true that a boy can become a man overnight in combat, then his talents can flourish at the same pace. I was amazed—and deeply pleased—at the sudden jump in my ability. And, after the war in Czechoslovakia, our CO (commanding officer) encouraged me and gave me time to finish drawings that I had not completed while in combat. I received art materials with the cookies and powdered milk from home, and I finished my drawings and produced paintings as well. Many of these works appear in this book.

The GI Bill provided me the opportunity to attend art school and commence a life of painting, illustrating, and doing mural work. I have lived in several countries and traveled extensively while executing art projects. Many years ago, I lost track of the portfolio of my war work, until it turned up in New Jersey in 1996. As my wife and I looked through the works, I realized how truly rare they are. I thought they eventually should be put in care of an infantry museum. In time, I decided to write the story behind the art.

My agent and friend, Eugene M. Amend, brought over retired Gen. Alexander Bolling to see them. By great coincidence, General Bolling had been a first lieutenant in my regiment's Cannon Company. To my surprise, he informed me that the 94th Division had an active association that held annual reunions. (Incidentally, Alex Bolling's father was commanding general of the 84th Division during World War II in Europe.)

I attended my first reunion in Albuquerque, New Mexico, in 1997. It renewed inside me a place of warmth and friendship untouched and almost forgotten since 1945. My war drawings and paintings were exhibited, and Bob Cassel of the 301st recommended that I design a mural of our division, which I did at the Massachusetts state house in Boston, our division's home. The concept became a legislative bill. After several years, a busy legislature finally delivered the bill to the governor, who signed it into law. I anticipate installing it on a seven-by-sixteen-foot wall in the state capitol at Boston, Massachusetts. The rotunda has several large murals depicting the fighting men of earlier conflicts. Now the collection will include a World War II pictorial symbol.

Stateside basic training has been amply described and dissected by others. So much so, that I feel free to move on to describe those awe-inspiring experiences that awakened the poetic mentality in me. I use the word "poet" in the universal sense of creativity. This living force of spirit manifested as pictorial illustration and now in the written work.

As early as I can recall, I had the ability to draw well. Every schoolbook that misfortune placed in my way served as testimony of my talent. Each photo, map, and diagram challenged me to bring out of it more than its editors or my teachers ever intended. The application of ink or pencil to a graphic of Washington's crossing the Delaware produced sea monsters clawing at his boat, more dangerous and intriguing than the British adversary on the Pennsylvania side of the river. I mentioned misfortune because, under my hand, algebra texts and English grammar rapidly lost their original meaning, subjected as they were to the barrage of inked-in cannon, soldiers, and aircraft. For this I paid often and dearly at home and at school.

In the '30s and early '40s, most students were herded scholastically toward a narrow menu of industrial choices, and I suspect the same archaic policy survives today. Rare indeed would a budding talent be recognized as needing special education in the arts, with a minor in learning to balance a checkbook. The result was a string of tutors who suffered my rebellion only a short time. Frustration drove a wedge between my good parents and myself, and this situation was especially intolerable because of the love and respect I had for them. For me, my father was a heroic figure—I admired him greatly. He had been an infantry rifleman in the 77th Rainbow Division during World War I, and he was wounded and gassed during that combat. The rare wartime experiences he related, and those of his veteran friends, opened my eyes to the horrors, insanity, idealism, and great moments they had experienced. I spent many hours with books, historical and fictional, on that subject. Through the passion of drawing pictures of heroic rescues in the barbed wire and shell holes, I struggled to reach my father in that no-man's-land.

But the actual rescue of our family relationship was infinitely more complex. From the age of sixteen on, I watched World War II begin to wind down toward an end that would preclude my serving in the ranks. Then, two months before my eighteenth birthday, D day grabbed the attention of us all. Legally of age, I applied for immediate induction with the draft board. To me, the phrase "immediate induction" was on par with "immaculate conception" as far as great and mysterious happenings were concerned. I was trading the intolerable scholastic stress and parental control for the possible stress of incapacitating wounds or death. But I never had any doubt that I had chosen the right course, because to remain confined to the menu of choices open to me seemed the road to mediocrity and boredom. I felt that society produced this condition, to some degree, in almost every adult I knew. Eighteen-year-olds often saw things that way.

These thoughts, written some fifty-four years after the fact, are obviously a retrospective by a somewhat more sophisticated "edition" of the eighteen-year-old who was groping for a place in the sun. And, part of that retrospection rejoices in the knowledge accumulated over the years that something of the spiritual interplays in the guidance of each of us.

I was due to get my physical and would be leaving home in the firm knowledge of my family's involvement in wartime-related activities: Mother was rolling bandages for the Red Cross; Father was in charge of the local Red Cross; and, my sister was working as a secretary at the Bendix war plant. Our neighborhood had a victory garden that I had to weed daily. This was another minor problem between me and my father who—upon returning from his office—would put in an hour loosening the earth around the vegetables. He felt that I should leave stones by the side of the path and not toss them a hundred feet to a bushel basket that I had nailed to a tree stump. So, when his criticism began to grow, I explained that in case I would find myself lobbing grenades at Germans in a few months, I figured I had better get all the practice I could. When he saw how accurate my demonstration actually was, the matter was dropped. Soon I packed away my Lionel train and model planes and got ready for the service.

At eight years of age I was diagnosed as anemic and had spots on my lungs. If those spots were still there, the medical staff never made note of them. They objected to my flat feet and commented that men in antiaircraft units did not march much. Lying through my teeth to prove that I could march forever, I convincingly described my hiking accomplishments as a Boy Scout (I had never been a Scout). The officer in charge looked up at me and asked incredulously if I really wanted to go to the infantry. I emphatically said, "Yes!" After that I headed for a short line of men choosing to be U.S. Marines, but another fellow joined the line right before I got there. Only three were to be accepted and being the fourth man in line, I watched fate take its course; in a matter of days, thousands of us arrived at Camp Blanding, Florida.

Shortened infantry replacement training nonetheless resulted in deeply calloused feet that forced me to walk painfully on the sides of those appendages. I never fell out of a march except for when I was seized by an attack of diarrhea during a night march through the Florida boondocks—I had a hell of a time finding my company again. The training was tough, and I enjoyed it but my feet disagreed. The only artwork I did in basic training was to copy sexy Betty Grable pinups from *Yank* magazine. These were for my buddies. And, of course, I did a Kilroy image in place of a postage stamp on my envelopes carrying letters home to 108 Grayson Place, Teaneck, New Jersey (servicemen were exempted from the need to use postage stamps during their service).

Then things became real. It began with the quick ocean trip on one of the *Queens* and then troop trains from Scotland to a wharf in Southampton (we never once set foot on English soil). Immediately we shipped to Le Havre, and on "40 and 8" trains, we pushed through the replacement depot. We drove through Thionville and some other small French towns, freezing on open six-by-six trucks. We knew we were near the front lines upon hearing distant thunder in January—it had to be artillery fire and not lightning. The knee-deep snow tended to cosmetically cover signs of war. Most villages still showed damage despite the local French citizens who were here and there restoring roofs and barns and mending walls that tanks had torn through. We were often held up while watching myriad army vehicles convoying their cargoes in every direction. Military police (MPs) at all crossroads, stamping their feet to stay warm, shouted terse answers to drivers who were asking them questions, and catcalls of "You'll be sorry!" rang out in our direction through the frigid air.

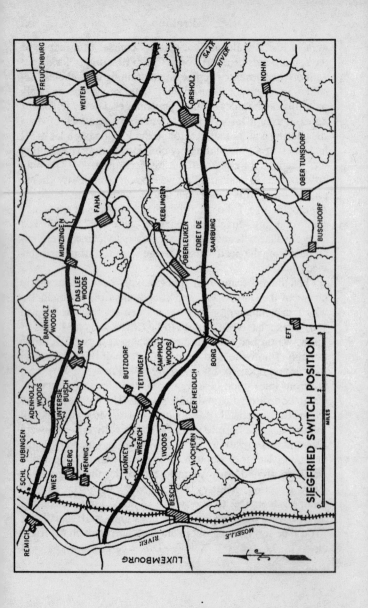

SIEGFRIED SWITCH POSITION

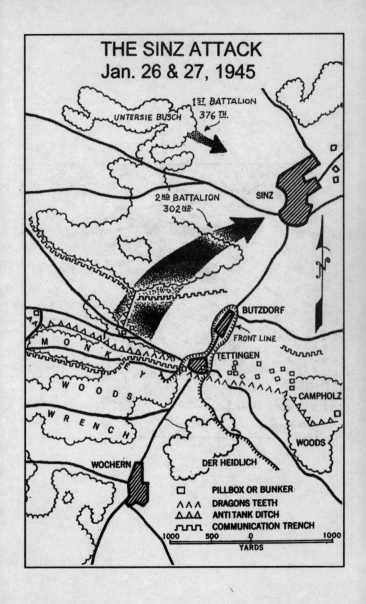

THE SINZ ATTACK
Jan. 26 & 27, 1945

UNTERSIE BUSCH

1ST BATTALION
376TH

SINZ

2ND BATTALION
302ND

BUTZDORF

FRONT LINE

M O N K E Y

TETTINGEN

W O O D S

W R E N C H

CAMPHOLZ

WOODS

WOCHERN

DER HEIDLICH

☐ PILLBOX OR BUNKER
ᴧᴧᴧ DRAGONS TEETH
△△△ ANTI TANK DITCH
ᶯᶯᶯ COMMUNICATION TRENCH

1000   500   0   1000
YARDS

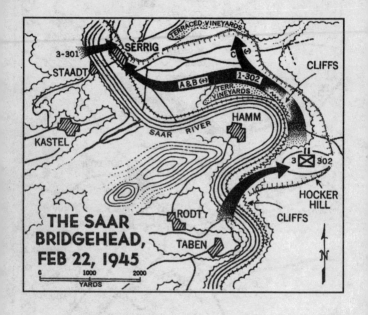

THE SAAR
BRIDGEHEAD,
FEB 22, 1945

0   1000   2000
YARDS

Map labels: 3-301, SERRIG, STAADT, KASTEL, TERRACED VINEYARDS, CLIFFS, C (-), A & B (+), 1-302, TERR. VINEYARDS, SAAR RIVER, HAMM, 3 ⊠ 302, HOCKER HILL, RODT, CLIFFS, TABEN

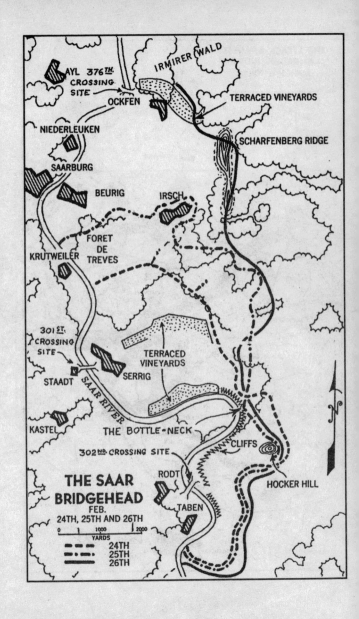

AYL 376TH.
CROSSING SITE
OCKFEN
IRMIRER WALD
TERRACED VINEYARDS
NIEDERLEUKEN
SCHARFENBERG RIDGE
SAARBURG
BEURIG
IRSCH
FORET
DE
TREVES
KRUTWEILER
301ST.
CROSSING
SITE
TERRACED
VINEYARDS
STAADT
SERRIG
KASTEL
THE BOTTLE-NECK
CLIFFS
302ND. CROSSING SITE
RODT
HOCKER HILL
TABEN

THE SAAR
BRIDGEHEAD
FEB.
24TH, 25TH AND 26TH

0   1000   2000
YARDS

- - - - 24TH
▪▪▪▪▪ 25TH
━━━━ 26TH

N

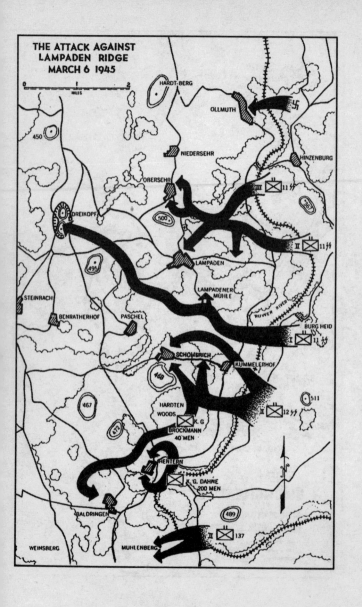

THE ATTACK AGAINST
LAMPADEN RIDGE
MARCH 6 1945

MILES
0   1   2

HARDT-BERG

OLLMUTH

450

NIEDERSEHR

HINZENBURG

OBERSEHR

III   11 SS

DREIKOPF

500

II   11 SS

LAMPADEN

495

LAMPADENER
MÜHLE

STEINRACH

RUWER RIVER

BENRATHERHOF

PASCHEL

BURG HEID

I   11 SS

SCHOMERICH

KUMMELERHOF

468

511

467

HARDTEN
WOODS

472

II   12 SS

K. G.
BROCKMANN
40 MEN

HENTERN

K. G. DAHNE
200 MEN

BALDRINGEN

489

II   137

WEINSBERG

MUHLENBERG

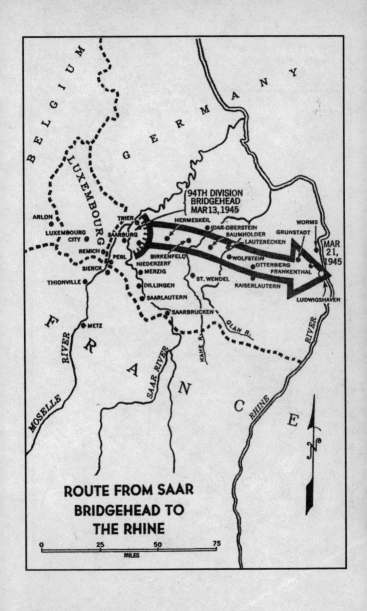

**ROUTE FROM SAAR
BRIDGEHEAD TO
THE RHINE**

1

Combat on the Siegfried Line

It was the 25th of January, and we were more than twenty cold and miserable recruits in each truck, bouncing around in our replacement convoy. We had begun losing trucks as one or two turned away to follow faint tracks that paralleled signal corps' wire strung everywhere. A convoy of huge 155mm Long Tom cannons passed us on their way somewhere—maybe going north to support Patton as he helped squeeze the Germans from the Bulge. As for me, I sat and shivered uncontrollably like everyone else, alternating my Hail Marys and Our Fathers with memorizing the serial number of my second- or third-hand M1 rifle. Why is it that half a century later I can remember "2506819," but can recall so few faces of the men I knew?

No conversation took place other than short exclamations of acute discomfort or to pronouncements of the need to remove a leg wedged between someone's pack and another man's rear end. Occasionally, a man desperate to relieve himself would pick his way to the tailgate. With one hand holding on to the seat back and the other digging out his penis, he would cause the truck following to back off a bit.

Before dark, our truck and one other pulled over, and a white-clad man materialized out of the snow, barking for everyone to fall out on the roadside. Stiff-bodied, groaning recruits dropped by twos from the lowered tailgate; many sank to their knees, unable to stand after the cramped accommodations. We were told to toss our barracks bags in a three-quarter-ton truck. Finally, we struggled into line and began moving through the snow as the trucks backed around. The men watched the trucks take off the way they had come.

The snow absorbed most sounds and made our voices sound strange. We had not seen any sunlight since Scotland. It was difficult to pick our way along the wheel ruts of the occasional traffic passing us—the gray light made everything look flat and foreboding. We knew where the road lay buried by following the strands of communication wire strung from trees, poles, and fence posts.

Noncoms (noncommissioned officers—corporals and sergeants) fielded questions from the curious, newly arrived soldiers. Broken trees off in the fields appeared as gray silhouettes, along with the shapes of abandoned vehicles and tanks. The falling snow became heavier, and noncoms increased the distance between each of us about fifteen yards, so any shells hitting near would claim fewer of us.

There was an obvious difference between the noncoms and us: Faces half-wrapped in scarves revealed raw, weather-beaten flesh. Their equipment and uniforms were caked in mud, but their weapons were clean.

The sound of boots crunching through frozen snow was the only sound now. And then my heart almost stopped, as off to the right sudden stabs of yellow light shot skyward, followed by a terrific concussion of sound—the loud, flat sound of cannon. Their projectiles made impressive rushing sounds as they climbed to the dusky overcast. We stumbled along, all eyes on the dimly seen guns and prime movers way off in a field bordered by woods. Some moments later, from miles to the north, came the sound of the shells detonating in several heavy and deep *crumping* sounds. This certainly brought home vividly the connection between our present location and the absolute certainty that the front line was near and that the German army was dug in three or four miles away. What could be a stronger introduction to the reality of what faced us than that demonstration?

The question was forcibly answered within a couple of

minutes. More artillery salvos off beyond a forest were followed by sounds of *Crump! Crump! Crump!* We stopped in our tracks to allow some self-propelled cannon to turn into a field. Farther on, we were introduced to the war's best cannon (not American), as the shells of 88s ripped through layers of wind and swirling air, constantly changing the pitch of sound. It was not unlike a great mile-long canvas being ripped from one end to the other by a giant hand. The shell from that long tube traveled like a rifle bullet; and depending on the distance of gun to target, from the moment it was first heard, a man had roughly a second or so to drop to the ground. But if the cannon was a few hundred yards away, its shell would arrive instantly, the sound of the cannon following the shell's impact in a double bang.

This evening's introduction proved to be a mere demonstration as the shells traveled several miles and detonated a half mile or so to the rear. This was the two-second-warning variety, and noncoms had everyone up and moving as fast as legs would move through snow and the icy wheel ruts. The shells continued streaking by overhead for a time. Closer and louder thuds and flashes of light down the road toward the front increased this excitement. Moving toward this new revelation was an unpleasant sensation: It was one thing to have shells detonate to the rear, but to be marching toward them was distinctly depressing, and men wondered whether they would be required to march directly into it. The shells dropping to the front were (according to one noncom) 120mm mortars, the largest of either army.

Several brilliant explosions close together revealed a town several hundred yards ahead, and our line was stopped and ordered fifty yards or so off the road. I found a seat on the ice-encrusted running board of what had been a truck. If the shelling moved up the road toward us, I could burrow underneath this rusting remnant. The other men squatted, watching a building on fire through the snow. There we remained until the shelling suddenly stopped.

The noncom hesitated a minute before shouting instructions that if the shelling would resume, once in among the houses, we should take cover in the nearest building and then form up on the street the moment it would stop. He added that he was responsible for everyone, and anyone getting lost would answer to him.

On the road, we doubled-timed into town along with traffic, which was moving again. This was the first German town that I ever was in, with France and Luxembourg a few miles to the rear; the town was Wochern. We moved along past trucks and jeeps in the street, and others were parked beside buildings and down side streets. Soldiers were moving in and out of houses and barns as they unloaded trucks. A wall stopped one tarp-covered six-by-six so that other traffic could get by. The six-by-six was pointed in the direction that we had just come from, and as I moved along between it and the wall, I saw GI boots stretching out of the back. I did a double take, because in the dim light it took a few seconds for me to realize that these were the mud-caked boots of dead soldiers. One limb was black, shriveled, and footless. The next man behind me closed up and I indicated to him what I had just seen. He turned to look, gagged, and then vomited against the wall as the line of replacements tried to squeeze past him. This was another graphic introduction to no-man's-land.

After this sudden glimpse at the reality of what we were getting into, we were assembled in a courtyard in front of a building that may have been a school. We were told to drop our packs in the snow and to file inside a large room with olive drab blankets over the windows. A lamp illuminated the interior. Following us in was a tall, thin officer who identified himself as a chaplain and informed us we were part of the 94th Infantry Division, XX Corps, Third U.S. Army, with Gen. George Patton commanding. We were going to line companies of the 302d Regiment. He told us the expected, "Come to me with any problems you might have," and then he proceeded with a brief history of the division including its training and combat record. He kept it brief, and then another officer broke us down into groups; noncoms led their group out to where we assembled at our packs. We were told to locate our barracks bags in the truck and bring them to our packs. We were to stow most of our gear in the bag and were told what to carry with us to our rifle company command posts.

Then our group followed a noncom to a house a few streets from our briefing. This was the command post of G Company. We entered from the rear into a stove-heated cellar. There, sitting at a table illuminated with candles, sergeants and a couple of officers were smoking. Men were sitting or sleeping on shelter halves on the floor. Gear and overshoes were scattered everywhere, with weapons leaning against the wall. The men at the table looked us over. They asked us when we had last eaten and took us out again to a barn in the rear.

The barn's interior was also warm and filled with the smell of food and kerosene. We had dropped our packs in the cellar and had our mess kits at the ready. The cooks were friendly and generous with seconds. The food was hot and tasted good after the cold trip and march. While we washed out our kits in GI cans filled with hot water, one soapy and the other clean (or nearly so), we heard several explosions nearby—six or eight in a row. A cook told us that regular shelling occurred most every day and night. The Germans knew this town was used as the regimental units' headquarters, plus supply dumps for most everything except artillery shells. Often, mortar fragments hit men as they moved between buildings. The mortars dropped in without sound or warning, in contrast to the rounds of artillery shells that usually could be heard rushing in, giving a few seconds of warning before detonating.

The hot food brought on drowsiness: But sleep would not come that night or the next. We were taken back to the cellar, grabbed our packs, and were led up some stairs to a room that was candlelit and the windows were covered with blankets. Two noncoms were there, one a platoon sergeant. Two of the replacements were here alone with the sergeants, and the other new men had gone elsewhere. I was told to trade my M1 for a BAR (Browning automatic rifle), but I took a risk by saying that I really wanted to carry the M1. The sergeant looked at me a moment, and I expected to lose the M1 and be given a reprimand, when the other replacement replied that he would take the BAR. That got me off the hook. He then asked whether we had been given orientation at regiment. We explained that we had been filled in on the division's Stateside training history and combat history in France. The sergeant then described exactly where we were located in Germany.

This town had been captured and held since the previous November (1944). The enemy penetration through the Ardennes had caused this section of the front to remain static for the most part. We were a few miles from Trier to the north, the southern anchor of the German penetration. The division arrived here less than two weeks earlier from the west coast of France, where they had bottled up German divisions at a couple of ports since August. Furthermore, this regiment (302d) had been on the southern flank of the Bulge penetration only a week earlier before rejoining the rest of the 94th Division. The 301st, 302d, and 376th regiments of the 94th were located in the Saar–Moselle Triangle. We were beginning to chip away at the Siegfried line, whose fortified positions began a mile to the northeast. In a matter-of-fact voice, we were told that the policy with replacements, generally, was to gradually commit them to combat. However, we would be going up to the line shortly. In this attack, the troops were to travel fast and light, without packs or blankets. Another rifle company would relieve us during the night, when we would march to an assembly point where we would be attacking before light. This news hit me between the eyes—it was true I had asked for combat, but by then I found myself wishing for a few days of gradual orientation toward actual frontline action. I was assigned to 1st Squad of the 2d Platoon.

The other noncom turned out to be the platoon guide, who took us down the hall where crates of small arms and rifle ammo in bandoliers, and crates of grenades, along with bazooka shells in their containers, were stacked against the wall. We were told to leave our packs at this point. We were each given three bandoliers and four fragmentation grenades (frags) and were told to form a carrying party of ammo and rations. I lucked out by getting a lighter box of K rations to shoulder. Then we joined the rest of the replacements and noncoms in the street in front of the G Company CP (command post).

In a short talk, the platoon guide told us if we would "keep our heads and follow our squad leaders, there was a good chance that we would come through the war okay." We were instructed to maintain a single file, well dispersed, and follow the white tape when it was reached. He explained to us not to deviate from the tape—even one foot on either side—because of mines buried under the snow.

The column of noncoms and replacements began moving down the icy cobblestones. We joined the line of men as we passed the last houses leaving town. The weather was miserable: We were hit by wind and stinging snowflakes. Several more mortar explosions sounded behind us in the town we had just left, bouncing echoes back and forth, followed by artillery rounds rushing down from the low-lying clouds. We dropped into the roadside ditch and some slit trenches. Flashes of light briefly illuminated broken roofs back in Wochern. The shells continued to roar in for some time, and although we were a couple of hundred yards beyond the town, we were concerned with the danger of shells falling short. The concussion was heavy. While the last of the bombardment was tearing up roofs and walls, we heard the flat sound of our artillery, well to the rear, adding to the shrieks of projectiles that passed each other high above.

Our outgoing artillery continued to fire as Wochern quieted. Relieved to be out of town during the shelling, we regained our place in the column and moved out. Shortly, we passed a jeep whose motor was running in order to keep it from freezing. We noticed men working with communication wire. Suddenly, arching through the night, a brilliant line of tracers appeared, and then it disappeared silently, long before the sustained burst of distant machine-gun fire was heard.

Who can fully describe the heady sensation and feeling one has when approaching, for the first time, an active battle-field most aptly called a theater of war. I had the feeling of entering a darkened theater whose curtain was going up. The place was charged with the anticipation of actors taking their places as the light intensified. The mystery of a great play about to begin was forged forever in my memory. There was a witness, deep inside me, drinking in this entire panorama, while the outer body shook with the intense cold as the wind carried icy needles around my scarf.

I had no way to adjust the scarf, because I was preoccupied with toting a crate of K rations on a shoulder that barely kept my rifle sling in place. My helmet was out of kilter against the crate, but I kept my legs moving to remain in position on the line. We listened to occasional sounds of small-arms fire that was carried on the east wind. Shortly thereafter, we left the frozen tracks of the road and followed communication wire and white tape to the right through the knee-deep snow. That white tape we followed into the fields kept getting lost in the dark because it blended into the snow. We ran the tape through our gloved hands and then inadvertently lost it where it was attached to a tree or bush and had to pick it up again on the other side. To lose the tape or deviate from its course was to run the risk of activating a Schü mine or a Bouncing Betty's trip wire. Inevitably this would cost at least a mangled foot. The path was well trodden, the snow beaten down by many men using it for some days. The snow was almost knee-deep on both sides, and we could follow along easily without the tape; but we held on to it anyway for safe measure, as we entered the woods.

Ahead, a password was given and a countersign. We moved up to a hole and were told to leave our loads there. This was the company forward CP (command post). Some of us were taken up to a line of foxholes on the leading edge of the woods. I was paired with an experienced man in his hole. The password would be changing soon, and he gave me the new one. We were to be relieved by another company during the night and march to another section of the main line of resistance (MLR) and would be attacking in battalion strength.

My body had barely handled the freezing temperature during the march up, but there I was trembling and couldn't stop. My feet were quickly becoming a major worry, as my boots and socks were soaked through. The combat boots seemed to absorb the wet as if addicted to water. I was about to pull them off and change to a double pair of dry socks, but the other man stopped me: We could be moving at any time. My anxiety increased as time passed, and I lost feeling in my feet. I was desperate to get up and walk about. I had heard all the stories of trench foot and frozen fingers, noses, and ears, as well as of men falling asleep and freezing to death.

I almost forgot my feet for a few minutes when an explosion down the line to the right caught all my attention. A machine gun fired several short bursts. Then another machine gun opened up, so rapid in its rate of fire that one could not count the bullets. Tracer rounds bounced back and forth in the trees. To our rear, we heard a loud coughlike sound and, seconds later, a shell burst some distance to the right front. German mortars responded, and shells began exploding off to the right. My foxhole companion explained that someone probably thought an enemy patrol was nearby and had tossed a grenade. A light .30-caliber machine gun opened up and a German machine gun answered, followed by a mortar exchange.

My new buddy was called Dan, and he tersely gave a label to every unnatural sound that we heard. I learned a lot from Dan in the next few days and nights. He taught me to distinguish the important sounds of the various weapons of war, especially the sounds of German weapons, which had not been available in training. Not long after, men were brought forward from the rear, and one by one, the foxhole positions were replaced. Initially, as our turn came and two men moved into our hole, I crawled out and could not make up my mind whether I should continue crawling. I felt that I could not stand on my feet. I was truly desperate and embarrassed. If I could not keep up, I would feel I was a malingerer. Suddenly, I felt a strong hand grip me under my left arm and lift me to my feet. I forced one leg up at a time to move myself forward. My rifle, held at the muzzle, became a crutch. I realized that it was Dan at my side keeping me upright. We began silently moving to the rear. I felt nothing in my lower legs and feet as we moved to the rear through the trees.

At the edge of the woods, we had to move single file through the minefield. I preceded Dan and had a sense of being suspended in space, not knowing whether I would lose my balance and topple on to a Schü mine. I simply gritted my teeth and moved as quickly as possible behind the figure of the man to my front. At the road, we were told in whispers to follow along, well spread out. I suppose it was an officer standing on the road who asked me what was wrong. I told him my combat boots were frozen to my feet. Incredulously, he asked what had happened to my shoepacs.

I flashed on the overshoes in the cellar and I replied that I was a replacement and never was given a pair. Another officer laconically advised me to "walk it off soldier, you will find yourself shoepacs before long." He was right. And if I thought that I was in an impossible fix then, it seemed worse after a half mile or so, because gradually the blood began forcing itself into my cold flesh. The pain was almost unbearable, yet it sure took my mind off my trembling body. As we moved along through the black and gray night, however, gradually most of the pain diminished, and I could walk almost normally.

Later we followed an antitank ditch. We were marching and stopping, marching and stopping over fields and through woods, but mostly through woods. We waited while another long file of men moved across our front, and then we moved over a communication trench. Farther on, I could make out what appeared to be dragon's teeth in the open. I realized with a sense of awe that the vaunted Siegfried line lay before us. If ever there could be such a thing as a romantic nightmare, this was it. I had received the great patriotic fantasy that I had imagined—the infantry. And all facets having fallen into place neatly, I arrived facing the German army in time to be a part of the big show before the final curtain dropped. And what a place to begin—Patton's Third Army, poised at the Siegfried line. The truth of my condition was not something easily unraveled and laid out to examine. This was what I wanted and had always aimed toward in my eighteen years.

We quietly filtered through these great concrete tank stoppers. Wading would describe it better, because the blizzard had wind-sculpted some fantastic snowdrifts around these reinforced concrete pillars, which were three to five feet tall. We moved along, in reserve, to the rear of E and F Companies of the 302d Regiment, who—unseen—were hundreds of yards to our front. We were in columns, Indian file, to not get lost. We passed a pile of great rubble that had been a pillbox until the engineers blew it soon after its capture. We suddenly and repeatedly stopped and started through the dark as our scouts kept us following the forward troops.

The sky gradually became lighter as we moved through Monkey Wrench Woods, which it resembled from an aerial view. The various units were organized and oriented, each in proper relation to the other. We had little doubt that German patrols and outposts observed these shifting movements. Automatic fire and mortar rounds searched the woods to our front where E and F Companies were preparing to jump off. Hundreds of men, with dry throats and thumping hearts, checked and rechecked half-frozen equipment and weapons. Then, outgoing artillery shells screamed overhead, descending toward the dug-in enemy soldiers.

Overhead, fire from our heavy machine guns joined the outgoing artillery, and German bullets popped. Then the amazing, spontaneous, and deep cry of hundreds of men made the hair on the back of my neck rise. It was the warrior battle cry, hidden in our genes, that needed to be released every generation or so. It meant that our guys were attacking, because the intensity of rifle fire increased even more. The force of hundreds of eight-round M1 rifles firing as fast as they could was so powerful that I was lifted to a psychological level I never suspected existed. Dan and I looked at each other wide-eyed. As the bullets hitting our area decreased, I found myself opening and closing my rifle bolt, prodding the ammo to prevent it from freezing. The platoon sergeant and several men moved by, shouting to get ready and instructing us not to shoot until told to do so. Meanwhile, our heavy machine guns continued intense overhead fire, the tracers streaming by. Then we were up and moving. Many of our troops were leaving the edge of the woods and moving abreast of us in the open field, trudging up a low incline. This was really my first sight of our company since joining it. And it was awesome to be part of this. But tracers came streaming and thudding into the trees nearby, some smoking and sizzling in the snow. A glance to the right revealed our men disappearing into the bushes and snow.

The automatic fire was coming from our right rear. Everyone dropped to the snow, seeking any cover available—there wasn't much—from the enfilading fire dropping in. Officers and sergeants ran around prodding the line to get moving. In sudden leaps and crawling, we did just that. The German gunners could not see us in the slowly thinning fog. Later, we learned that the fire came from pillboxes at least a thousand yards to the right, on the far side of the village of Butzdorf. Their guns had been preset to fire in this direction, and their gunners were informed by radio of our movement.

As we neared the edge of the woods, we could see a field to the front and, several hundred yards beyond that, another wooded area where troops from the forward companies could be seen moving into the trees. What looked like a ditch turned out to be a tank trap. Men were coming out of it, walking wounded heading for the rear. We were herded in that direction. The tank trap was wide and deep, extending to the other wood, which appeared to afford some protection. Snow and smoke erupted from the field as mortar shells searched for targets. We could see several bundles in the snow—they were the dead or wounded. Medics were pushing through the snow. Men were shouting not to bunch up and to take turns running for the tank trap. A column of our company moved across the field to the right where there was some concealment at the tree line, mainly in the form of bushes and broken ground. In places where earlier shells had made craters, fresh snow then covered them; but there were other craters, black with recently blown earth flung over the white blanket of snow. Driven into the deep ditch, we were almost unaware of bullets plowing up the snow. Our excitement built to such a fever pitch that I felt impervious to the flying lead all around us as we jumped, by twos and threes, into the ditch.

I had a momentary glimpse of many, many mounds of bodies buried in the snow, along with arms, legs, and equipment protruding from the white powder. The drifts had been trampled and compressed by the movement of the men who preceded us. We struggled over the frozen dead partly hidden in the snow. They all seemed to be Germans.

We pushed past walking wounded who were moving to the rear and a line of men in long field-gray overcoats, who wore long-brimmed caps and had their hands behind their heads. These were the first live Germans that I had seen—prisoners of war. Throughout this passage of time, shells were still throwing up snow and smoke awfully near the trap, and we could distinctly hear the buzz of fragments overhead. A traffic jam formed and progress slowed as men behind shouted, "Get the lead out, move it, move it!" We stopped momentarily, and I glanced back to see men leaping and diving for the trap as others, bunched up on the top, tried to move around and get in. I saw one man knocked sideways and another slumped over. I heard screams of agony as Dan pulled me forward, forcing himself through and over men bleeding in the snow. Farther on, we found more order and less traffic— and minutes later, we reached the end of the trap to find a comparatively shallow trench running to the left. Our squad leader was there; he guided us away from it and out to the forest where the forward companies had preceded us.

Here the woods carried a heavy smell of cordite from shellfire and small arms. The sounds of exploding shells and hollow shouts of men reverberated strangely in the forest. Men who I did not know, but who probably were in our platoon, were scattered about behind trees. Bullets still flew and popped through the underbrush. There were foxholes and a great dugout at the wood's edge, with all sorts of equipment and weapons that I did not recognize, but knew to be German. And here again, were dead Germans and many wounded— with medics, German and American, working together. Noncoms called out to their squads. Ours was one of them; our squad leader caught up to Dan and me and the men lying in the snow near us. "Anyone see Peters?" he asked. One of our squad said that they saw him go down hard before the tank trap. I had an inkling that Peters was a replacement who arrived with me. In single file, the platoon moved to the right toward the edge of the woods, but remained in the dark of the trees to avoid being spotted in the open. We moved sporadically several hundred yards through the trees, as shells burst in the branches too close for comfort.

Then, to our shock, small-arms fire crashed around us, and we hit the snow. Dan dropped so hard I thought that he had been hit, but his BAR began chattering. There were screams of pain nearby. But before I could even begin "to get my act together," shouts of *"Kamerad!"* caused the fire to cease. Another surprise was to see Germans, donned in white, rising up with arms vertical, only yards away.

We had overrun them. Our other company had bypassed them to the left. I realized we were no longer in reserve and had arrived to the extreme right of the attacking line. With hands held high, the POWs were rounded up and relieved of their white jackets; and eight or ten of them were sent to the rear under guard. One of our men had a slash across his cheek where a bullet grazed him. Another GI lay wide-eyed, his pierced body spasmodically pumping blood vertically. Nothing could be done for him. It struck me how composed and calm he became—I believe I saw him die. We were formed up and again moved forward so as not to cause a gap in the company line. The edge of the woods to the right was fortified with bunkers and dugouts, well constructed with logs and earth. Dan was wading through snow twenty feet in front of me. Captain James W. Griffin, our CO, came trudging by with the executive officer, Lieutenant Kelly, and the first sergeant. I believe a runner with a radio was also part of the group, which was headed for the front of the line.

Soon we fanned out and began digging in near the northern edge of the woods. To the right front, we could see out along the edge of the trees to a town that was sitting under low dark clouds and smoke. It was a foreboding sight, with much open ground between the town and us. The ground sloped down gradually and then rose somewhat to the town. The distance was about a half mile. We lost no time chopping and digging through the icy turf to the softer earth below, and the labor helped keep us from freezing. The town was called Sinz, and I would never forget the place.

Later, as we deepened our foxholes, we heard the ominous sound of heavy diesel engines and creaking metal carried on the wind. The sound faded in and out, but gradually the noise seemed closer. Men called out "Tanks!" Simultaneously, shells began popping in. Off to the left front, we saw movement in the snow and underbrush. There, several enemy tanks moved toward the line. Their machine guns began raking the woods. A muzzle flash from a tank's cannon was followed instantly by its shell bursting in the woods. Another tank appeared closer to our area and fired a shell that exploded just to the right of our hole, some twenty feet away. I had been too fascinated by the majesty of these monsters to drop down, and fragments whizzed past me. Immediately, I dropped to the bottom of the hole that was only two feet deep, where I heard the vicious drumming sound of the ground being beaten by bullets and the loud smacking sound of bullets hitting trees. Screams of agony and constant calls of "Medic!" came from our right. Dan was white-faced and wide-eyed as he quickly peered out into the smoke. Someone called out a warning, "Kraut infantry behind the tanks." Other cries of "Bring up bazookas!" and "Fall back, fall back!" and "Fire your weapons for Christ's sake!" were constantly shouted. Dan slapped my arm and said, "Let's go!" and we grabbed our weapons and shovels. It was apparent that almost every man was falling back. Firing broke out sporadically along the line from the left and to the right; Dan's BAR chattered as he and I moved backward.

During this time, I have absolutely no memory of firing my rifle for the first time in combat. But, as we headed for protection on the other side of a little hill to get some earth between us and enemy fire, I burned my left wrist on the hot barrel. Crouched behind a tree, I blindly fired a couple of rounds—emptying the clip, which clanged out. Quickly and with shaking hands, I pulled an eight-round clip from my suspenders and managed to let the bolt fly forward. I was concentrating on this exercise so acutely that I never thought to get lower than the kneeling position, convinced that the lead flying around would not hit me. Men were shooting weapons from every conceivable position while moving back. I saw two men shouting into a walkie-talkie, but could not hear what they were saying. The tank never let up firing its weapons. In my imagination, I saw a hundred huge tanks and battalions of German infantry moving up, pushing us from the woods.

Some men ran up, and it looked like Captain Griffin was one of them, shouting to hold up. The men with him were moving to the right and to the left, shouting, "Hold here!" Other men crawled up to him with bazookas, and together they ran to the left; I lost sight of Dan but heard his BAR and additional rifle fire around me. Again, I had that unfamiliar lift that I experienced earlier. If I had learned anything in basic training, it was the value of firepower to convince the other side to back off—and the enemy soldiers were beaten back. This we understood minutes later as our artillery screamed in, kicking up the snow and earth a hundred yards in front of the woods. That, plus the small-arms fire, had broken the back of the attack.

When the artillery ceased fire, we were again brought forward to our half-dug holes at the edge of the woods. I passed the incredibly bloody body of a man with no face. One of the tanks was burning with its ammo exploding like the Fourth of July. Captain Griffin quickly moved past us with his bazooka team warning us to get underground fast because they might hit us again. I had never even seen the German infantry. Someone said that they wore white camouflage snowsuits. Someone else bitterly remarked that we should have had more sheets than we had—it was true that some of us stood out against the snow like black bull's-eyes. Therefore, at every opportunity, we liberated German jackets of white material to add to the few sheets that we possessed. And there could be no doubt that, while our rifles had difficulty lining up sights on the white-clad Germans, the unseeing artillery did its work quite well.

I prayed as I chopped into roots in the hard earth, while Dan spaded the loose earth to the front. Building a barrier between direct fire and us, we worked like madmen, not stopping even when the shriek of incoming artillery fire plowed into the ground and trees. Then something—I never knew what—pushed my face into the dirt. I came up spitting; I could not understand why I felt so light-headed until later someone tossed a helmet to me. Groggy, I looked at it and decided it was mine; a near miss had blown it off. A tangle of orange and brown oak leaves was caught in the netting of the helmet. I left them there. They offered little in the way of camouflage but, like men around us, had been cut down by shellfire. Mostly brown with touches of orange and yellow, they were survivors of the peaceful summer of 1944. Thousands of their generation lay scattered in the snow or still fluttered in the trees above. My deafened ears were slowly losing the ringing sound as my head cleared. I picked up my shovel and saw Dan staring at me.

Smoke and the stink of burned powder made men sneeze and curse. Someone was saying over and over in a strangely calm voice, "Medic, medic!" I wondered why if he was hit, he did not shout so he could be heard. But the voice trailed off, and someone was crying.

Dan and I went back to chopping roots, ever going deeper, but working from the prone position. The mortars were the worst, I think, because we had no warning—they dropped in silently. Again, we were delivered small-arms fire from across the field of snow. Several times, bullets dropped into the snow after bouncing off trees and branches. And again machine-gun fire came from the right rear from the Butzdorf–Campholz Woods area.

We hugged the bottom of our holes, and I do not believe a man could ever suffer more stress than this without losing it all and breaking. We were out on a limb—a mile in front of the MLR. To our right was nothing but open fields in the shallow valley, and I had no idea how much protection was on our left. I had a panicky feeling that the other companies had fallen back and the enemy would move around to our rear. We were in a cross fire of automatic weapons from the front and right rear. Their mortars and big guns were dropping their shells directly on us. The shouts of "Medic!" came so often from near and far that it seemed certain none of us would survive. All they had to do was continue what they were doing, and in a matter of an hour or two, there would be no attack on Sinz and these woods would have more dead and maimed GIs than the German dead.

I wanted to take off running to those beautiful dugouts the German soldiers had constructed. There at least we would have protection from the fragments that literally sizzled and buzzed toward wounded trees, where they made a noise that sounded like "Pock!" Since the war, similar sounds always bring me back to the woods of broken trees.

In those moments when the fire slacked off, we could hear the moaning of wounded men. Dan crawled to the foxhole to our right, some twenty feet away, and was gone for some time. For my part, I never ceased from deepening the hole. I planned to go down six feet and then excavate a tunnel so that the only way we would get it would be a mortar shell right in the hole.

Dan showed up after ten minutes or so with a pair of shoepacs. Bless the man: They were for me. They had belonged to one of our neighbors who died that afternoon from the same mortar shell that blew off my tin hat. His foxhole mate had absorbed most of the blast, and his shoepacs were too messed up to bother with. Dan was wiping blood from two dog tags, then put them in his pocket.

The boots he gave me had required much effort to pull off due to the frozen condition of the fasteners. I lost no time in pulling off my ice-caked combat boots and wet socks. I pulled on two pair of dry socks, and massaged my feet, before pulling on the shoepacs. It was a luxury to sink my feet into the felt-lined boots. Fortunately, the size of my feet matched those of the recent occupant. The boots still retained some of his last body warmth. Immediately, my feet felt a few degrees warmer, and as I tucked my OD (olive drab) pants legs inside the boots, the warmth crept upward. Later, as the temperature dropped, the warmth would again descend, but not as far as combat boots allowed.

I do not know whether body heat caused slush and melting snow to raise the water level in the bottom of the hole, but it became a constant battle to stuff branches and pine needles between our rear ends and the rising liquid and mud. Dan had scrounged a shelter half—that was a godsend. We sat or kneeled on one end and arranged the other end over our heads. I suppose it kept some wind out and some body heat in. The coming night would be the coldest. The night before—as bad as it was—had been full of physical movement and some warmth.

Once my trembling began, and as the cold penetrated all defenses, my muscles automatically stiffened against the invasion. This muscular reaction achieved nothing against the cold and, in time, the stiffening became painful. The winter nights are much longer than back in the United States. Unable to sleep because of the cold and shellfire, our misery only intensified as the hours dragged on forever. The thinner a man is and the less flesh on his bones, the greater his physical suffering. And the cold would continue into April.

Intermittent shelling dropped in as the gray daylight gradually faded toward night. Across the open ground to the left front, men of the 376th Regiment sometimes could fleetingly be seen near the Untersie Busch Woods. Tanks of the 8th Armored Division moved along the road bordering those woods; it ran from Nennig to Sinz and then climbed up Munzingen Ridge. There had been considerable action in the woods during the day.

Immediately to our front, we heard several cries of *"Kamerad!"* Two storm troopers, in whites, materialized out of the snow with hands held high. Both appeared to be wounded, as they tentatively approached. But a BAR let go a burst that blew both men back into the snow. After a shocked silence, anguished cries were heard. Our squad leader, his voice laden with sarcasm, said, "You're an asshole, Moore. Get your tail out there and finish it!" Several men echoed his sentiments in various and colorful ways. Apparently, it was not so much that he had shot men who were trying to give up, but that he was sloppy and failed to do a clean job of it. Moore responded emphatically that he was not, absolutely not, leaving his hole.

Off and on, we heard the crying and moans of the wounded men. The voice of one of them suddenly rose to a shriek—anger or pain or both, I did not know. I did know that I had never heard so devastating a human sound as those high, guttural notes as they spun wailing down. It might have been the kind of response the last man on earth would give as he viewed the ashes of his world. I had never before then experienced hopelessness. The cry frightened me. The flash and bang of a potato masher (German hand grenade) in the deepening atmosphere was so absolutely a correct act that the logic of it terrified me even more.

It was a good thing that I did not know Moore's face or who he was. I never heard him mentioned again. I assume he found his way out of the snow the next day. He was either several feet under it or ended up in between sheets with army nurses fussing over him while a Purple Heart would be pinned to his hospital gown.

Of course, my reaction to what happened was a typical one for someone of my background. However, in the space of merely one more day, the objectivity—numbness we called it—would set in. Survival demanded it. By this time tomorrow I would not even bother to wonder about the person I had been the day before. And by the war's end, the person who left his family in October (as Thomas Wolfe learned in the '20s) would not come home again. From Normandy to the Elbe River, bits and pieces of discarded personality lie, unseen, among the cartridge casings and K-ration wrappers.

The night of gray and black, occasionally pierced with crisscrossing tracers of different colors, passed agonizingly slowly. I could swear the hands of my luminous dialed watch, if not treacherously moving backward, were at least locked in place. Instead of serving me, the timepiece appeared to take orders from a god: a maker of mischief, misery, and confusion. He played with me and only inched the minute hand forward as I was about to rip the traitor from my wrist and toss it away. Dan appeared to sleep at times, and I kept watch for an eternity. I had to change from sitting to kneeling many times due to muscle cramping.

Occasional flares popped here and there, and I watched them descend in sparks to die in the snow. The automatic fire from the right rear in the Campholz Woods petered out at dark, and fires burned in Sinz and in tanks across the fields. The tank our CO knocked out still glowed fifty yards to the left. Several times, the swirling wind blowing fresh snow in my face carried the smell of burned rubber and hot metal. The disturbing smell of roasted meat puzzled me for a time. But I figured that one out, too.

Over time, the uncomfortable growling in my belly grew and finally drove me out of the hole. I heaved myself up, over the rear, and onto my back. Undoing the cartridge belt, I wrestled my clothing down and the wind went through my body like acid through wax. It totally cancelled the urge to defecate; and again, as during the march up, I felt helpless, foolish, and freezing—unable to shit or even pull up my pants to get my tail back under the tarp. But then, the urge returned big time, and a violent flush emerged. I had "the GIs," a common affliction. Most every man experienced it, often over many days. And men had to dig deep for the energy and guts to force a weakened body to do what was required.

Afterward, pulling up my pants and returning to the shelter out of the wind, I felt almost warm. I put my canteen back between my legs and my rifle's working parts inside my jacket, moving the operating handle every so often. I checked the luminous watch more frequently toward 4 AM. So, when our artillery shells began roaring in the direction of German lines, we all snapped to awareness that more than likely we would be attacking shortly. High above, the large-caliber shells sounded like an express train rushing toward Sinz. We checked our weapons and gear and decided to leave the shelter half behind. I replaced my canteen in its insulated container.

Our squad leader ran from hole to hole, and reaching ours, he told us to be ready to follow him and stay with him. At the ditch in the field, we would pause and then keep moving. He gave us more directions: Use marching fire and keep the weapons hot. Get into town and attack buildings next to each other—do not get cut off. He dropped a pair of ice-caked shoepacs in the hole and told me to get them on as soon as possible. He could not see my shoepacs deep in our hole, and there was no point in explaining that Dan had already gotten me a pair. I would later thank him anyway. The noise of German shelling came from Untersie Woods to our left front. We continued to get our share of fire and casualties.

Time passed, and the order to jump off was delayed. Hours passed, as we never ceased to improve our hole and keep our weapons ready for the movement across the field.

That was another day of intense cold. The night had been terrible—dark by 5 PM—and seemed to last forever until the sky became light again by 5:30 AM. We ate K rations and waited. Shelling was sporadic. Off to the left and left front, a considerable battle was ensuing involving the 376th. We heard tanks and could occasionally see Germans in the distance.

Finally, in the afternoon, we were given word to get ready as our artillery again screamed into Sinz. This time, with my heart pounding and leaping in my throat, I knew we were going: And to think that my greatest fears as a child centered on going to the dentist. I flashed on my family, and just short of whispering goodbye to them, I instead worked my rifle, pumping the unfired rounds on to the tarp and working them into the clip, thus reloaded. I was desperately unready, but we were to go.

The signal to move out must have been given. No whistle blowing, no shouted commands. Men simply began moving out of the trees and onto the field on our right, and we moved with them. Almost immediately, I walked past the two white-clad Germans lying in the snow almost invisible. They had held each other and exploded the grenade between them. But the burned clothing and blasted flesh, along with their faces and hair, had frozen cosmetically white.

Not twenty paces from the trees, tracers began darting across the open field, followed by the ripping sound of their machine guns. It was the totally different ripping sound from 88mm cannon fire, whose shells erupted smoke, snow, and clods of frozen earth into the air directly in front of our advancing line.

No words can describe the utter vulnerability one feels in this maelstrom of vicious sound and vision beyond understanding. Whizzing shards of hot jagged metal caused me to dive to the frozen ground. I heard several hissing noises nearby as fragments of shells burned through snow. I turned toward a shout in my ear to see Dan next to me yelling, "Go! Go!" I heard other voices mixed in with the pounding explosions. "Move out second platoon—Move it! Move it!" Then, within seconds, we heard screams and shouts of, "Medic! Medic! Over here!"

Dan and I ran on side by side. When he dropped to the snow, I dropped. As he scrambled to his feet, I followed. Staying erect, one could leap over the knee-deep snow and make progress, but I felt less exposed forcing my legs through the white powder crouched over, before lying flat again. Tracers whipped past just overhead, and we dropped to the snow, gasping for air, looking at each other. An ice-caked gloved hand was in the snow right behind Dan. I became aware of several bodies—Germans half-buried in new snow, who were probably hit during their attack with the tanks the day before. The machine guns' bullets thumped like an exaggerated popcorn cooker. Their rate of fire, so much faster than ours and with much longer sustained firing, was more than impressive. The corn popping chose another zone of influence. Dan shouted something about the bodies providing good cover, and off we pushed through snow again.

As far as I could tell, we still were pretty much in line with our squad. But, increasingly heavy clouds of smoke began drifting over us, and visibility was good or bad, depending on the direction you chose to look—which changed constantly as new explosions erupted. I spotted tanks—ours—on the road, with their machine guns firing tracers. The direction of the guns' aim seemed awfully close to our men.

I lost the scene in the smoke while my eyes went to a large explosion some seventy yards to our front. Someone to my left shouted, "120 mortar!" Instinctively, everyone ducked as they moved. Men disappeared in the snow—to reappear, moving. It was impossible to determine how many men were hit or how many lay hidden in the white stuff. We moved through areas of burned powder, gray on the snow's surface, as well as shell holes of black earth and debris tossed over the white and gray. Dan and I paused in a shallow shell hole, as though lightning never struck the same place twice.

Another 120 dropped behind us, and we snapped our heads around to see two men of the weapons platoon sink to the snow and a third move to the rear. I saw other men in the distance heading that way. Glancing to the front, I had no doubt we were still attacking. Two men moved past us, one toting a bazooka and the other carrying rockets. I started to get to my feet, but Dan restrained me. Then, thirty feet in front, a blast took the air from my lungs. It was a lick of flame and boiling smoke, flying crap everywhere, as a smoking piece of OD cloth—with singed flesh attached to it—dropped near us. The smoke lifted to show a helmetless figure sitting in the snow. We crawled to him, passing a smashed bazooka that lay by itself. The man, black and smoking, settled on to his side, dead before we reached him. The bazooka rockets had been set off by the third 120mm mortar shell. Dan took off with me right behind him.

The antitank ditch suddenly appeared in the smoke, and with all the metal flying around, I unhesitatingly jumped in. It was much deeper than I thought it would be, plus I plunged into a foot of water and surface ice. Dan and a couple of other squad members dropped in, splashing ice water on me. A noncom way off to the left kept shouting, "2d Squad! 2d Squad, 2d Platoon, over here!" Our squad leader splashed over to us from the right with the platoon sergeant behind him. He sent two riflemen past us to the shouting sergeant who had only a three-man squad until others turned up.

Quickly, the noncoms gathered their squads together and counted noses. The sloping walls of the trap were fairly well beaten up by erosion and shellfire. I had not noticed that our engineers installed bridges a night or two before. Men were trotting across as we shoved and hauled each other to the top. Two men were hit, however, as they left the trap. Shouts indicated that our own tanks were firing on us. We flattened ourselves in the snow, and some men jumped back into the trap. A lone rifleman worked his way to the tank and slammed his rifle butt against the turret until he got the tanker's attention and they broke off firing at G Company. I would see this happen again weeks later.

At this point, the advance resumed with orders for marching fire. The one advantage we had over the German five-shot, bolt-operated rifle was our eight-round, semiautomatic M1 rifle. Our tactic of marching fire with the M1 and the BAR enabled us to move, in rushes, to close with the enemy, thus sustaining fewer casualties than German infantry attacking against our M1s.

At first, the sound was a ragged crackle of our rifle fire that, within seconds, became a roar. Again, the hair on the back of my neck stood at attention. The psychological effect on me was that I felt a real lift, a confidence boost. Two rapidly depleting companies of American infantry continued their movement over the field. The rate of our fire rose and fell, almost drowning out the incoming shellfire, and our own shells burst on the town a quarter mile ahead. I no longer heard individual sounds—not even my own rifle. A concussion broke heavily in my head like storm waves breaking on rock.

Closer to town, haystacks and farm equipment were scattered about. Men tended to use these—anything more than ten inches high—as cover. A bazooka fired a rocket at a haystack, which immediately burst into flames. Snow and wet posed no impediment to the intense heat of burning powder. Then I noticed a long shape protruding from the hay and, as I realized it was a cannon, several figures appeared running from the fire. Excited by targets I could see, I lined up my sights, probably too quickly, and jerked—not squeezing the trigger. The running figures toppled to the snow, probably riddled by many .30-caliber bullets—none of which were mine. We could then make out the tank; it was on fire.

I had lost sight of Dan as I dropped into a small depression that also shielded another rifleman. Together we shoved in clips of ammo to our M1s. Wherever the smoke thinned and I could see the town, I squeezed off rounds that kicked the rifle into my shoulder. I could hear nothing, and although I was feeling the concussion, I did not realize until later that I was deaf.

Snow was erupting in three-foot fountains immediately in front. The regularity of hits indicated a machine gun, because shell fragments struck differently. The firing shifted away. Some of our men were moving ahead and I could no longer shoot safely. I slapped the arm of the man next to me as I got to one knee. He did not respond, and I saw he was without his helmet, the top of his head a pink mush. I think I leaped to my feet and ran so instantaneously that I left my panic behind.

I caught up with Dan, who was shouting, but I could not hear the words. He and others were firing to the left front. Germans, one hundred yards away, were exiting a trench and running to the buildings. All five or six were tumbled to the snow in a couple of seconds. I never got my rifle to my shoulder.

About one hundred yards from the blackened and broken walls and roofs, our artillery shifted its fire deeper into town. Now we were racing to get in among the ruins before the Germans who were sheltering in cellars would reinforce the Germans above. A low stone wall spanned the edge of town directly ahead. I pinned all my hopes on arriving there in one piece. Lungs ready to burst, I threw myself behind the wall's temporary protection, along with our squad leader. Dan plopped down, looking at me wide-eyed. A man he called Salazar arrived next to him. I became aware of my agonizing thirst and the fact that I was hot and sweating. However, our squad leader was talking, and I could not understand his words—I could only hear the voice. He was pointing at Dan and me. Dan pulled a grenade from his suspenders, and I followed the move.

Our squad leader bent down on his knees as Dan pulled the pin, and I followed suit. I flashed on my bushel-basket accuracy and drew back my arm. But a live potato masher, looking as large as a baseball bat, dropped from the upper window of the house right across from us. We ducked, although I knew it would explode beyond the wall on the road. Then I let the grenade sail through the upper window, while Salazar and the squad leader fired at the same opening. Dan next sent his grenade into the lower window.

Broken window pieces flew down from above as we hurdled the wall and crossed the dirt road to the front of the house. The house's entrance was through a broken latticed gate, and our sergeant sprayed the garden area with his Thompson submachine gun. Dan rushed in, firing into the closed door of the house. I was next and understood I needed to shove the door open. This I did by grabbing a handrail and delivering my best kick, which swung the door open. Dan burst past me and I followed him in. Straight down the hall, a staircase littered with rubble rose upward. As we began moving down the hall, another potato masher appeared, bouncing down the stairs, and we ducked into doors off the hall. I heard that one explode in the enclosed space. The other three began firing their weapons through the ceiling, and thinking that was a great idea, I joined in.

I noticed my hearing returning because I heard the German soldiers shouting *"Kamerad!"* several times. The sergeant shouted, *"Kommen Sie hier!"* (You come here!) We watched the jackboots appear, and then the rest of three snowsuits descended the stairs with hands behind their heads.

I finally learned the sergeant's name as Salazar spoke to him; it was Langley. Salazar knocked the helmets off the white-clothed men. We watched as they were searched and then relieved of their white jackets for our use. We also stripped the white covering from their helmets. I stuffed one in my field jacket.

Upstairs, Salazar and I found and deactivated their weapons the best we could. Bent out of shape, the M42 machine gun lay on the floor next to a broken table—maybe my grenade caused it. Platoon sergeant Baker called from downstairs, and we kicked rubble from the stairs as we descended. Baker was with his runner carrying the radio. We were told to take the prisoners next door and go on to the next house behind this. Langley had no answer to where the other men of the squad were. I hoped we were but briefly separated; yet that was doubtful. I flashed on men I saw hit near me. Going out the door with the three enemy soldiers in front, Baker told us that the CO was wounded near the woods and Lt. Peter R. Kelly took over, but a machine-gun burst killed him minutes later.

The conversation, brief and hurried, left me with the impression that our casualties were heavy. The three POWs had pulled out their long-brimmed caps to replace their helmets and were hurried out the door to the dirt road we had crossed coming over the wall. As the first POW emerged from the latticed gate, a burst of automatic fire slammed into him. I was still walking out of the house and did not see it, but I certainly heard the bullets' impact. Langley was shouting, "Cease fire!" An answering shout from down the street reminded me of Moore, the BAR man. Whether this had been deliberate or an error, the POW lay in the snow with blood pouring from his chest and mouth.

Salazar pointed out the shortest route to the next house, through the garden and a near wall. He was detailed to watch the two surviving POWs, and Dan led the way to a large hole in the blasted wall. I followed in his wake—but backward—watching every window and possible hiding place I could see. As I backed over the rubble of the wall, I slipped on something other than ice or snow. Glancing down, several seconds passed before I could classify a shredded mass of cloth, flesh, and bone, as posthuman. I continued moving to get behind the wall to better cover, but my eyes could not leave the strange snow patterns: The shell's explosion had instantly splashed hot blood onto freezing snow, creating forms rare and unbelievably beautiful.

For a long moment, my focus had removed me from the scene of the human hunt. The constant explosion of shells and grenades provided background for an incessant enemy machine gun. I looked down an alley, past Dan, to a street where snow was being turned to mist by bullets. Lying in the center, a jumping, flopping figure of a man was being ripped to pieces. The sound was vicious—whacks, thuds, and screaming ricochets. Dan turned his head and shouted for Langley, who had passed me, to join him at the end of the alley, where Dan already was firing his BAR up the street toward the machine guns. The German fire ceased, but not before its final burst popped an object high into the air—the punctured GI helmet fell nearby. Both Dan and Langley shot complete magazines up the street, with only short M42 bursts responding. Langley hollered a question to another GI across the street at a window. He answered the words indistinctly in the noise of battle. Later on, I learned Sergeant Nowak was the man killed in the street, and the battalion CO had been wounded. Our company had lost three or four officers, 60 percent of its personnel.

Dan returned down the alley to the other end, finding no safe way around the house. He paused at what appeared to be a broken cellar window and heaved a grenade in. The muffled explosion puffed smoke into the alley.

Behind us, the first house we had entered received a mortar shell on its roof, which sent broken roof tiles around. Langley yelled to Salazar in the garden who, with all the noise, could not hear him. He shouted again, "Shoot the prisoners, and get over here!" For expediency, I automatically relayed the message. As several rifle shots sounded, I realized numbly that my voice had carried the death sentence through Salazar to the POWs. Langley cried out for us to get through the cellar window, as a shell hit the garden and splattered the wall above me with fragments that powdered my shoulders with cement dust. Salazar practically dove through the window, followed by the others and me. In the darkness that smelled of cordite and potatoes, Salazar's flashlight showed a ladder dimly illuminated by an open trapdoor above.

Another shell hit violently outside, this time puffing smoke and crap into the cellar. Langley poked his tommy gun up the ladder and ascended, followed by Dan, who got a boost from me, burdened as he was with twenty-two pounds of BAR and all that ammo. As I pulled myself up and out of the trapdoor, several bursts of Langley's Thompson sounded off. Dan flew out of a door, followed by a diving Langley, as a grenade exploded in the room behind them. Langley rolled to the side of the door; pulling and de-pinning a grenade, he let the handle fly. After waiting a dangerous few seconds, he flung it into the room where hobnail boots had just hit the floor. Burp-gun bullets splattered wood splinters and gesso from the wall near us, and the grenade flashed with a deafening concussion in the closed space. There was a brief scream as smoke and dust filled the hall by the trapdoor. We heard an excited exchange in German, and then—except for our breathing—total silence.

Langley entered the room, sneaked a look out the window, and came back and told Salazar and me to check upstairs. Before I could comply, Dan handed me a stack of empty magazines to fill. Shoving them into my jacket, I followed Salazar to the stairs. They were strewn with rubble. Smoke was heavy upstairs, and we found burning furniture under the smashed roof.

We moved to the side of the house where the German soldiers had jumped out the window. The smoke was so thick that I pulled my GI handkerchief over my nose as a filter and cautiously peeked out a window at the broken wall and roof of the house next door. It was fortunate such a volume of smoke was pouring out the window because, not thirty feet away, a group of white-helmeted soldiers were focused on the lower window of our house. All held burp guns, and one held a device unknown to me. In tones I could barely hear, Salazar told me to stay put: "They've got a *panzerfaust* [anti-tank rocket]; be back with firepower."

He quickly returned with the others who took a look at the group in the shell-holed house opposite. Langley kept his eyes on the foe and said, "Okay, the biggest bunch is in that shell hole where the *panzerfaust* is, and a couple just moved to the window on the left. We do it fast and head for the stairs. *Panzerfausts* scare me. Foley and Dan, grenades in the left window. Salazar and me toss to the hole. Then empty one clip and take off."

Dan and I stood behind the others crouching by the window. With weapons between our legs, we all pulled pins; and at Langley's terse "Now!" we launched them from the smoke. Most of us were up with our weapons and firing as the grenades went off. Bellowing and screams mixed together with the background noise of house-to-house fighting in the town.

I probably was the first to head over the debris for the stairs, only pausing long enough to insert a fresh clip before descending through the litter. I had the uneasy feeling that other enemy soldiers had entered the house while we were upstairs. Salazar and I descended about the same time and cautiously moved around the corner to the front of the house, checking rooms as we moved. He went to the extreme front to look at the street while I stopped at the room Langley had dived out of. I could picture a German in there bleeding to death and a burp gun aimed at the door. But a quick look showed the room empty, with only a few odds and ends of furniture. I walked to the wall next to the smashed window where bloody hands had gripped the sill. The floor had blood on it. I just stood there alone and began to pull Dan's empty magazines out, using M1 clips from a bandolier to reload.

I heard occasional German voices in the house next door, and several bursts of burp-gun fire splattered and bounced on the walls of our house. Some slugs blew the whitewash from the inner walls of my room. I heard Dan and our squad leader clumping down the stairs and kicking aside bricks. Dan took up position on the other side of the window and remarked on the bloody damage outside. Below the window were several formless bundles: bodies, clothing, equipment, and weapons—a testimony to Langley's work with his Thompson and grenade. From behind the shadows of the splintered table, Dan came up with a burp gun, and I pointed out the bloody palm prints on the windowsill.

An increasing amount of smoke and welcome heat were emanating from the house next door. The crackling of flames in both houses mixed with the sound of small arms and the *crump* of mortar shells. Occasionally, artillery fire screamed in both directions. In general, it seemed the small-arms fire was dying down. Langley sent Salazar back the way we came to coordinate with the rest of the platoon wherever they could be found. He had gone only as far as the cellar window when the platoon sergeant and his runner came in and followed Salazar through the maze. Joining us, he received a report from Langley, who did not mention shooting the POWs. We learned the company was down to less than one-half strength, from 178 men two days ago to 80 effectives left. E Company was in similar shape. I learned it was true that out of the original eight in our squad who began the attack two days before, four of us remained.

Suddenly, Dan (at the window) cautioned us to be quiet—and we froze into the shadows as a figure materialized out of the gloom and smoke outside. Langley was raising his tommy gun to take him down, but Dan pushed his barrel down, not taking his eyes off the figure. He whispered, "Medic" and motioned us back. The German went to each still bundle in turn; then he followed the blood pattern—so black in the snow—to the window, and he spoke in a low voice, looking for wounded, I assumed. Then he faded away. After a few moments, Dan explained that if the medic had known we were here, Dan would have captured or shot him because the medic could have reported our location.

The platoon sergeant said he was pulling us back to the first house where we could better hold and tie in with the rest of the company. The burning houses would no longer be shelter anyway, and their light would help us defend in the approaching dark. I gave Dan the reloaded magazines, and we headed to the cellar and back to the first house, moving past the dead bodies and the equipment.

The platoon sergeant informed us of our casualties—one-half the company was missing. Most of them were hit in the field while moving on Sinz. The tanks had almost been more help to the Germans than to us. We suffered some killed and wounded by our tanks, and they failed to adequately support our attack in town. German tanks had been firing on us from Munzingen Ridge all day. He and his runner left us, and the four of us began setting up our defense of the house.

I managed to eat most of my K rations before we received a big barrage of heavy mortar fire—probably 120mm—which was followed with machine-gun fire. We had huddled in the cellar during the shelling, but we rushed to windows when the machine guns started.

We repulsed a strong counterattack in the eerie light of burning houses and tanks. I can remember only frenzied minutes of intense firefights, *panzerfaust* and grenade explosions that resulted in more white-clad bodies, screams, moans, and all sorts of strange sounds—human, animal, mechanical—I could not identify. I remember the postfight aftermath of heavy anticlimactic sound and silence more than I remember the action: It almost seemed as though reality had given way to a surrealistic dream state.

We were totally flabbergasted to learn that rather than having reinforcements show up during the night, we would be pulling back to the woods. We were to pull down doors for stretchers to carry wounded back. Half-tracks arrived to transport the most seriously shot-up. It was an order I could not conjure in my worst nightmare.

The walking wounded were distributed among the able-bodied. Many wounded were being transported on the doors, four able-bodied men on each door, weapons slung over their shoulders. The exhausted column led the march northwest. The rest of us fell into extended columns, well dispersed, and trailed after. We left the burning ruins of Sinz behind us and followed a well-trodden path in the snow toward the woods we had left the previous afternoon. I experienced the totally unreal sensation that we had attacked out of those woods at least a week ago. Intermittent shellfire, mostly mortars, briefly flashed in the dark.

As intense as basic training was, it was in no way comparable to this. Evacuating Sinz and approaching the woods, I found myself stumbling along, almost falling at times, and I realized that I had never been this exhausted. It would be my third night with no sleep. I felt despondent and slowly I began to comprehend in my numbed mind that, as one of our four companies, we had attacked a town. Two companies had been stopped in the woods to the left, and our two had attacked alone, taking the full impact of enemy fire and leaving 60 percent of our men in the snow. By this time, we had pulled out and were back where we began a half day earlier.

All of this pain and suffering had accomplished absolutely nothing. Tomorrow, or the day after, we or some other outfit would have to go through the same hell and pay dearly for possession of a pile of rubble that had once been a town. I had experienced in my first couple of days on the front line most everything that could be thrown at an infantryman. I had used grenades and fired many rounds of ammunition— some of it at enemy troops only a short distance away. The one thing I had not actually experienced is seeing a German soldier get hit by my rifle fire. Even the firing at the groups of men at the window in the house happened so fast and with so much smoke surrounding the action that I did not know whether I hit someone.

The sporadic shelling trailed us back to the woods we had

emerged from the afternoon before. And, where we had been two men to a hole, twenty feet apart, the day before, on this night we were two men forty or fifty feet apart. Many men still lay out there in the shell-torn field: some yet alive, physically shattered, their lives hopelessly ebbing with the icing of their bodies. In the wind, I sometimes seemed to hear the cries of those men lost under the deepening snow. I was aware of the movement of litter-bearers moving to and from the battlefield. Dan, huddled next to me, snored. Our shelter half was elsewhere as we occupied a different hole dug by men who may have died or perhaps were on their way to an aid station or field hospital.

Despite the shoepacs, the combination of exhaustion and cold caused the worst muscular pain yet. My tightening of tissue in trying to control the shakes turned to pain—pain from being in the grip and control of inward-creeping icy temperature. I did manage to escape the misery for a couple of hours. I awoke to the shifting of Dan's body as he heaved himself out of the hole. I heard teeth chattering briefly while he fumbled with his clothing to relieve himself. He settled back into the hole, and we said nothing as the dawn of 28 January gradually revealed the eastern sky to our right front.

The gray and black never disappeared even when it reached midday. The grays only increased toward dirty white. I cannot recall ever seeing pure white snow that January. We hugged our knees to our bodies and hunkered down our heads into our field jackets. The winter nights in North Europe were much longer than New Jersey nights. Then we had the conflict of wishing the night suffering to end coupled with the fear that light would again send us into greater danger. We stayed put in our holes until the next day, 29 January. My feet, if they could have thought, would have by then been thoroughly disenchanted with shoepacs as a cure-all. Sweat from the day's activities had turned to damp cold, and trench foot remained a true threat.

Langley appeared out of the gloom and mist—the platoon sergeant with him. They spoke of relief by another outfit and passed out several C rations, frozen solid. We stowed them inside our sweaters; the food would take hours to thaw. They talked of a hot meal later behind the lines and asked questions about feet, mainly about feet. So Dan and I had to pull off our helmets and remove our gloves to pull out the socks above the webbing. They were actually dry. In removing our shoepacs, we had little feeling from above the ankles down. We changed socks and could feel nothing of their dryness or anything else. I pushed the wet ones into my helmet liner and replaced the tin hat on my head. Dan pushed his wet ones deep inside his sweater. We massaged each other's feet. My body was stiff as a board and painful to move—all the more reason to move.

On the one hand, I felt as though a different person was emerging in me; in fact, it had emerged. I felt capable to do all that was necessary to be considered a *combat* veteran, an integral part of an exclusive fraternity that only one in seven or eight men of the ETO (European theater of operations) gets to join. On the other hand, I felt confusion about being ordered out of Sinz after we had paid the price of capturing and holding part of the town. I guess my confusion had to do with the guts of two companies of men that were cut to pieces and, despite all odds, had been forcing themselves over the open ground to push the enemy from those houses. So why were we pulled out? I had the gnawing fear that we would be ordered to attack again that day, and I thought the chance of surviving a second attack under the same fire received the day before indeed doubtful. By then, I had seen enough to inspire me to offer up prayers to the almighty—I requested that the platoon sergeant be correct that we would be relieved. Somebody would have to do it again, and I wondered whether the town would be held this time.

Little remained of my leaf decoration in the webbing of my helmet. I glanced upward to see scattered clumps of leaves—gray and black—in the trees. A mass of leaves surrounded a deserted nest, the feathered occupants long gone. And something was extremely wrong, something was missing in the leaves: For the life of me, I could not understand how, in only two days, the brown and orange had become gray and black. From September to late January, the leaves had gradually turned from green to brilliant autumn tones; in the space of two days, they had lost all the color. Then, from the periphery of my mind, the insistent thought pushed front and center that *it was not the leaves that had changed, I had*.

Later that day, information filtered down to us about the 1st Battalion of the 376th Regiment, who were supposed to have attacked with us from our left in Untersie Woods. German infantry with tanks had hit them just before their attack commenced. Their attack stalled, they had to repel the German thrust. As a result, all of the other German fire could be directed at our two rifle companies. To top off a bad day, the 8th Armored tanks, receiving their baptism of fire, were pulled out at dark, their forty-eight-hour loan to us having expired. With our two rifle companies reduced to less than one, we were pulled out to prevent our being wiped out by a strong German counterattack.

Much later, we learned that when the 8th Armored was taken away, the remainder of a new plan to clear Sinz of the enemy had to be thrown out. The 7th Armored Infantry Battalion was to have been committed to our left in Sinz, and together with our 2d Battalion on the right, we were to clear the town. The street down the center of town was to be the dividing line between us. Unable to proceed against the 11th Panzer Division's heavy tanks without our tanks, we were withdrawn.

Sometime on the morning of 29 January, men who I viewed as saviors filtered up to our holes and took over as we grabbed our stuff and headed back. The 2d Battalion, 376th, relieved our 2d Battalion, 302d. The relief was slow due to the enemy's well-timed shelling of our area. Again, I could barely feel my legs and had little feeling from the knees down. I was not alone in this: Dan stumbled from tree to tree, as did most everyone else I could see. Langley was leaning stiffly against a tree, his tommy gun slung over his shoulder. Slowly, men moved to the rear, using weapons as canes and crutches. Through the smashed trees, I saw men slumped in the snow, some pulling themselves along as I had begun doing my first night on the line—until Dan had pulled me to my feet.

An officer and runner moved past and told Langley to move his men to the rear or be left behind. As shells harassed us, everyone moved like Frankenstein's monster in slow motion, stumbling along to the rear in a ragged column. At first, men cursed and moaned as we attempted to filter through the trees, and squad leaders had to be careful no one be overlooked. As it was, one man was overlooked; he could not move and froze to death, and his body was found a week or so after the snow melted.

On the way out, I saw something that devastated me. I witnessed a group of litter-bearers through the trees, carrying what appeared to be stiff and distorted bodies. Other bearers, carrying folded stretchers over their shoulders, were passing them while heading to the front. Then, farther on, I saw the long lines of shapeless bundles lying in the snow, bordering a farm track. The six-by-six trucks were being loaded with the dead of our battalion. I flashed on photos and newsreels of the white crosses of American graves from World War I— row upon row of them. The symbolism branded a deep impression, those pale ranks fading almost to photographic infinity.

I knew that some, if not all, of the replacements who had arrived with me a few days ago were lying there under the trees. The dead kid in the road, whose ammo I'd taken, had trained with me. Fifty-two years later, I would visit them at the cemetery at Hamm. My wife, Nadia, and I spent hours moving through those crosses—acre after acre—reading the names of dead infantrymen and remembering a few of them.

2

Accidental Combat Drawing

Men were hit somewhere behind us—I heard the shouts for "Medic!" as I passed by scattered men who had dropped out of the column because their feet could no longer hold them up. Some men were held erect by two others—one on either side. A noncom pressed me into service to help him support a man who had fallen out near the dragon's teeth. I could not answer that I was not capable of ten more steps: I just did what he asked. But we had to help him only along a few hundred yards to the road, where tarp-covered trucks were collecting the men who could not walk. Near the communications trench, a chow line was forming, and pulling out our mess kits, we joined the line. We ate the hot food, a profound blessing, near the trench—just in case we would be shelled. But the shelling was hitting the woods behind us at a good distance. No one spoke, or could speak, and we consumed the food quickly before the intermittent drizzle could turn the solid food to soup. The platoons formed up and began moving across the road in single file. The food had been enormously welcome, and it did wonders for both our morale and stamina. A slow cadence enabled most everyone to keep up, and those who could not climbed into a truck.

Either the German soldiers had a hidden radio operator nearby who reported our position, or they could see us in the trees from the high ground at Munzingen Ridge. We were shelled several times as we struggled more than six miles to our new area of the front. I think we lost another ten or twelve men—some hit, and some to frozen limbs. Several men, including myself, limped along in agony because of our near-frozen feet. Hours later, we left the woods, crossed a field, and were assigned to houses in a village. Our group chose a room, dropped our equipment, spread blankets, and pulled our shoepacs off. To the sound of artillery fire in the distance, I massaged my ugly, almost black, feet, and in time, fell unconscious with the luxury of having a broken roof overhead.

The next day was 30 January, as gray as the days before and as cold. We heard that of the 176 men who began on 25 January, G Company had 44 men remaining. A rifle company normally has close to 200 men at full strength. We heard that replacements were moving up, but we never saw any.

That day, the G Company survivors who could move about heated water and attempted some cleaning up. Much attention was given to feet and stomachs. We had a real breakfast and another hot meal at midday. We checked equipment, cleaned weapons, and drew ammo, grenades, and rations—some received mail.

In the dark, moving along a slippery road in weather that alternated between sleet and snow, we detoured through the woods to a line of foxholes and dugouts. It was from here that the extreme right flank of the division front, the 1st Battalion, 301st, had lost almost two companies attacking Orsholz. That town was a mile or two to our front. To our immediate front, a road ran along between the lines.

After we had settled into our holes, the order came alerting us for a move farther to the right. I had the dubious honor of being selected as first scout, and Dan was to back me up with the BAR. Another outfit relieved us, and we filtered back through the trees. I noticed that every time we moved, something between a few mortar shells to a barrage of artillery or rockets would hit us.

The front lines in World War I were continuous trench systems well manned for several hundred miles, and it was dangerous in the extreme for even small patrols to try sneaking through these trenches to the rear. But in this war, both armies often established strongpoints and placed small groups in isolated points in between. They ran contact patrols to their right and left to check on their security and to try to intercept any enemy's attempts at infiltrating a patrol to the rear. Both armies used patrols to actively probe and locate weak points and then would attack in strength. If a breakthrough occurred, the attackers would attempt to roll up the lines to the right and left, as well as penetrate the rear. In general, one-third of the defensive force was located to the rear of these weak points. If a breakthrough happened, this reserve was employed as a counterattacking force. The U.S. Infantry of World War II was a triangular design. One of the three rifle platoons in the line company normally was kept in reserve. The battalion having three rifle companies held one in reserve; one battalion of three in a regiment was in reserve; and, of course, one regiment of the three in a division was held in reserve. All of these units were rotated in turn so the men in the foxhole line could rest and refit in the rear for hours or days.

Officers, noncoms, and machine gunners were the most apt to be hit by something because they moved around more than members of a squad. Machine gunners called considerable attention to their noisemakers, which make bright, sustained muzzle flashes and fire tracers immediately pointing out their position. They usually packed up and moved to an alternate position fairly often just to confuse the other side, and they tended to operate much as the antitank gun did (these 57mm cannons would fire a few rounds and quickly move elsewhere).

But the man at the point, the scout, moves to unfamiliar territory, leading a patrol or heading a column of hundreds of men strung out behind—his second scout often moves thirty yards to his rear. The scout's job is to choose the best route possible and to see or hear the enemy soldiers—or even smell tobacco smoke (if the wind is right)—before he is seen. He must use arm-and-hand signals to warn and instruct. Either a sergeant or officer joins him where he is concealed; or, when he senses danger, he moves to the rear fifty yards or so to confer with the decision makers.

An alert enemy always has the advantage. They are usually concealed and dug-in while he is in the open and moving. The enemy knows his area and the scout does not. An experienced outpost or MLR will allow the scout to move past and then quietly will take him prisoner. Perhaps the second scout would meet the same fate. Therefore, the rest of the column unsuspectingly could move up and into devastating small-arms fire and mortar shells. No matter how you looked at it, a scout had heavy responsibility and an awfully good chance of having his punctured body tossed into the back of a six-by-six truck.

My feelings were definitely mixed when informed I was to be scout. I met the sergeant's eyes, and controlling my fear, I nodded and said, "Okay, Sarge." And while hoping it would be a one-shot deal (no pun intended), I was inwardly thrilled at the prospect of the experience. But I would have been happy to see someone else do it. Also, the platoon sergeant neglected to tell me where we would be going. Not knowing where I was going, I was preparing myself for a move to another area of the front and then an attack, which I would lead.

However, it turned out that it was not that heavy a task: G Company was in the wrong place, and we were to move a mile to the correct position, and then my stint as point man would be over. Thus, our platoon, which consisted of nine men instead of the normal forty, moved to the head of the company. In passing, I was glad to see Captain Griffin in his trench coat. He still had an obvious white bandage under his helmet.

I left Dan near the beginning of the column and limped on, glancing over my shoulder at our platoon sergeant, who gave me a signal to keep moving on the track through the woods. It was easily followed—the snow beaten down by the passage of many men and vehicles. Mortar shells dropped somewhere behind me. It never failed: Move as carefully as we possibly could, and the enemy knew where and when, and they had the expertise to drop stuff on target.

I had noticed some of the men wearing white camouflage, either on their helmets or upper bodies, so I pulled out my white cover and donned it over my helmet. Several times a minute, I glanced back to check on my distance from Dan and the main body, or to pick up any signals aimed in my direction. I moved past a battery of 81mm mortars off the track near a farmhouse. A weapons carrier was parked there, with men lifting a wood-burning stove from it. I envied them, as they smirked at me and carried it to the house. There was no dearth of cut firewood—everywhere were twigs and shell-torn branches to keep them warm.

A couple of officers in a jeep sped past and stopped fifty yards back to talk to our platoon sergeant, and I was signaled to hold up. Another mortarman with a carbine slung behind picked up an armful of stovepipe from the carrier and asked what outfit we were. I told him G Company, and he responded he was D, the heavy-weapons company of our battalion. I learned their heavy machine guns were scattered throughout the rifle companies on the line and that they were a quarter mile away.

At this point, the platoon sergeant came up and the company followed us a short distance to a crossroads. There we turned left and followed the road north, staying in the woods. No traffic moved on the road; there were only knocked-out snow-covered vehicles scattered around. We arrived at a clearing where several jeeps and other vehicles were spread out in the trees. The first sergeant and several men miraculously appeared from the earth—a dugout covered with logs and earth was hidden in the snow. Our platoon sergeant received brief instructions from the first sergeant, and Captain Griffin joined us. As the company passed through, each man was handed extra rations and a blanket. We then walked up a white-taped path through the gloomy pines near the edge of the woods.

We were spread out, and we waited. When it was almost

dark, we were guided forward a few hundred yards to our holes. It was a wordless relief, as we replaced the miserable and tired men, who quietly faded to the rear.

For once, we were spared shelling while we moved about. Dan and I lost no time in sneaking around in hopes of improving our accommodations. A few yards away, we found a dugout we could sit or lie down in—in a V-shaped slit trench, with its point oriented toward the northeast. Around eleven feet long, the middle part was well logged over with a heavy earth cover. It had an entrance from either side and two firing ports; the bottom was covered with a thick layer of soft pine boughs, which left the mud and water well below.

Langley showed up and explained the schedule for contact patrols. There were hundred-yard gaps between some of the manned holes. But worse than that was the news that he would be taking Dan and me on a reconnaissance patrol to locate the Germans' positions and, if possible, bring back a prisoner. The idea of my first patrol scared me. I listened as Dan discussed his twenty-two-pound BAR and heavy ammo belt, a definite hindrance during this type of patrol. Langley had fallen in love with the burp gun we had found in the Sinz house, and he wanted to carry it, along with four hand grenades. But common sense dictated that if he were captured with it, bad news! We would use the white hoods and jackets, and Langley appeared later with a carbine for me and a grease gun for Dan.

Already knowing the password, and the rest of the line aware that we were going out, Langley took a compass reading and told us what he knew about the terrain to the front. We would move through fields and try to get into the forest, keeping north until we found their lines. Then we would memorize all we would see and hear. And if we would find an outpost, we might try to get a prisoner. It was almost 8 PM, and we were to move out at 10 PM. Langley said he was given hot food at the CP. I was told to take Dan's mess kit along with me and get the food; only one of us could go because the line was so undermanned. Davis took me back as far as the woods to see to it that I traveled the mine-free path marked with white tape—I had to run the tape through my hand because it often could not be seen against the snow in the dark.

Back at the CP area, my stomach did flip-flops as I smelled coffee and food. A mess sergeant doled out the food in the dark into our mess kits, which I carefully sealed with the lids. I emptied the water canteens, except for whatever ice rattled around inside, and filled them with hot coffee. I scalded my lips and mouth drinking some of the blessed mud. Going to the crates of small-arms ammo, I found some phosphorus grenades and frags to bring along, and also more carbine mags that I checked to make sure they were full and not totally frozen. In the dark, no one saw me grab a couple more blankets for Dan and me.

While arranging the food and ammo wrapped in one of the blankets and getting set to tote my supplies forward, I saw several stretchers being carried in and placed on a jeep that was marked with red crosses. I found this curious to see and was surprised when I was called by name. I approached a stretcher being lifted to the hood of the jeep. The man had his head partially covered with bandages, but his eyes were free to see. The dark prevented me from seeing who the man was, but he identified himself as Burke from Camp Blanding. So he had come up here at the same time I did. His ears, nose, and fingers were frozen, and he had lost parts of them. But, he considered himself lucky to be out of this. Although I could not place him, he knew me. I wanted to see what the other evacuees had suffered and who they were, but I couldn't stay—our food was getting colder by the minute. I wondered how he recognized me in the dark and decided he must have seen my profile against the sky as he was lifted up.

I arrived back at the hole about 8:50 PM, and Dan and I ate the food, which by then was cold. Our artillery continued to fire missions sporadically; every so often the enemy would unleash a salvo or two, just to let us know they were awake and to keep us sleepless, too. Occasionally, machine-gun tracers flashed through the dark. The sky was drizzling and sleeting all day. And, as the time approached for our patrol, the sleet became mixed with snow. We were pretty well-off in the dugout, and Dan, as usual, had come up with a shelter half that he arranged over the right entrance where most of the wind entered. The drips from the log ceiling had frozen with the coming of dark, and there were no more leaks to plague us. The bad weather could only help us—providing some cover as we moved. And the Germans would more than likely huddle under something and, we hoped, be less alert. At about 9:30, Langley crawled in, and we reviewed our touch signals and the compass azimuth we would use. Finally, we checked our equipment and left our blankets and other weapons, already frozen, wrapped up and stuck as high as was possible in the log ceiling. Salazar came in to fill in for us and cover the gap our absence would create.

We had donned our white jackets and hoods and then the equipment. Staying close enough for visual contact, we moved north, away from our lines toward a row of trees that bordered the road we were to cross. At the trees, we squatted and checked out the other side. We remained quiet, not moving for several minutes. Looking back to where we had come from, I tried to spot a terrain feature standout to guide us back, but it all looked the same—forest background. However, to the front, in open ground, was a shape I could not identify; I decided to look it over if we would go that way. Langley was leading, and Dan and I brought up the rear. Earlier, Langley had said that he had some info on minefields, but that it might well be out of date. The 301st, several weeks back, had gone through hell a mile north of this point. One by one, we crawled across the road and through the ditch. Not hearing anything, we continued north, squatting when there was cover, and stopping to listen. I often cautiously operated the freezing operating rod of my carbine and hoped the fifteen-round mag would cooperate if needed. Off to the left were the silhouettes of tanks obviously knocked out and abandoned. They could provide a reference point for our return. We continued on toward a wooded area. To our left front, fields went on for some distance. I did not feel especially cold, although I continued to shake a little. I wondered why we saw no flares from the German lines, and it occurred to me that they had patrols out here as well. Flares would be a danger for their own scouts. But if they were to sense us crawling around, I did not think they would hesitate to shoot one up.

Our sounds were covered by the shriek of shells roaring along high above, but if Germans were nearby, we also could not have heard them. Entering the woods on our bellies, we moved a distance and stopped, listened . . . crawled on through the snow . . . stopped and listened. Then I smelled tobacco—strong tobacco. I hit Dan's boots twice to signal him to stop, but he had smelled it, too. The wind was coming from the east, our right. Davis slowly moved in that direction. We followed, moving silently through underbrush and in between trees. I seemed to see movement everywhere. The light was dim, and from time to time small sounds reached us, such as a metallic click of a weapon connecting with a helmet or the checking of a machine-gun bolt. Strong tobacco smell again—stronger than ever. *What in the hell did they smoke?*

We pressed deeper into the knee-deep snow as a distinct crunch of boots moved in our direction and stopped. My mind flashed on a fast chain of unhelpful thoughts bordering on panic. A voice not fifteen feet away whispered a sound instantly answered by another whisper; these were followed by the dim scraping sounds of soldiers moving about and a few indistinguishable words in German between them. I grasped that this was the relief-taking place. More crunching in the snow faded in the distance, and we listened to the new men settle their bodies in for this frozen tour of duty. The question was, How many enemy soldiers were in this position? Was it only an outpost? Or was it a part of their MLR extending right and left? Were we lying near thirty or so Panzer grenadiers?

I felt Dan's boot move twice in my hand: "Don't move." A short time later, I sensed Langley slowly moving off to the left. I retained Dan's boot in my glove and froze, literally and figuratively. The snow froze my clothes, but my body re-

mained dry for the most part. I feared that when it would become necessary to move again, my uniform would crackle. I
wondered whether Langley would discover occupied holes
nearby. If so, I would find it hard to believe it possible to grab
a prisoner and escape in one piece.

One important lesson I learned was how easy it was to
learn the all-important password of an enemy. If I had understood German, I would have been able to approach any
position there. The future would reveal how Germans, who
understood English, successfully took GI prisoners by doing
just what we were then doing.

A German voice was answered by a different one. The
words over the next minutes seemed to indicate there were
two men there. Were others asleep in the same hole? The luminous dial of my watch showed 12:25 and Langley had
been gone almost twenty minutes. If he did not return soon, I
would be up for backing away. I was shaking uncontrollably
and afraid to be heard by the enemy. Then, ghostlike, Langley was there again. As it was too dark to see what he was doing, we could not communicate intentions other than "don't
move" and "move." Within a couple of seconds, I heard the
low sound of a voice: Was it Langley? Then came sounds of
equipment dropping to the ground, the scuffling noise of
clothing and boots, and Langley whispered just loud enough,
"Dan, cover this guy" and "Foley, this one. Follow me." I
came to my knees as the other men passed me toward the
edge of the woods, and I followed with my carbine prodding
the back of a German soldier. He had his hands knotted together on the back of his neck; he wore a long-brimmed cap,
and I smelled sardines. I had just learned some German,
"Hände hoch!" (Hands up!)

At the edge of the trees, with Langley's tommy gun in the
back of the other, he motioned us down while he studied the
open ground we had to cross. We were a mile or a little less
from our lines. When we were about to start out of the
woods, a firefight suddenly broke out across the field, and we
instantly hit the snow with the prisoners. Machine-gun fire
grew in volume as many different weapons joined in, fugue-

like. Sharp sounds, which I took to be grenades, punctuated the cacophony and light show. Tracers ricocheted—arching instantly high to the left of where we wanted to go. It looked as though G Company's right flank had been hit.

Then a bright light, a flare, burst way off to the right and floated—sparks falling. I realized that the burst of the flare had instantly pushed us, prisoners included, even flatter, a good combat reaction. Any Germans behind us would have been able to see our outlines in the light of the flare had we remained any higher. Somewhere to the German rear, mortars coughed, and seconds later their shells silently burst in and around the scene of action—followed by the *crump*. A minute or so later, our own mortars dropped shells well behind us, trying to finger our opponent's mortars.

I flashed on H Company's crews leaving the comfort of their newly installed woodstove to warm up their 81mm tubes. Finally, we crawled out of the woods and carefully felt our way across the field. Langley did not take the same route, but led us farther to the right. After a while, I decided he was being canny. If a German patrol had spotted us coming up, they could be concealed and waiting to ambush our return.

At this point, Langley moved the prisoners to the front, and we followed in their footprints. If there were to be mine casualties, better it should happen to those who planted them. When we arrived at the road, we paralleled in the ditch until we came to a tree that Langley apparently recognized, and I could again see the dark shapes of tanks to the left. Then we moved up to our hole, where we were challenged; we gave the password and found our platoon sergeant, Roberts (who was the platoon guide), in the dugout. Langley went with them and the prisoners to the rear to make his report.

Dan and I both performed a long and thankful piss at our latrine, an abandoned mortar pit. My urine smoked to the snow. I envisioned being found the next day, frozen and securely connected to the ground by an arched icicle of pee. Great photo for *Life* magazine on life and death at the front.

I buttoned up and was in the dugout before Dan—there I

pulled our weapons, ammo belts, and blankets down; worked bolts; and got organized. We sat close together for warmth, wrapped in four blankets around us along with our weapons.

Dan took first watch. It was 4 AM when he awoke me. At 6, he took our mess kits to the rear to see whether there was any breakfast. A steady drizzle came down as daylight increased from black to gray to gloom. It hovered at gloom all that day. But not everything was so dark. Something especially exciting and enlightening began in me: This illumination, once begun, has shown me my lifelong path.

Alone, I stood in the trench outside and took my first look at the harsh scene we had entered at dark the evening before. I studied the terrain to the front—the road and burned-out vehicles. I counted seven, but there could be more half-buried in mud and snow, behind ruined farmhouses, and among the scattered groups of trees. My eyes roamed over the woods where we had snatched the enemy outpost. I studied the ground to the right and left and thought of Laurel and Hardy, who continued to man their trench—not knowing the first war had been over for years. Then I took in the snowy mounds of abandoned equipment and whatever decaying horrors were cosmetically masked over around me. I saw movement to the right—a helmet just above the snow. I called out, and the head turned. It was Salazar, who seemed no taller than his M1; his small bullet head seemed lost in his helmet. This same guy had led me to the cellar window in Sinz. He gave me a big smile and salute. Then other heads popped up here and there to see what was going on. They did not stay exposed long in the lousy winter weather. Thanks to the 301st, most of us seemed to have a roof of sorts. I crawled back inside, positioning myself to be able to see out the nearest gunport.

I realized I very much needed to get off a V-mail to my family. I had written from the replacement depot (Repo Depot), and that seemed as though it were weeks ago, but it was actually only six days before.

I found the V-mail form and a pencil, and I tried to compose something cheerful, knowing the censor would chop out words I should not be using. I had not done any drawing, or even sketching, in the ETO—except for a drawing on the railroad freight car, capacity forty men or eight horses ("40 and 8's"), coming through France.

So, with thought not yet forming words, I doodled on the form; and in the pencil lines and smudges, I began to see images of my squad slowly appearing out of graphite and into a long ragged line of foxholes. Other shapes took on the forms of rifles and, yet others, shovels. Working quickly with an enthusiasm that I never before had in drawing, I filled in the bullet-and-shrapnel ripped trees. In a few minutes, I had established the design. My filthy hands, at first accidentally, and then deliberately, smudged the smoke of burning buildings and a tank in the background. The face of the foremost figure, with shovel in hand, was strong, and he looked real soldierlike under his helmet and knit cap.

In the past, I had always drawn pictures of subject matter from an immature mind; I rarely had anything to say pictorially—until that moment. The pencil slid out of my hand: I realized my fingers were frozen, or close to it. I blew on them, got my gloves on, and with a genuine sense of accomplishment I had never before felt, I sat there and stared at what was clearly expressed on the V-mail form. A basic ability to make two-dimensional paper give the appearance of three had been mine from earliest memory. But all that had been like placing on paper random words that expressed nothing. This was different.

From somewhere in me, a surge of self-esteem welled up higher than the lift I gained from proving I could, so far, take infantry combat. Nothing would ever be the same after that day. I had not arrived at the point where I could call myself an artist; I knew only that I could do this drawing thing well, and I was excited.

Quite hungry, I was relieved to see Dan cautiously move up to the dugout, still sporting his grease gun in place of the BAR. It made little sense to carry more than twenty pounds of weapon just to get breakfast. He must have made a fast trip, because the food was still warm. He filled me in on the action on the right of the line just after we started out of the woods with our prisoners. A large German patrol tried to infiltrate 1st Platoon, which then let its raiders get close and let loose with everything they had. The enemy soldiers went to ground with casualties. Some of them gave up and brought in their wounded.

I had been controlling my excitement over the artwork—waiting for Dan to notice. I'd propped it up between two logs. Removing his gloves, Dan took the V-mail form and expressed admiration for the drawing. His eyes held mine as he shook his head slowly from side to side. He seemed to grope for words. I suddenly felt grateful to this soldier, who had been so good, caring, and instructive to a replacement. I was moved to give it to him, and he carefully stored it away with his stationery wrapped in plastic waterproof. I could see he was pleased.

Salazar visited. After admiring our living arrangements, he hurried off to see about breakfast. Then Langley popped in to talk about last night's patrol. We wanted to know how he had gotten the drop on the Germans. He explained how he crawled some distance to the right, and not finding anything, decided it was only a two- or three-man outpost. Crawling to the rear of their hole, he poked one of them in the back of the neck with his tommy gun and whispered, *"Raus mit du."* The soldiers froze, raised their hands, and that was all there was to it. I commented on his choosing a different route back, and we discussed the pros and cons of patrol work. As he crawled out of the dugout, he said that patrol work was normally spread around as fairly as possible. But, when a squad got a reputation for consistent and positive results, the tendency was to use the same group more often. And, until we received replacements and trained them in our ways, we could expect a heavy workload. One bit of advice proved extremely valuable later on. Never split a night patrol—stay together and keep the number small for better control. In a sense, we had split last night when he left us for twenty minutes, but it had been necessary.

Not a minute later, we received a hard wallop, as a mortar

shell hit terribly close, its concussion rearranging loose dirt and mess kits. Dan thought it had to be at least a 120. Three more followed within a minute, and I seriously questioned the thickness and stability of our overhead protection. Dan muttered something about our dugout becoming a hangout and some great German optic lenses watching the movement around our location. As the last shell hit, sending dirt and debris into the trench next to me, a totally different sound—a large automatic weapon—was pumping shells precisely at us. They exploded with heavy thuds, slower than the machine guns of either army. We hugged the floor under the firing ports as the shells raked and tore up snow and earth all around us. The acrid stink of cordite filtered through with the wind, and the pounding stopped as suddenly as it had begun.

The silence following this was as deep as the shelling had been loud; we remained frozen on the bottom of our hole, looking away from each other's eyes. If just one of those 20mm shells had come through a port, it would have exploded against the back wall, spraying us with splinters. Neither one of us stirred. I know I had no desire to lift my head or a finger any higher than where they were then. And that was good, because the canny gun crew had purposely waited a couple of minutes, hoping to catch a head or two poking too high after being fired on. Their next burst of fire was longer. It drummed loud, but not long at us, as the gunner opted to ride his gun down the line of the 2d Platoon—scary, but no cigar.

We had little doubt that German observation of our movements was excellent. Aside from suspected radio operators hidden behind our lines, much of what they observed was seen from the high ground of Munzingen Ridge that ran northeast and was the backbone for the Siegfried Switch line. And the Siegfried, as explained earlier, was the line of bunkers and pillboxes behind the woods across the open ground. These forts were all over the ridge and throughout the small towns and woods between the ridge and the Moselle River.

Their fortifications averaged two miles in depth, and with

typical German efficiency, the triangle had been carefully designed for defense. Their observers sat in almost complete security in reinforced concrete and steel forts, with the best German binoculars and telescopes. Their communication lines to rear artillery emplacements were deep underground, safe from our shellfire. The crews from our own signal corps were constantly on the move, repairing our communication wire, strung aboveground everywhere and exposed to shell fragments that mindlessly cut through and into anything mechanical, electrical, or human.

These forts were warm, dry, and often equipped with bunks, showers, and kitchens. The Siegfried line was legendary. I had heard about it for years—long before joining the army. Its interlocking defenses were cited as able to cover all approaches: not only to itself, but to its neighbors as well. Deep tank traps were dug that could not be crossed by tanks without our engineers putting bridges over them. And this was costly in the extreme, because the bridges were always covered by machine-gun fire, cannons, and mortars. Everyone has seen photos of the dragon's teeth that connected the traps to other tank traps. Minefields were often placed where you would expect them, and often where you would not.

Berlin believed no army could penetrate these defenses. Of course, they were wrong; but the fighting to break through was some of the hardest and costliest of the entire ETO. And this is what the 94th faced, with occasional help at times from units such as the 5th Ranger Battalion, the 2d Cavalry Group, and the 8th and 10th Armored Divisions. It was the 94th, however, that broke through.

If we had held on to Sinz, we would have come close to that final breakthrough to Munzingen Ridge. But we didn't. One of our other regiments did, at terrible cost, finally retake it and the woods around it.

Then, the night after drawing my first war sketch, we were alerted for an attack before light the next day to hit some of the pillboxes and bunkers at the edge of the woods across from us. Reinforced by a platoon of antitank company armed as riflemen, and some engineers, we quietly moved across the open ground while our artillery threw a bombardment out in front of us. I do not recall that any of us in the attacking companies, reduced to one-half strength and less, even got close to the pillboxes. The German infantry probably lost few inside their forts. The only result was medics and litter-bearers bringing back the dead and wounded, and we were further reduced in number. Where were the replacements we were hearing about? One wonders what the big picture was that would cause strategists to throw such depleted numbers against such fortification! Perhaps, as Hitler did, they saw unit designations on their maps, but not the existing unit strength.

Weeks before, the 301st suffered so heavily here because they were sucked into the German defenses, and with support effectively sealed out, two companies were lost. In time, I came to understand that our failed G Company attack on the pillboxes was—in the eyes of higher authority—a necessary probe. It was one of many probes that eventually helped plan our all-out division drive to tear through the forts and storm Munzingen Ridge.

After the early morning attack that failed, we limped back to our holes to sit, wait, and be shelled. Our number-one activity was to constantly improve our dugout; keep weapons operable; treat cracked lips, feet, and skin; reinforce the roof; and bail water.

I recall hot meals (when possible), a few carrying parties, and many contact patrols. Some relief arrived, and our platoon went back to the village where our CP had relocated away from the woods. The kitchen, which was located in the village, sent the food jeep to the old CP behind us in the woods. We spent a night or two off the lines in that village—I remember warmth and a shower. Months usually passed between showers or a change of clothes.

Compared to the dugout, constant contact patrols, the shelling, and the wet mud of melting snow, the house in the village was heaven. The building was 80 percent livable, having sustained artillery damage before we arrived. But every time we returned to it, it seemed to have more holes and to have lost more roof tiles. We occupied only the rooms on the southwest side, because the occasional shelling came from the other direction.

Because the upper stories had been reduced to rubble, the last time we stayed there everyone piled into the cellar, and we found our woodstove was moved down there. The cellar was crowded, but had we been a full platoon of forty men, we would have been living as we did when we were herded into a freight car traveling from one front to the other. The only time being undermanned was an advantage was off the line where there were fewer men to grab the available beds and a lot more food to go around. I suppose the kitchen received rations for two hundred men.

My newfound passion for drawing our experiences drew considerable attention and support from the other men. All sorts of paper and pencils, looted here and there, began to fill my art pocket on the lower right side of my field jacket. Someone came up with a bazooka rocket tube I utilized as a vastly improved container for my artwork. Having to unroll and flatten the paper was a bore, but it was worth it, giving my work much greater protection. In the beginning, I kept the drawings flat between cardboard that was stuffed inside my sweater over my chest. Much later, I found a larger cardboard tube from an 81mm mortar shell. The timing was good because I wanted to do larger drawings. I exchanged my GI blankets for German field gray ones—larger and warmer. I kept the tube well insulated in that blanket roll, which was then rolled into a shelter half, tied, and carried over my shoulder and at my side. These were always with me except during patrols.

I believe we traversed that area about eight days before moving back to the Borg area and Campholz Woods in support of 1st Battalion, 302d.

One other incident occurred while on contact patrol between our dugout and another to our left, a night or two before we were relieved to move back west to Campholz Woods. In the gap between our two dugouts—a distance of well over a hundred yards—H Company had a heavy, water-cooled

.30-caliber machine-gun emplacement some seventy yards behind the dugout line. The two dugouts and the heavy-machine-gun position formed a triangle. The machine-gun position had the gunner, assistants, and supporting rifleman. Our route was to angle back to them and then angle to the left front to the other rifle dugout, and then we were to reverse the route to our dugout. This time, Sanders went with me: He was in his early thirties, a steady soldier who had been with the division a long time. Contact patrols with long gaps between manned holes could be anything but routine. The 11th Panzer Division facing us was vastly battle-wise and had been active for years on many fronts. They probably knew how depleted our ranks were. They probed our lines nightly as we did theirs. Contact patrols intercepting the enemy were operating catch as catch can; and the more often the patrols were run, the better was our chance of ambushing their patrols—conversely, they could also ambush ours. And although we had outposts with field phones located between fifty and one hundred yards to the front, they also were spread too thinly.

We ran our first patrol soon after dark settled in. We chose a route to our left, through sparse underbrush and a few shattered trees, about one hundred feet to a trail that followed a low fieldstone wall in the direction of the machine gun. We had agreed I would lead off, with him following a short distance, and then reverse the lineup upon return. That was a fine arrangement—except we never got that far together.

Much of the snow had melted, making it debatable whether to use white camouflage or olive drab, and I'm sure the enemy soldiers had this to consider, too. The ground was frozen hard in places and muddy in others. The ground we encountered dictated our movements, yard by yard. We would negotiate a stretch of icy crackle sound and, then, the soft sucking noise of thawing earth. Slowly picking our way, we passed a couple of deserted dugouts and moved on through the best concealment I could see in the gloom. Then we arrived at the trail and wall. The wall provided good cover, and we crouched there a while.

We were set to continue on after a few minutes, when the

sound of movement in the field beyond the wall grabbed our undivided attention—we heard muffled footfalls and a low voice, and then silence. We could see their movement about ten or fifteen yards away. Then they seemed to fade into the dark earth, and all was quiet. We whispered to each other and decided they had to be Germans, and that it appeared they had occupied some deserted foxholes between our dugout and the other ones we were to contact. We decided one of us should keep an eye on them and the other slip up to the machine-gun emplacement to alert them to the enemy and maybe get some mortar fire on them.

The result of our deliberations saw Sanders back off from the wall toward the dugouts we passed for some overhead protection, in case I could get mortar and machine-gun fire on the enemy. So I followed the wall toward the machine-gun position, expecting to see a German or two come over the wall at any time. After all, we had no guarantee that they remained where we last saw them. Without knowing how many there were, it was impossible to know their mission—recon, prisoner raid, or the probing point for a larger attacking force waiting down the road.

When I saw the stand of trees where the machine gun was located, I tried to get as close as possible to the gun crew before being challenged so my voice would not carry too far. Actually, circling to the rear of them, I whispered the password twice before I received the countersign. I quickly laid out for them what we had seen, and someone cranked up a phone and whispered his call sign and target location.

The moment we heard the cough of a mortar behind us, the same man lifted his arm with a weapon that turned out to be a flare gun. He fired as the first mortar shell burst in front. Light from flares, although necessary, can often distort what you think you see. A quickly descending flare creates rapidly shifting shadows from objects, especially trees. Eyes can not always read accurately what they perceive. But, with the sudden burst of the flare, the machine gun began its twelve-round bursts, traversing the ground to the front, with the tracers' brilliant ricochets.

The "fire for effect" order was given to the mortars. Meanwhile, the other men were laying down rifle fire to the front. For this night patrol, I had opted for the grease gun that I fired once in basic training. With so much firepower to the front, my eyes anxiously swept my right flank for movement, and holding the grease gun sideways as had been suggested, I ripped several bursts through the dancing light and shadows. The bursting mortar shells were so close—I felt panicky as several fragments whizzed past. One flare after another was fired. These hung higher longer.

At this point someone shouted "Grenade!" and I ducked. A series of loud bangs and the buzz of fragments flying around kept me even lower. I heard the gunner curse desperately and jerk the operating handle of his machine gun. A burp gun raked the forward edge of the position, and men were shouting. The one phrase I heard that energized me was "Lob grenades." Several of us pulled pins and let fly. The gunner was giving up on his machine gun and pulling pins. A bright flash and a scream came from the trench. I felt claustrophobic keeping my head down and knowing the enemy soldiers were moving closer. With all the metal flying around, it took all I could muster to quickly glance to the front. Someone was loudly talking into the phone, while overhead bullets whistled. What I saw were muzzle flashes and several figures in the light of the flare. The nearest German was about fifteen to thirty feet away, so I ducked; then I came up, grease gun first, squeezing the trigger. No time for aiming—only raking the jumping weapon from left to right.

Some of the shouting sounded enough like screaming that I could not really differentiate yelled instructions and encouragement from the exclamations of shock and pain. But the machine gun was firing again, and I had a taped magazine reversed and into the grease gun. Still worrying over my right flank, I saw movement just outside our stand of trees in the underbrush. I flashed on Sanders, but knew it could not be him. I shouted to watch the flanks and added "Grenade!" as I tugged the pin out of my last frag and carefully let it fly to immediately ahead of the movement I had seen. After the sharp bang, I rose up and expended half a magazine in that direction. But I froze my finger at the panicky shout of *"Kamerad!"* Someone behind me shouted, *"Kommen Sie hier,* son of a bitch!" Meanwhile, all shouting ceased as several more cries of *"Kamerad!"* were heard from out in front.

With the total silence and drifting acrid smoke, I stood in shock, shifting my gaze from the front to the right, where I waited for the capitulating German to emerge. The light of the flares was dying down, leaving only small fires to the front. The shock I experienced was caused by the sudden shift from total violence and desperation to the immediate and maddening cessation of it: I was alive, unhit, and full of suspicion about the enemy soldier on my right.

Hollered instructions in bad German from our gunner or his loader initiated movement and guttural responses from the enemy out to the front. The mortar fire was shifted, walking the explosions toward the German lines to harass and discourage any attacking units that might be out there.

Suddenly, small-arms fire crackled from out in the field, with our machine gun responding with a short burst. Shouts back and forth—the Germans were again prone, hugging the mud and shouting *"Kamerad!"* Then, in bad English, one of them tried to explain that his dead comrade on fire had his ammo belt explode.

Again, the German soldiers were told to come in, and they lost no time in doing so. The clearing smoke and a round from the flare gun showed men supporting wounded and heading our way. They approached and appeared to be four relatively unharmed prisoners, supporting others unable to walk. They deposited the injured in front of the trench, and two prisoners went back for another whom they picked up and carried in. The moaning was dreadfully disturbing, pitiful.

That was when I heard a voice say that a GI was lying in the trench, dead. A grenade that came in had killed him. The machine-gun loader had taken a piece from the same grenade in his ass, possibly achieving the proverbial million-dollar wound. He could limp out and recover slowly from such a wound if it were deep enough. Of course, if it went too deep, it would no longer qualify as a million-dollar wound.

I reminded the man on the phone about the German off on the right, and he ordered the tallest prisoner to go bring in the other one and told me to cover him. Dark had fallen again, with only flickering tongues of fire in the field and a really bad smell wafting up to us of burned meat, hair, cloth, and powder. I remarked that we needed a flare, and the gunner complied.

The big German soldier strode around the edge of the trench, his silhouette and peaked cap clearly etched against the sky. The sudden flare burst revealed his equipment belt bearing a knife. The prisoners had not been frisked, and I lifted myself out of the trench and followed just far enough to keep him in sight. He bent down and, after a muffled exchange of words, came toward me backward, dragging another man who complained bitterly, apparently in much pain. I lost no time in dropping into the trench again, realizing I had wounded him with either .45-caliber slugs or my grenade. The phone man had explained the successful conclusion of the action to his CP and requested medics and litter-bearers.

Sometime later, men with stretchers appeared, and our man with shrapnel in his ass headed for the rear with the others, followed by advice of a ribald nature: "And remember to write and stay in touch!" The dead GI was lifted out of the trench and laid out to the rear for later removal.

A drizzle was turning to snow. It occurred to me I had better finish the contact patrol to the other dugout. They would need to know the result of all of the activity just to the right. To avoid any itchy fingers, I approached extremely carefully and my password was alertly answered. I crawled inside, where we compared notes. They had responded to the first flare with a grenade and rifle fire.

I returned to the heavy-machine-gunner's trench and remained there as water rose in the bottom of the trench. The machine-gun crew was short a couple of men, but no one had asked me to hang around. They were crowded under the shelter half, and I was becoming saturated. Although I seemed to be resisting the weather better, I decided to return to my dugout. When I lifted an end of the dripping shelter half and said I was taking off, I received a friendly slap on the arm and an invitation to drop by any time but not to invite the Krauts in the future.

I crawled out of the trench, stepped over the dead man, and groped my way to the right until I found the equipment of the prisoner I had hit. Curious to discover exactly what weapons he would have used on us given the chance, I found a bouquet of potato mashers with his belt and ammo pouches. Then I picked up a weapon, a machine pistol. I was too miserable to grope around in the muddy dark for souvenirs, but I was mildly disappointed at not finding a Luger or P38 pistol on the belt.

When I returned to my dugout, Sanders challenged me. He and Dan pulled me in and arranged blankets to include me. Then my energy deserted me: All I could do was shiver a while until some warmth began spreading out from my core. I told them what had happened as briefly as possible and dropped into a deep sleep.

I awoke to Sanders operating the squad stove. It was always a pleasant sound—the intense yellow and blue flame. Powdered eggs, fresh from the kitchen jeep, were warming up for me. They had theirs earlier. After eating the eggs and working on some K rations, I did considerable work on several drawings.

Occasional shelling, including mortars and Screaming Meemies rockets, struck the area. (Screaming Meemies gained the name by their raucous screech of rusty barrel-like sounds.) Sometimes the closer shell bursts shook mud and dirt from our roof and made it extra-difficult to keep my paper dry. The melting snow did not help at all. Twice during the morning, 88s screamed overhead to explode in the area where the CP had been and where the kitchen jeep parked.

Then, around midday, something ugly occurred that really shook us. Dan and I had carefully moved to the trees, thirty feet behind our dugout to use our latrine. Crouched over, we were returning to the dugout when a voice called out from the trees well to the rear. We turned, and a soldier, apparently an officer, asked whether we had any cigarettes. We dropped into our trench, and Dan asked Sanders if he had an extra pack on him.

Dan pointed out several bodies to our left front that were hit by the 81's walking fire at the conclusion of last night's action. I turned as the young officer, in a spotless uniform, approached in full view of the German lines. He was saying something about H Company and I interrupted him to shout, "Get down, don't you know where you are?" He stopped twenty feet from us and looked confused.

The shriek of the 88 shell gave us just enough time to duck down; then it exploded immediately. The smoke and crap settled down, and I took a look around. The shell had passed only a few feet over the dugout. Sanders poked his head out the entrance with a pack of Camels in his glove, saying, "Christ, that was close; you guys okay?" I nodded, wondering where the young officer had gone. I knew he had had no time to hit the dirt unless he was a superman. Dan and Sanders craned their necks, but there was no one nearby. Finally, my eye caught something moving on a branch of a tree nearby. I recognized the object, but my mind refused to accept the visual evidence. I asked Dan for his German binoculars. The tree had been nude of foliage for months, but I was seeing stuff hanging there. I focused the optics, and my mind was forced to accept the obvious. A pair of red dog tags hung on the branch, swinging in the wind. The other things were shredded cloth—black and bloodied. I handed the glasses back to Dan, telling the others what I saw.

We could not leave the dog tags there. They had to be turned over to the first sergeant. Normally, we left one of the two on the body, but here there was no body: It was as though the man never existed. I realized there had to be boots and body parts scattered around, but I was not about to repeat the man's mistake by exposing myself while looking about. I fired one round at the branch with my M1, and the branch dropped to the ground with the dog tags.

Later that evening, we were relieved; and, on the way out, we picked up the dog tags to turn over to the platoon sergeant. Before we left the dugout, we clued in the relief about the area—the layout of the holes, the wall, the heavy machine-gun position, and the numerous bodies. It was the least we could do.

3

Patrols and Pillboxes in Campholz Woods

Another platoon pushed its scouts out and our 2d Platoon just slogged along, following through the mist. It struck me as significant that we were not shelled at all during the eight-mile trek. Jeeps and weapons carriers, including H Company, passed through our ranks. I thought I spotted a stove and its pipe stashed in among mortar tubes and crates.

My feet never ceased hurting, but by carefully placing them step-by-step, I winced only one out of ten or fifteen steps. The skin of my hands, feet, and lips was tough and cracked. But all in all, I was staying about even with the weather then: I was not winning, but neither was the winter.

I was relieved to know that the platoon alternated scout duties to some degree. A ways back from the van of the company, our squad followed along, well dispersed. The night deepened, arranging its basic tone of black and not quite black. The men settled into individual cadence, their movement forward always focused on the interval between them and the dark shape of the men forty or fifty feet in front. No one spoke. Each man hunkered down inside his woolen wall against the elements.

With wool-knit cap pulled over my ears and scarf wrapped around my face and neck, only my eyes kept watch. My thoughts revolved in a vortex, always pulled to the center that flashed on the drawings I had done. And I wondered when I would have mail from home. Would a certain girl write as she had promised? (She never did.)

I realized our battalion had by then wrapped up about a week of what would be considered rest in a quiet sector. After Sinz, events had been quiet most of the time, comparatively speaking. Some abnormalities intruded on our rest, such as the contact patrol to the heavy machine gun. One major concern was the depleted ranks and continued absence of replacements. Whatever tomorrow would bring, could we do it in our current numbers? I noticed that I no longer thought past the next few hours. Certainly, I had ceased to consider the day after tomorrow, and my thoughts often returned to what I'd seen and felt in the recent past. Mental pictures formed on the silver screen of my mind of the best way to portray what had touched the artist in me.

I felt a new yearning that could compete with a long-established horniness that tormented me at times: This new sensation seemed propelled from my heart area to the fingers of my right hand. I experienced almost a thirst in those appendages to grasp a pencil and record a vision on paper. It was a nervous twitch, not unlike the feeling, promise, and thrill of sex stirring in my belly and balls. The irony was that I remained a virgin in one area and suddenly superactive in the other.

It is said the opera singer attains true color of voice only after having experienced a wondrous affair. In a perverse sense, the artist in me was having an illustrious affair with war—and war was *devoid* of color. This realization had me doing a quick rerun, in reverse, of my short tape of combat experience. I no longer received images in the colors I used to perceive; I saw only black and several values of gray (falling well short of the white of snow). How many times had I seen snow coated and recoated with smoke and burned powder? I tried to project red blood onto my scene—and try as I could, I saw only blood, black as night moss, on burned limbs and gray-muddied cloth. The fresh olive drab color of my uniform and equipment quickly was absorbed into earth tones like a sponge dropped in ice-cold coffee. Man became indistinguishable from the mud that covered vehicles and weapons. These winter gray forests, with areas of shattered and blackened poles (once trees) stretched from Switzerland to the North Sea.

We walked on through the dark with patches of fog rising and drifting through the land. The wind rose and carried stories from the east: the familiar stink of burned things and the sound of wind-driven metal against metal off in the unseen field to the right. Burned rubber mixed with the smell of overcooked meat—all against the background sound of gunfire.

My mind was almost overwhelmed with thoughts and images too new, coming too fast, to record them in an orderly way. Neatly, however, the thought fell into place that I was not limited to my stubs of pencils, stenographic lined paper, or U.S. Army stationery and V-mail forms. Of what use would colored pencils and paint be in rendering this no-man's-land, where color, like the birds and deer, left for greener pastures?

My movements over the ice and mud became automatic in the wee hours. I no longer felt pain in my feet, but I was only indirectly aware of this. With no feeling of discomfort from the cold, I dreamily visited my parents in our living room: My father dropped the *Bergen Evening Record* to the floor, revealing Buff, the cat, nodding on his lap. My mother's birthday was 31 January.

An ugly nightmare jerked me as I collided with the man in front. I tried to get my thoughts together of how I came to lose my concentration, my place in line. Then, immediately I was hit and shoved from behind, as the truth of our situation broke into my cobwebbed mind—I was sleepwalking. We merely stood there in the mist until we got the word to fall out on the side of the road and "take ten." We rested, although it might have been better to let us go on undisturbed, to let us sleep and cover the miles while dreaming of better places.

We arrived at Campholz Woods beyond Borg on 5 February and were moved directly up the hill and through the firebreak. We were placed in existing holes and dugouts to the right side of the woods. E Company was on our left. H Company's heavy machine guns were scattered throughout our perimeter; its 81mm mortars were placed behind the village of Butzdorf.

After Sinz, we had 44 men left in G Company; at this point we had 34. On a couple of operations, we had 8 or 10 men from other units loaned to us for short periods. And the days had turned into weeks that G Company was put in the line and did its best without replacements. This situation continued in Campholz Woods, where we relieved the 1st Battalion, 302d.

With much difficulty, one of the most important pillboxes had finally been captured by C Company, 302d; but when they were relieved by A Company, 302d, someone failed to lead the relieving unit to that particular pillbox. The enemy discovered this and reoccupied it. This lapse led to several failed attempts to recapture the pillbox and also led to many more casualties, including deaths—a major foul-up.

Many men paid dearly for the mistake, and now G Company was slated to make its assault and take the pillbox back. Its importance was due to its location at the northwest corner of Campholz Woods, where it overlooked Tettingen and Butzdorf and had been used as an observation post to bring down all kinds of fire on the towns below. It had also directed the enfilading machine-gun fire from the right rear while our battalion advanced, in my first action, through Monkey Wrench Woods toward Sinz.

I do not think we lost anyone all that day and night after arriving in Campholz Woods. There was a lot of noise, especially off to the left in the open fields between Tettingen and Campholz Woods. We assumed other units were trying to clean out the bunkers and pillboxes on the hill. On 8 February, we were relieved by the Pioneer Platoon of battalion headquarters and we pulled back to the south edge of the woods. We were to assault the elusive OP (observation post) pillbox by hitting it from two directions.

The 1st Platoon, with attached engineers carrying flamethrowers, was to circle around behind the OP in a pincers movement while part of our 2d Platoon would sneak through the communications trench that led directly to the objective. The rest of our platoon was led away to the left to hit bunkers on the open hillside two hundred or more yards beyond the OP.

We filed through the path marked with white tape, through the dragon's teeth, and entered the communications trench. The trench was about three feet deep, and the bottom was sucking-mud, with snow and ice. Where shells had obliterated its form, we had to wade through deeper, iced-over puddles. In much of the woods, mud-colored carcasses of soldiers sinking into the ooze resembled gruesome bas-reliefs—half in, half out of the earth. They were American and German. Only a piece of equipment on a cartridge belt, or a helmet sticking up from the wet, would provide a hint to the nationality. Broken branches, blackened tree stumps, abandoned equipment, and rusting weapons were scattered everywhere. I saw fins of mortar shells sticking out of the muck, unexploded, thanks to slave-labor sabotage or the soft mud. Small oblong box shapes revealed their deadly form as well—Schü mines, planted under earlier snow, now melted. Having become the same color as the surrounding dirt, they could—and would—kill and maim more good men today and in days to come.

A pretty good battle was going on beyond the trees to the right. Finally, the word to move out had Dan and me moving through the trench, the rest of the men following well dispersed. We arrived at the edge of the woods where a pillbox, supposedly empty, straddled the trench. It stood just beyond the trees, and I approached cautiously. Sergeant Baker called out to keep moving. After the snafu involving the OP, I took no chances and carefully checked the position out before continuing on.

Beyond the pillbox, I could see the big OP near the edge of the woods a hundred yards down the trench. I stepped on the remnants of a German overcoat on the trench bottom, but it felt more as though I were stepping on an inner tube that then released an ugly sound and a stink beyond description. After stepping beyond this corruption, I turned halfway around to Dan and pointed down, but the expression on his face told me he had already gotten the message floating on the wind.

I halted about one hundred feet from the rear of the big fort. I could see men of the 1st Platoon moving up and firing their weapons, but I was not sure they wouldn't make a mistake and open up on us. I had seen friendly fire before, and I certainly did not want to be fried by a flamethrower. The engineers with the flamethrower were right behind the attackers rushing the OP, but they did not get to use it. The firing broke off and we left the trench and milled around the fort as some German prisoners were brought out of the pillbox with some wounded. About all our squad could do was provide support.

Captain Griffin organized us, and soon Baker had us digging in around the concrete box. This fort had cost a great price in our regiment—we were not about to lose it again. In the end it turned out to be a pushover, and we lost not a man. I managed to look inside later on, and gazing out of the firing apertures, I could see the surrounding country amazingly well. The two little villages of Tettingen and Butzdorf could be seen in every detail a thousand yards down the slope. I saw groups of GIs milling about other pillboxes and bunkers scattered on the slope below. Although several hundred yards away, I recognized several from my platoon. Lifting my gaze, I could see Monkey Wrench Woods just beyond Tettingen and Butzdorf, where I had seen my first action. Sanders and Salazar joined me there, and we could see Sinz off to the right.

After the weeks of hard fighting in the villages and Monkey Wrench Woods beyond, G Company finally had taken something from the 11th Panzer, and it looked as though we would hold on to it. I looked out at the chewed-up terrain torn by thousands of shells and strewn with the rusting and burned-out hulks of German half-tracks and tanks, along with American tank destroyers. I saw an 88mm cannon with its long barrel and complicated recoil mechanism dug in nearby.

The fields were chewed up by tracks from the armor and shell holes, clumped mostly around the villages, roads, and pillboxes. Empty cartons and crates of all sizes, shell casings, and dead bodies rotting into the mud appeared from the last patches of melting snow. This had not been a war of movement here in the triangle. In many ways, it reinforced my impressions of a World War I repeat. I caught a fleeting vision of my father in his English-style tin hat, as filthy—head to toe—as I.

The seesaw battles of villages and woods and fields began here—with a lot of movement of company- and battalion-size attacks and counterattacks. Soon the 94th would break through the Siegfried only enough to launch a full-division attack, for the first time, up and over Munzingen Ridge, which loomed over most of the front to the northeast.

We settled into our holes for another cold night. After dark, we visually tried to identify the various flashes of light behind the German lines. The idea was to time an exploding shell by the number of seconds back to a particular flash or glow and then locate their mortar in a map grid. We phoned or radioed the coordinates to our mortars or artillery. Sometimes we would plaster them on the nose.

Some of us managed to pass an hour or two inside the OP that first night. Baker came out of the pillbox at dark with a pile of German blankets, rain capes, and other items and distributed them. Because they were larger and warmer than GI issue, I used two of the field gray blankets.

The weeks of dark skies and constant wet would soon give way to several days of clear skies, which would enable our P-47s to take off and give us a helping hand. We would see them bombing and strafing the German-held woods and villages, seeking out artillery and tank locations. Movement of any size on the roads brought the planes in on strafing runs. As a result, the enemy did most of their moving after dark.

Dan and I did a recon patrol out of G Company's position

one night and took a recent replacement along. Blanchard, twenty-five and a male model in civilian life, was proving to be a good guy and a good soldier. We were to move north until we would hit the Germans' front line and then try to find out what they had. Traveling light, we left our helmets, packs, and the like in the hole; our wool knit caps were less noticeable.

I led off with Blanchard behind me, then Dan. The night was full of mist and drizzle as it usually was. We slipped and slid down the north slope of the woods, checked out at our outpost, and took off. Before reaching the east-west road, we waited a while listening; then we crossed the road and moved several hundred yards through windbreaks of tall bare trees—we used all the concealment available. Munzingen Ridge, barely seen, loomed closer. We covered several hundred yards more and heard the sounds of digging.

Moving through a ditch that ran along a farm track, we listened to the sounds of entrenching tools to the north. Dan whispered we should move right to see whether more digging was going on. Then I saw a shape moving through the dark: Two men, making faintly clicking metal sounds, crossed the dirt track and ditch to head in the direction of Campholz Woods. After they disappeared in the mist, we had another conference. If we could capture the two, intelligence (G-2) might learn what they wanted to find out—or nothing. We decided the men were either on patrol or an outpost. Dan wanted to capture them, if possible; I wanted to explore along the line. To my surprise, Blanchard agreed with me. I would have thought a man new to combat would prefer heading back sooner rather than later.

We continued moving east through the drizzle but lost all contact with enemy activity. A building appeared in the gloom, and we checked it out, finding it roofless and deserted. We moved on a ways and walked beside a low hedgerow and farm track we stumbled across. A couple of things happened then: An angry voice some distance to the left dropped us to our knees; and, simultaneously, a flash and explosion occurred right behind me. Either a small mortar shell or mine, I guessed. A grenade's four-second fuse makes noise—I had not heard any then. Hearing sounds of physical distress, I turned back and met Dan over the writhing form of Blanchard. A flare burst directly above, illuminating Blanchard's shredded and smoking lower body. Vomit and digestive acid burned to my throat but no farther. Tracer bullets loudly popped and ricocheted overhead, but we were in defilade. I could see we were lying in a sunken road. Immediately I covered his mouth with my hands to prevent any outcry—his teeth sank through my glove, and I had to control myself from crying out. Detonations, mortar shells, or potato mashers: I could not tell or care, as Dan and I tried to hold Blanchard down. The next flare revealed what could only be Schü mines scattered on the edge of the track. A mine lay partially sunken in the mud a couple of feet from Blanchard. Instantly, we moved him toward the middle of the road, not knowing whether we were moving onto other mines. I had let go of his mouth to move him. The third or fourth flare popped open and I quickly glanced around and under me, but saw nothing. I remembered the morphine in my rifle stock and pulled the weapon to me. Blanchard was trying to talk. I think his lips formed the word "cold," but I could not hear him. He was shaking badly, and I had the syringe in hand but did not use it . . . because he was quiet.

I realized he had gone to ground directly on top of a mine. He was so badly shattered in the legs that I assumed that his knee had set the damned thing off. I felt completely helpless and overwhelmed. The only chance we had was that the Germans would suspect a pig or other farm animal tripped the explosive. If Blanchard had screamed, the story would have had even a worse ending.

Dan fumbled under Blanchard's clothing for a dog tag and said, "He's gone, let's go." I took a few seconds to relieve the dead man of his grenades and a bandolier, and to sling his M1 over my shoulder. The emotions caused by Blanchard's death were relegated to a closet in my mind. The enemy would not get to use this rifle. I needed these seconds to recover myself. I crawled past Dan, keeping a lid on all feeling, and I felt confident I could crawl us out on the path we came in on.

In the then-quiet night, we crawled along the middle of the track the way we had entered. We walked past the house and finally turned south toward our lines in the woods. A dark shape behind the trees proved to be a landmark of mine—a burned-out Mark IV tank sat sinking into the mud. We squatted on the shattered bazooka skirt that lay next to the vehicle and stared into the dark, not speaking. I was fighting the heaving sensation all the way back from the German lines. I bent over and let it go, as quietly as possible. To me, and I'm sure to Dan, my noise threatened our own survival. After a while I settled down. Neither of us made a move to get to our feet and cover the last fifty yards to the outpost. The only sounds were shells whispering high above the clouds and occasional small-arms fire in the distance.

I recall remaining there a long time, my mind a blank. Eventually, like a recurrent nightmare, the images of Blanchard's death returned with a vengeance, pulling in guilt and anguish I had never known before. My body shook convulsively; I grieved but could not cry. I felt Dan's arms around me, and I wondered why the tears would not come. I knew the older man was trying to form words to speak to me. Dan never did speak much. After a bit, I made a stab at it and said, "You were right in wanting to take those Germans prisoner, Dan. Blanchard would be here right now." I added, "I took us right in to the Schü mines." Dan thought about it for a long moment and replied, "We don't know for sure if we could have taken them prisoner easily. Blanchard, any of us, could have been hit. It looked to me like they carried burp guns. Frankly, I was a little relieved when Blanchard voted with you."

Soon after, we approached our outpost and gave the password. If they had heard any retching, nothing was said. We reported to Captain Griffin (who never seemed to sleep), and turned in Blanchard's dog tag and the approximate location of the body. I worked out an overlay on Griffin's map showing where we figured the enemy soldiers were dug in and where the mines on the track were located.

My throat burned red hot from digestive acid, and my mouth tasted like rat meat. Blanchard's teeth had bitten through my glove and broke the skin in several places. Was it punishment? The captain asked about my artwork—offered to keep it in the headquarters platoon. The offer was tempting, but I declined with thanks. He told me to make sure my home address was both inside and outside the tube. We returned to our hole and my helmet, blankets, and tube of drawings.

In the afternoon of the following day, and on into darkness, eight men were mutilated, not just wounded. Schü mines not far from us killed one man. They were men from Company B, 319th Engineers, moving up with demolition charges to destroy the OP, adjacent bunkers, and pillboxes that had just been captured.

The first three men who inadvertently tripped a mine were wounded. A group moved to rescue them, and as they placed one man on a litter, another mine exploded wounding another three men. A second party of rescuers put their lives on the line and tiptoed in. They safely brought out three and returned once again to the footless men lying in agony, not daring to move—for the mines were everywhere.

It was almost dark by then and, as I explained earlier, even in the daylight it was difficult to spot these things, because so many lay just below the surface of the mud. The men did succeed in reaching the wounded still lying there but, in placing one of them on a litter, another mine detonated, killing a medic and wounding two more rescuers.

One private first class with this group carried his wounded lieutenant out and returned twice more to safely carry out the last two. And this was not an isolated incident. Our division history recalls many Schü mine and Bouncing Betty episodes; a bad one happened in Company F of our battalion in Monkey Wrench Woods on my first day in combat. All of these incidents filtered down to us over the months.

About the same time we lost Blanchard, the platoon was given a different kind of mission. The company executive officer, Lt. Joseph P. Castor III (Lieutenant Kelly's replacement), was with us, along with a 300 SCR (Signal Corps Radio). This was not an ordinary patrol in that we wouldn't be out there looking for a fight, taking a prisoner, or doing reconnaissance. We would be doing our utmost to remain unobserved, find a location to hide in, and just listen and report. We were to dig a defensive position near German-held Oberleuken. It was known that the Germans launched attacks from this town. Beyond this town began the large forest called the Foret de Saarburg, which reached some miles to Orsholz to the east and extended south to behind our lines. The exec was especially concerned that Dan and I understood the network of roads where we would be located and observing from. Because of my ability at drawing and visual imaging, map reading and map making were easy for me. Another plus was my instinct for knowing my whereabouts. I've lost most of that instinct, though, over the years.

It is one thing to fight and move in conjunction with other units on both sides of you and another to establish an isolated listening post in the middle of no-man's-land near the enemy's lines. We realized the danger of encirclement and capture, or worse. Judging by the amount of extra ammo and rations we were carrying, I could only conclude we would be gone a while. This really was a scary proposition. A small group might remain out of sight for a day, maybe two, but the German patrols were exceedingly thorough in combing everything in their area.

I do not recall the number of 2d Platoon men who went with us to establish the listening post—at least ten, maybe twelve. I doubt that the platoon had more than fifteen in total. We sneaked out of the woods after dark, however, and down the hill, with Dan and me at point. We followed clumps of mud that were footprints. I knew this was, in all likelihood, a trail used by German troops and thus probably was mine-free. Also, there was the chance of meeting a German patrol on that trail.

Behind Dan and his BAR came McKay, who for some reason had become our squad leader. Probably it was one of the times experienced men were shifted to other squads to help new men. We preferred Bill McKay, who was a staff sergeant and an especially steady, well-trained man to be with in combat. Just behind McKay was Lieutenant Castor. Whenever I had doubts about the route, three or four of us would confer in whispers, decide, and move on. When we came to a suspicious haystack, we circled around it to make sure no tank or machine gun was lurking there.

Later, I saw the silhouette of a ruined farmhouse ahead—a logical place for German soldiers to hole up. But we were not looking for them. The lieutenant had us cut to the left, and we made it around the building and its outhouses. At the road from Borg, we went to ground for some minutes. We listened to jackboots making sucking noises in mud and sharp clatter on the icy patches that remained. In a few days, all of the snow and ice would melt as the sun appeared. Soon the sounds of what was probably a squad of men faded away as they headed for our lines.

Dan went alone to the road and returned in a short time; we followed him across. Meanwhile, Castor had pulled a raincoat or blanket over his radio and informed battalion of the enemy patrol. McKay remained stationary to see to it that we crossed at exactly this point. He explained that any tracks we left could be noticed, which in turn could provide a clue leading toward our elimination. McKay later told us he had done his best to eradicate any sign of our having passed that way. I was always learning new stuff.

From there I became extra careful picking a route toward Oberleuken. I do not think we left many tracks. We were one-half mile or so from the town and could hear diesel engines in the distance. We moved right and then left looking for any rise in the ground where we could hole up to both see and hear. The big backpack 300 SCR—when working—would be our lifeline to battalion and the means to channel information to the artillery. Then we squatted in the shadows of a windbreak of tall poplarlike trees, while the lieutenant and Dan left us to more easily scout for our best location.

Ordinarily, you do not split a patrol, especially at night. This was not an ordinary patrol, however, because the main group was stationary and the two men moving off had arranged a careful I.D. signal upon return so that itchy trigger fingers would remain calm. When they returned, they led us to a row of haystacks on the edge of a field. The lieutenant arranged a defensive perimeter in a rough oval around two of the haystacks at the south end of the row.

Immediately we began digging two-man holes where our automatic weapons covered the terrain around us. The field was scattered with hay and some farm implements, so it was easy to camouflage our position and stuff hay in the bottom of our holes to keep the seeping water at bay. And, as the approaching dawn began to reveal the landscape, I could see we were located on a slight rise that provided us with a view of the local road network.

But the increasing light made us aware of how close Munzingen Ridge loomed over us to the north—the ridge held the pillboxes and entrenched gun positions. We adjusted camouflage between our holes and the ridge with care. Observers, with some of the greatest telescope optics in the world, were up there. They would not be looking for us here, but we could take no chances. The lieutenant and his runner with the radio had created a sort of foxhole on top of one of the haystacks, which could only increase their visual observation of the area. The daylight revealed trees and ground all around us for hundreds of yards. Because the area had not yet been touched by artillery, I felt we could not have chosen better for our purpose.

Directly to the east, shellfire, and a lot of it, was falling on the town. Tit for tat; within minutes Borg was getting hit and later the shelling shifted to Campholz Woods one-half mile behind us—120mm mortars again. The days we passed in those holes were nerve-racking. The danger of discovery and capture was constant. Here we were on an island surrounded by beasts that had not quite smelled our meat yet. The only thing that appealed to me was doing to our adversaries what I always suspected they were doing to us: infiltration behind our lines, with radio contact to their artillery. They almost always knew where we were. Technically, we were not behind their lines, although exposed as we truly were, we may as well have been. We were not in a forest blending into the undergrowth; we were on a windswept rise in the middle of open country.

The wind turned and came at us from the east that afternoon. Simultaneously, from behind, a burst of sunlight swept over us like a celestial searchlight. Turning to see, I was momentarily blinded by the phenomenon—I had seen no sunlight for so many weeks. This shockingly powerful ray of light carried a hint of warmth. And then it left us and swept over the desolation. It briefly pointed up the landscape and trees lifted from the gloom, and then dropped them.

Later in the afternoon of 14 February, the sun broke through the overcast several times. Then, finally, we saw more clear sky than clouds. We had had little air support during the bad weather, though: On occasion, we would see our small artillery-spotting planes putt-putting around and getting shot at. Enemy artillery tended not to fire when these light craft were above. When they fired, a concussion ring was often observed from the air, even if the gun was hidden. So for our infantry on the ground, the putt-putting overhead was always welcome.

But what really was a dramatic show would come in the clear weather of the next few days. Meanwhile, after establishing our listening post, I took advantage of the clear light the first day. I sat in our hole and drew pictures of anything I could remember of recent events of the 2d Platoon.

Some of the holes were situated where men could slip out and urinate. Ours was one of the holes that could not be left until dark cut observation. We had to do our necessaries in our helmets and toss the contents downwind. It was tough not being able to stretch our legs.

After dark on our second night, 14 February, we again heard diesel engines to the north in the direction of Kirf, beyond Munzingen Ridge. We passed the night—two hours on watch, two hours trying to sleep. While awake, we watched the by-then-familiar flash of the suspected 120mm mortar position. We would hear the report, do some timing, and then turn our heads to try to see the flash of the exploding shell on Borg or Campholz Woods. Calling artillery fire on the mortar did not seem to knock it out.

The sunrise on 15 February was brilliant, and the air was terribly cold. But we forgot about the temperature later, as the roar of P-47s of the XIX Tactical Air Command came roaring overhead. They formed a breathtaking scene as they made their intentions known by circling their targets once, peeling off, and following each other down. One group hit the area around Sinz. Great clouds of smoke rose from the forests there. The ground shook with concussions although the bombs were exploding several miles away. Planes seemed to be everywhere we looked to the north and northwest, and they were bombing three or four other targets. After they pulled out of their bombing runs and climbed, they again dropped in shallow dives, lining up their gunsights. The tracers could clearly be seen as they strafed their targets. It was all I could do not to shout with joy—not to spring from my hole and laugh, dance, and scream "More! More!" For men with little or no tank support, we no longer felt as though we were alone.

The formations of planes headed away, except one group that flew past at several thousand feet heading east. One by one, they made strafing runs on the Orsholz area. We saw tracers rise from the ground, but the antiaircraft failed to bring down any of the tough P-47s. We looked around at the horizon and saw heavy columns of smoke rising in several places.

Breakfast was K rations as usual. And, of course, I drew a picture of two dogfaces in a hole cheering on the P-47s. Meanwhile, behind us between Borg and Campholz Woods, a noisy battle ensued: Some bunkers and big pillboxes were situated on the open slope of the hill leading up to the woods; the other companies of our battalion were engaged in some ugly and bloody combat trying to drive the Germans of the 713th Grenadier Regiment out of these positions.

The battle went on all day and into the night. Comparatively speaking, we had it good. But sometime after dark, we again heard diesel motors, and this time they were approaching from Kirf in the north. It was easy to know when the tanks—if indeed they were tanks—finished descending Munzingen Ridge. They changed gears and the motors were quieter then. Lieutenant Castor and McKay squatted next to our hole and told us to join them in a patrol. We were to set up near the road the enemy would have to use. The lieutenant's runner hoisted the radio to his shoulder, and the five of us headed west several hundred yards to a ditch a safe distance from the road. Then we heard the heavy squeaking sound of German tanks—the absence of ball bearings caused the squeaking. I felt we were too close. If they had flank guards in the fields, we would be in trouble, and I quickly told Castor what I thought. But the situation was even worse than that. Apparently, thinking the road was zeroed in by our artillery—which it was—the enemy was fifty yards east of it on a parallel course. They would be overrunning us within minutes.

We grabbed our gear, and staying as low as possible, headed back east at least a hundred yards. Castor got everyone down, and in less than a minute, we watched tanks and infantry pass in the direction of Borg, where our lines and battalion CP were located.

Because of the clearing weather, the starlight, and distant flares east of Campholz Woods, we gained a fairly accurate count of well over 170 infantry in three columns, with ten Mark IV tanks and four self-propelled guns. Castor had the coordinates all set for transmission to battalion. The *moment* battalion received the message correctly, Castor got us heading back to the listening post double time.

Well before we arrived, the first salvo was rushing through the frozen layers of air, like an invisible freight train, moaning and rattling through the night. We dropped to the mud before they hit, not because of fragments at this distance, but to avoid being seen by a possible German patrol in the sudden illumination. At a distance of three or four hundred yards, we watched while shells began striking in and around the open self-propelled guns and tanks. Shellfire, exploding ammo, and fuel lit up the scene of bodies blown into the air. The salvos repeated for a few minutes in a devastating display of artillery fire. And while they lost some armor and had many infantry casualties, the German soldiers went on with what they had left.

Years later, the official division history filled in the picture of that night. After the shelling, the surviving German force continued on toward Borg, until they arrived opposite the pillboxes and bunkers on the hill outside Campholz Woods. They wheeled about and deployed. They moved up against the American fire to support their beleaguered storm troopers, who continued to hold out in some of the concrete positions. They recaptured two pillboxes and several bunkers. That happened several hours before midnight. Eventually, the German tanks and infantry were pushed off the hill by an American counterattack and dug in somewhere between the hill and our listening post.

Around two in the morning, they attacked again. The Americans, after another wild and bloody fight, drove the enemy back again. These understrength companies, E and F, were comparable in size to our G Company. They had no tanks to put into the fight; and, even if they did, our Shermans were often—too often—unable to match up with the Panzers in thickness of armor or firepower. I must note here how dissatisfied I am in finding it necessary to write so briefly about those events where I was not present. Great nobility and courage were demonstrated by the men who wore both uniforms. The one fatal and false note involving the German army was the regime they represented in battle: Most German soldiers knew little or nothing at that time of their leader's base intentions.

A division is a big entity, and every day and night men were engaged in overcoming horrific odds along that ten-mile front. I regret, more than I can ever say, that the vast majority of those events will die in the hearts of men who did great things and could not bring themselves to enlighten others as to the nature of their deeds.

After the artillery fire we had brought on the German column, we returned to our holes and listened to the fight—we saw the flares and flashes on the hill where E and F Companies were fighting for their lives. Wrapped in blankets, I slept despite the noise. But sometime in the wee hours of early morning, hours before dawn, McKay shook Dan and me awake. Battalion wanted a patrol to locate and destroy the 120mm mortar tube that was so accurately zeroed in on the battalion and battalion headquarters.

Without helmets, traveling light, and rubbing oozy mud with our fingers on every inch of visible skin, the three of us moved east on our predetermined azimuth. We proceeded almost one-half mile to a row of trees that bordered a field. At that point, I was relieved of point duty and followed McKay. He moved agonizingly slowly, prodding the earth with a thin metal shaft at a forty-five-degree angle—mine searching. He carefully cut his way through barbed wire, and we followed. The occasional flash of the big mortar guided our direction. We waited until we all were through the wire.

McKay spotted a manned German position that we avoided, crawling through slush and mud, hoping it was a lone outpost. Later, maybe a hundred yards or so, we heard movement—voices. We slithered to within stone-throwing distance of a pillbox close to a group of buildings near Oberleuken. Off in the other direction to the left was silhouetted what seemed to be another pillbox.

We had not observed the flash in some time, and of course our own artillery was staying clear of this area until after our patrol returned. It would have been helpful, however, if we could have requested a shell to drop into the flash area just to give us a reference point. We hunkered down wondering in which direction to move. There we stayed for a period of time, until a flash, followed by a slight rushing sound and the considerable bang of the 120mm, gave us the direction to move. It was off to the right front, behind what appeared to be a pillbox. We resumed our crawl, aiming between the two points—the bunker on the right and the one on the left. Coughing and voices came from inside the right pillbox. On the way up to it, we crawled past exposed Schü mines lying in the mud; all over this triangle, the melting snow exposed the plastic or wooden boxes. Seventy pounds or so was sufficient pressure to detonate one. We were able to move them to the side with great care while single file we snaked among them.

We realized the need to memorize our route and return the same way, because if we were spooked into running, our weight could set off one or more of the mines. Adding to the urgency, dawn was due to break. McKay directed us to cover the back door of the pillbox where, in between shoots, the mortar crew apparently took shelter from our artillery and the weather.

Once in position, McKay crouched over and disappeared in the direction of where he assumed the big mortar was dug in. Later he described following the gun crew tracks to the mortar pit, where he dropped a thermite grenade down the tube. This was followed by McKay racing from the path and hoarsely whispering to Dan and me to "take off!" This we did seeing no Germans emerge from the fort. Within three to four seconds, we hit the dirt at the edge of the exposed Schü minefield and, as fast as possible, crawled on hands and knees between the deadly plastic boxes. In the growing light, we dropped to our bellies to crawl through the wire. We were then walking fast, when surprised German voices brought us to a stop almost in the midst of three men who apparently were asking in German what in hell we were doing. We lost no time before probing the startled Germans with our weapons. We quickly disarmed them, had them carefully put down the cases of Schü mines they were carrying, and herded the three in a direction away from the outpost. The return to the listening post went a lot faster than when we had left hours earlier. Arriving at Lieutenant Castor's haystack, we frisked the prisoners more carefully and put them out of sight by the haystack with a guard watching them. They were from the 416th Infantry Division and freely answered questions; they thought the 11th Panzer had been withdrawn from the lines some days earlier.

The night of 17 February, we were instructed to return to Campholz Woods and deliver our prisoners. We had not lost a man. Our 120mm mortar patrol must have really pissed off the gun crew, finding their melted down tube. I had done a number of drawings I liked and saw one hell of an air show. And, although we had escaped the hellish battle for the pillboxes just south of Campholz Woods, we did whittle down the attacking force going after E and F Companies of our battalion (and I hasten to add) with the help of the artillery.

4

The Reduction of the
Saar–Moselle Triangle

After midnight on 18 February, 1st and 3d Battalions of the 302d relieved us in Campholz Woods, and our 2d Battalion found itself marching to division reserve in Eft-Hellendorf, a couple of miles behind the lines. We were jammed into the buildings of the village to rest and refit. Replacements trickled in. The big push was to jump off at 0400 on 19 February, and it appeared that 2d Battalion, of all nine battalions in the division, would just wait in the wings as division reserve.

We had lost Sanders for a minor wound a week or two earlier—it was good to see him show up when the replacements came in. Salazar also was gone for some days with frozen ears and fingers and then returned. The value of experienced men mixed in with the new guys could not be underestimated: Squads were reorganized to some degree with the mixture of old soldiers and the new. I had settled into my role as one of the seasoned men although many new men were months and even years older. Certainly my uniform was exceedingly well worn and showed signs of every scrap I had found myself in. My helmet lost more and more of its original rough texture, and the net—held in place with elastic— had a large hole on top from using it as a seat. I could no longer distinguish the dried blood on my jacket and OD pants from the mud.

Blanchard's body must still have been lying out beyond

Campholz Woods. If the big push would be successful, all those bodies would be picked up. Yet, I worried it would sink into the mud over time—or else suddenly be compressed under the tracks and wheels soon to be employed in the push to the ridge. Over several days, I had seen bodies flattened and blended into the mud until they became a permanent part of a road, and undoubtedly they remain there today.

Those invisible powers that make armies move around were up to some innovative decisions. Before this time, the 94th had been held in leash with only limited company- or battalion-size attacks permitted at any time. Therefore, every time a company or battalion moved aggressively, the enemy could put most or all of their defensive artillery and mortar fire in the relatively small area of our attack.

A case in point was our 2d Battalion attack on Sinz. We lost 60 percent of our men during that two-day attack. If the two companies of the 376th had not been held up by the German attack and had crossed that field with us, the shelling would likely have been distributed more equally between four companies than it was with two. So it follows there would have been roughly 30 percent casualties in our battalion and 30 percent in the battalion of the 376th.

So, big changes were in the works at this point, because the 94th had penetrated enough of the Siegfried line and destroyed more than one-half of the 11th Panzer Division and much of a couple of other infantry divisions. The 94th had performed well in its role of pinning down German units and preventing them from reinforcing the bulge attack just a few miles to the north.

Patton decided the moment to unleash the entire 94th Division's three regiments had arrived. We were to drive up Munzingen Ridge, roll up the flanks, and keep pushing to the Saar River. This would put the entire Saar–Moselle Triangle in Allied hands.

Back in the town of Eft, our 2d Battalion rested, refitted, and integrated the replacements. We had plenty of hot food. I did get some clean clothes, but I kept my field jacket. My OD pants had become stiff with Blanchard's blood and so had my field jacket, but a good scrubbing helped greatly. I also washed my double layer of green flannel pajamas—could not stand woolen long johns against my skin. My flannel pajamas had elastic on the wrists, ankles, and neck. I wore OD underpants, two sets of OD pants, two OD shirts, two sweaters, and a scarf under my jacket. We all had knit caps under our helmets, used at least two pairs of socks in our shoepacs, and carried a rain cape and gloves. A few times we used an overcoat over everything—cartridge belt and suspenders always on the outside. Eventually, as the season changed, I discarded some of the interior clothing, but not much. April was cold. The shoepacs were discarded in early March and replaced with the much-better-for-walking combat boots. I managed to hold on to two field gray German blankets scrounged from the pillbox we had so easily taken just west of Campholz Woods.

I finished several drawings. One was a request from one of my H Company machine gunners, and I walked the cobblestones to their warm house to deliver it. But his team was elsewhere, and I left it with their CP for him. Also, Captain Griffin dropped by and encouraged my artistic efforts. His head wound from Sinz no longer posed a major concern. I figured he was eight to ten years older than I was, but I had turned him into a father figure and deeply trusted and admired him. He often wore an officer's trench coat—I remember well his distinctive face. I felt flattered when he asked me for a drawing; I wonder if his family still has it.

By then I had gotten to know more men in the company, and I had more than a nodding acquaintance with a few men of other companies. Several times, I ran into the H Company machine-gun crew I was with during the contact patrol near Orsholz and was once invited to eat with them around the corner in their commandeered house. They had a letter from that guy who got the million-dollar wound. Unexpected infection had prolonged his hospital stay. The general tone of the writing seemed to hint that he had engineered the infection himself, and his old gun crew apparently admired and envied this.

G Company had some rambunctious parties. The one I remember most happened the night of 18 February during this reserve. The standout was a guy in the weapons platoon who not only resembled Jerry Colonna (the motion picture comic), but also had the crazy eyes and big black mustache to go with it. He had picked up a top hat somewhere and was the life of the party. The hat must have been collapsible and storable, because he appeared under it at other times. Alcohol often turned up from hiding places used by German citizens who had been evacuated from the combat zone.

Well before dawn of 19 February, we were awakened by the thunder of division artillery announcing foreboding events. Fifteen thousand rounds were fired at the ridge, towns, and road intersections beyond. A battalion of tank destroyers, the 778th, moved up the ridge in general support. The 376th jumped off on the left, moving through Sinz and Banholz Woods—which had been won and painfully lost several times before—while the 301st moved from the center. The 302d's 1st and 3d Battalions jumped off from Campholz Woods on the right.

I hoped our mortars already had taken out the German machine guns and minefield we located on the recon. The mine that blew away Blanchard's legs revealed precisely the gun's area. Having sketched in landmarks, roads, and other features, I easily made a map for Captain Griffin after the patrol. I hoped the map and report went through channels and worked its way into division artillery's fire plan, as well as to the unit moving through that area. Several times during those months, my maps were used along with many others by patrols up and down the line.

The entire ten-mile front was extensively patrolled in the two nights before the push. One patrol from the 376th moved behind the German lines to the town of Munzingen itself, discovering enemy tanks there and returning with the information.

Some of us headed for attics to see the action, but the growing light revealed little of the ridge because of smoke and mist. Occasionally, the wind carried the sound of small arms over that distance. Overall was heard the constant roar of shelling. Later in the afternoon, the smoke thinned and we could see more. Many vehicles were moving up the ridge. Dan's field glasses enabled us to spot figures against the skyline that had to be GIs because they were mixed in with American vehicles. Other men crowded around us begging for the binoculars.

Shouts from below alerted us to hot chow and also the news that we would move out within the hour. Although my colorful underwear was still damp from laundering, I quickly dressed to let body heat dry it. After dark on 19 February, we moved beyond Eft to the same east-west road we had traversed several times. We passed through Borg, and with considerable traffic, headed northeast toward Oberleuken. We moved past the burned-out German tanks and half-tracks that we had spotted with Lieutenant Castor's listening post out here in the dark fields to the right.

Blanchard's mutilated, once-handsome body lay off somewhere to the left. I doubted that they had gotten around to recovery of the dead yet. They likely would start the next day—there must have been a big increase in casualties this day. We wondered where we were going and how far the division had broken through.

We moved beyond Oberleuken and began the exhausting trek up the south face of Munzingen Ridge. A lot of activity was going on: signal corps laying wire, engineers working, MPs directing traffic. Many small fires burned along the ridge, and a few big ones. More ambulances moved down the ridge than did other vehicles.

We got a rest break on top of the ridge—fell out on the side of the road near a pile of wreckage that in the dark seemed to have been an 88mm cannon. We left the road numerous times to wind around bulldozers filling in holes or stalled traffic. Little, if any, shelling occurred as we moved through the night and found ourselves moving into the town of Keblingen. We stumbled over dark ruins and shell-blown rubble. Fire glowed down side streets and crackled like small-arms fire. With some stop and go, wait and move, we eventually rested in some relatively intact houses. Guard duty went to the new men as G Company fell asleep to the occasional sound of small-arms fire in the distance.

The next morning, 20 February, we were on our way early, having eaten cold rations because our kitchen jeep had not worked through to us. Our 2d Battalion spread out for miles, company after company following the 3d Battalion. The 3d was to assault the town of Weiten some three miles from Keblingen. Our 2d Battalion was then diverted along a farm track to the southeast, and 3d Battalion, 301st, followed us. These two battalions heading for Orsholz were called Task Force Gaddis. G Company was in the van. The point man spotted three horse-drawn wagons and quickly got the drop on the Germans—bagging about twenty prisoners.

We were held up a while. Ahead I could see a solid roadblock composed of logs across the road. Later, another fifteen to twenty German prisoners trudged past us to the rear. So far this day, I heard no small-arms fire. The town lay just beyond the roadblock. We were pulled off to the left, and some sort of coordinated attack eventually began that afternoon. We encountered a minefield and worked through it carefully. Gaining the outskirts of Orsholz, we began clearing the buildings.

Officers seemed in a great hurry, and we were pushed hard. When in doubt, we grenaded and fired at windows and doors and took some casualties when we encountered snipers. We began collecting prisoners, most of whom showed little fight. By late afternoon, we had cleared the town. Tanks of the 10th Armored Division joined us late. Setting up a perimeter for the night, most of us found decent rest again.

Falling asleep wrapped in my field gray German blanket, I reflected on my first patrol a mile or so west of here. Tense as it was, in retrospect, it was merely routine—returning safely with prisoners. At that time, Orsholz was out of sight beyond the woods and the name carried the stigma of being the town where the 1st Battalion, 301st, had suffered the loss of most of their men. The two companies were virtually destroyed and many of their wounded froze to death. Some tried to break out, and more men were lost.

Long afterward, those men who became prisoners of the 11th Panzer told their story of what took place. Some details emerged during the following summer of 1945. As they were repatriated and sent to the States, some of them wrote to buddies in the 301st stationed in Czechoslovakia, describing what they had gone through in the woods and following their capture. They had to march hundreds of miles under guard with almost no food. They ate snails and dug in fields for roots. They were subjected to strafing from our fighter planes. From the pilot's point of view, everything moving on the roads looked like a target. On occasion, pilots recognized and avoided strafing our POWs.

During my first reunion, in 1997, I met some of those men and succeeded in opening up a couple of them. It was during these conversations that I learned the deep value of these reunions. Of all the fine friendships I had formed over the years since my military service, none had ever reached the closeness that we dogfaces achieved. We had been part of something that took us to the limits of what men can stand, and in surviving, we came to understand and trust each other as no outsider could.

One former POW of the 301st confessed to me that, after repatriation, he left the army and just bottled up his emotions and memories. For generations, he lived with a sense of shame because he had allowed himself to be captured and felt he let his battalion down. Then, a few years ago, he finally decided to attend his first reunion. He finally achieved considerable peace of mind by completely letting go when talking with members of his regiment. He discovered that their point of view had always been that they themselves failed because they did not break through to relieve their trapped buddies. They too lived with guilt, although each concerned had given his all.

The next day (21 February), after clearing Orsholz we split into patrols to search the entire area. It was slow work because of so many mined areas. Many Schü mines sat aboveground, revealed by the melting snow. Some blended into the mud, taking on the same coloration. Bouncing Bettys were the worst, having been buried with only their wire tentacles aboveground. Some had their trip wires strung from the mines to trees. Snow was still plentiful within the shadows of the pine forests.

Engineers were scattered about toting boxes of explosives to destroy the pillboxes and bunkers. Day after day, dreadfully heavy thuds often sounded from near and far as the men went about their work: Many weeks ago they had learned to blow these boxes the moment they captured them, because at times the enemy had counterattacked to reoccupy them and had to be pushed out again.

It was becoming clear that the German army was using delaying tactics to move all they could to the east of the Saar River. Those units that ran into strongpoints encountered scattered heavy fighting. But for much of the division, it was a matter of clearing out snipers, flanking machine-gun teams, and eliminating 88s throughout the woods and towns west of the river.

The 94th had finally bellied up to the Saar. The German army, as usual, skillfully withdrew across the river. Three days earlier on 19 February, when the division swept over Munzingen Ridge, 611 wounded passed through the clearing station. Next day, the number was 344. Then on 21 February, 173 were wounded. That is 1,128 good men out of the line—some to return later—some, burned or limbs gone, doomed to go sight unseen in veterans' hospitals for the rest of their lives. This list does not include deaths. The division history provides the total combat death figure, but usually does not give a casualty count for the particular incidents and battles.

After clearing the Orsholz area, our 2d Battalion hit the road east through the woods and fields. We picked our way through the shattered remains of a German convoy. The debris of their unit was scattered in every direction: smashed wagons, trucks, and dead horses lying in harness—bloated and stinking. Live horses stood trembling in the trees with their heads down, not noticing us passing through. Some men tore through baggage until called back in line in case of booby traps. Many dead men lay along the road and in the woods. We passed several 105mm artillery pieces and burned-out vehicles. We did not see shell holes, so I assumed the column had been strafed by P-47s or artillery airbursts. Any plane firing eight .50-caliber machine guns would create a devastating event for the other side.

Platoons tended to hang out together socially as a unit. But as casualties mounted and replacements came in, men from one squad or another platoon would be shifted around to bring experience where needed. Then old friendships crossed over all the squads. Friendship was an interesting problem with the natural tendency for men to reach out and bond with each other. But, by then, so many of the original company that had trained together for years in the States had become casualties that some "old" men became aloof or standoffish—to get too close and then lose a buddy would create more pain for a lifetime. Yet, the pain could not be avoided—men came to depend on one another, and certainly their performance in the field demonstrated most accurately just whom you would want next to you when the bullets would be flying.

Over the months, we had no difficulty identifying those men we could not trust. A squad had to have teamwork, especially during the majority of time when the normal twelve-man squad was reduced to only four to eight men. Whether in a defensive position, a patrol, or an attack, each man knew who was to support and back him up. One man almost always ran away under artillery fire. Another could not stomach machine-gun fire and either refused to leave his hole or took off. Yet, when we were cut off by the 6th SS Mountain Division later on in Schomerich, he volunteered to take a jeep and trailer through the German lines. He miraculously returned with a trailer-load of vital ammo and rations, with several new holes in the jeep. This guy we protected. The other, because of his totally selfish attitude that put us in harm's way, was court-martialed and, I believe, spent years in Leavenworth prison.

Then there was a replacement who had great night vision. At first, I thought he was inventing things he claimed to see in the dark because I too had great vision. But I soon discovered we both had 20/20 daylight vision, yet he alone spotted nighttime German combat patrols sneaking around our perimeter when I saw nothing. I did not trust him, however, because he was constantly nervously talking at night on the line and mainly because he feared raising his head above ground level. He had been paired with me, just as I was paired with Dan when I joined G Company. When I became aware of his unusual vision, I kept those night eyes in my two-man hole. Problem was I had to remain awake all night because he could not be trusted to do his two hours on, two hours off fairly. The worst part of this was my having to body-punch him so often to force his head up where he could scan the area around us. I used snarling threats when the punches wouldn't work, threats I knew I would not follow up on, and probably could not, anyway—he outweighed me by twenty or thirty pounds. There were a few others who could not or would not pull their share of the load.

I had heard it said that a platoon guide's primary purpose was to keep a bayonet fixed to his rifle and follow close behind his attacking platoon to keep everyone in line, and the guide should be ready to probe any man's bottom if he'd appear to falter in his duty. I certainly do recall Bill Roberts as platoon guide when he followed us one early morning. We were suddenly caught by machine-gun fire in the open and were taking casualties as we went to ground. Roberts found himself alone in the rear and sufficiently elevated on the landscape to have a clear shot at the machine gun. He pinned the German soldiers down, and we were able to crawl close enough to grenade the crew into surrender. Roberts saved those of us who survived.

Normally, only a minority of men of all ranks displayed aggressive initiative in the attack. And I have found since the war that the ratio of minority brave to majority timid remains roughly the same in most human activity where guts and commitment are called for. I went through inspiring moments—both in war and in peace—when I shared in the experience of an entire group so riled up that they surpassed their normal capacity for courage.

Once again, I feel the hair on the back of my head stand up as I recall those times I heard the spontaneous roar of hundreds of men around me while we moved toward Sinz. No one having had this experience could ever forget the powerful lift and sense of indestructibility felt as that battle cry burst from their throats. The memory of this spontaneous cry always puzzled me. It almost seems as though humankind carries this unique sound stored in their collective genes only to be given voice when war times' passions cause it to rise to the surface. Courage, like fear, is contagious, and at times, the timid can be transformed into lions. Sometimes this psychological lift was accompanied by a strong feeling of wild joy in the very face of hot lead and steel shrieking through the ranks.

I must add the unifying effect this battle cry had on our troops. It gave a clear message of arrogance to any entrenched enemy within hearing distance. The Germans sometimes also did this, and I suppose the Russians and Japanese did so, too. It is something warriors in extreme acts have always done. Men do it in bar fights sometimes, and come to think of it, so do women.

Another factor in the battle-cry phenomenon relates to the barroom fight: When available, the Germans filled their canteens with schnapps or brandy before their attack. This helped ward off the cold and created a more daring and aggressive storm trooper. The British had their tote of rum. Some GIs indulged when they scrounged a bottle or two.

Too often, those half-boozed German soldiers stood erect when they should have hit the dirt, or they kept to a straight run when they should have zigged or zagged. They made too many bottle-courage moves in the face of coolly directed small arms and shellfire. The smell of booze, blood, and eventually rot created a mixed miasma drifting together with the smoke and stink of burned powder.

Not having experienced alcohol up to that time, I never even thought to try it until after the war, and then I often drank too much of German bootlegger's potato schnapps. Some of the guys made a practice of snatching canteens from bodies, along with anything else of value. For a while, I was fascinated with the dead Germans' paybook I.D.s and personal photos I found. It became morbid—connecting pictures of families with the blasted flesh lying at my feet—so soon I stopped at finding a pistol or watch.

5

Saar River Crossing and the Second Siegfried Line

In the dark on 21 February, we trudged along the road toward Taben on the river. Traffic was heavy; we heard motors everywhere. We were constantly stopped by all types of vehicles jockeying for position, and some trucks were off-loading at supply dumps. The off-the-road activity—heard, but mostly unseen—was impressive. River crossings caused bottlenecks, and German artillery from east of the river continually searched the few roads that led to the crossing sites.

During various stops, we questioned anyone nearby who might add details of what was happening across the Saar. Several MPs were wrapped up inside sleeping bags and sitting in a jeep next to the road. I joined Sanders and some of the 1st Squad who were gathered there. From snatches of conversations, we learned that 1st Battalion, 302d, had passed through there the night before.

C Company had crossed the river first, right before dawn on 22 February, in thick fog. They surprised the enemy and cleared several pillboxes, killing and capturing a good number of the soldiers. Farther on, a signal corps wire team told us the river was high with melting snow and a seven-mile-per-hour current running to the north. The three regiments had their own crossing sites, each one roughly two and one-half miles from the other.

We did not hear much news about the other regiments yet. But in this sector, the twelve-man assault boats had arrived

98

an hour or so late. C Company pretty much exhausted itself, carrying the thousand-pound craft down the hill next to Taben and to the right of the blown bridge. The following troops of the battalion got a break, however, with a decision made to quietly roll the big boat-carrying semis (motors switched off) down the long hill. Then the infantry could offload their assault craft and more easily and quickly haul them to the river.

They would need all the energy they had to paddle, climb the cliff, and fight. A few boats loaded with mortars and ammo capsized in the strong current: These men had little or no experience paddling boats. Some men drowned. Others were swept downriver some distance and, upon landing, had to cut through barbed wire, negotiate mine-fields, and then work their way up the foggy river through enemy positions to rejoin their units. On the way, several firefights broke out when they ran into German OPs and bunkers.

So, as far as I could determine, the 1st Battalion was across and clearing out the pillboxes and bunkers. Word filtered down the line that our 3d Battalion, 302d, was crossing at the present time—and our turn would come next.

Outgoing artillery missions often roared and fluttered high overhead going east, and occasionally German shells hit the road to our front. We could see the flash of the bursting shell and figure the distance by the three to five seconds before the sound reached us. In our stop-and-go forward movement, we passed through that area. And from the sound of exploding shells farther east, we figured the boat-launching site was occasionally being peppered, too.

A big semitrailer slowly inched past with a cargo of twelve-man assault boats. The craft were so constructed that several were stacked one fitting inside the one below. In the dark, I could not count how many were compressed in this highly practical method.

As far as I could tell, G Company was not shelled on the road ahead. We moved along, stop-and-go, inching closer to a boat ride over a fast-moving and icy river—George Washington on the Delaware must have flashed through those minds that had a modicum of U.S. history in school.

Fog patches appeared and all shapes became ghostly. Ambulances and jeeps moving to the rear between the spread-out ranks of marching men simply showed up out of the gloom and disappeared again. Voices and machines sounded unnaturally loud in the fog and then less so as we passed through the mist to clear areas.

Finally, one could somehow sense the vast open and deep geographical void as we rounded a curve and left the trees behind. The night was halfway over and dark. Against the sky to the front was a massive shape, perhaps less than one-half mile away—a ridge or a hill. The road under our feet began dropping away and the air was even damper. Then I picked up the sound of water moving somewhere below. Yet, all lay hidden in fog with the ridge on the opposite bank rising far above the misty river bottom.

Any doubt about our guys being over there dissipated at once as tracers of different colors streamed through the night. No one could question the rapid rate of German machine-gun fire and the slower rate of our heavy .30-caliber's response. We descended into the fog, thick as a smoke screen. Eventually, we worked our way to the river's edge where the sound of moving water was loud, the air colder and especially damp.

If the winter temperatures were only mildly less cold than during January (when I had been sure I would freeze to death), my body and mind had gradually acclimated and resisted these conditions considerably better. And this was true of the diet, and often the lack of diet. My digestive system had fewer breakdowns that manifested in explosive bouts of diarrhea.

I still used the shoepacs—which showed considerable wear and tear—and left my combat boots in a foxhole before an extensive patrol from Campholz Woods many days earlier, along with extra bandoliers of M1 ammo. After that patrol, we returned to a different section of the line, and I never saw my boots again. The way my feet felt, I figured I would be walking on the outer edges of my soles and heels for the remainder of my human existence. The calluses in the center of both feet were deeper and quite painful if I put my foot down wrong. And, of course that happened about every ten steps, and more often when the ground was rough or uneven, which it usually was.

But I was becoming more stoic physically and mentally. I think I handled pain better than before. I experienced it vicariously as I saw men suffer from wounds. In the beginning, I empathetically took on the pain of others like a husband feeling his wife's birth pain. But I came to understand objectively that I was handling the pain of others and my own better. I suppose "mind over matter" expresses it best. Rather quickly, I learned to relegate most feelings of pain—physical and emotional—to a remote chamber of my mind. Over the years, though, I have found that memory is permanent and that all things repressed will be dealt with down the road. I figured the day of reckoning could be put off. I had enough stuff on a daily and nightly basis to contend with at the time.

It was 23 February, and these thoughts raced through my mind and were concluded with the realization that dawn was beginning to show through the fog. During the half hour or so I huddled in the water-filled shell holes near the riverbank, I felt the frustrated inner artist despair over being unable to view the battle site in the dense fog. This was my first (but not the last) river crossing.

We were not being shelled directly. The Germans mistakenly thought we were. But their shells hit upriver fifty or a hundred yards away. Without seeing them burst in the gloom, and with the confusion of sound in mist, it was a nerve-racking half hour. And we had not even seen the boats yet. One or two big shells screamed in to our left downriver, and then the word was passed to our group to move the last fifty or sixty yards to the river. We passed all sorts of equipment, rolls of coiled cable, and smoke pots for creating chemical smoke screens. I saw smashed boats from earlier shelling and machine gunnery.

Boats pulled into the riverbank, and men climbed in, placing weapons in the center. Everyone was facing forward and hoping to do well with unfamiliar canoe-type paddles—ten riflemen and two engineers to a boat. We clambered in ours as quietly as possible, followed by the engineers; they held the craft as steady as possible in the current, and riflemen helped so the boat would not be swept away. Other boats appeared out of the mist from downriver and were being man-handled with much effort by the engineers to bring them to the embarkation point.

It was obvious that once we had paddled from shore, we would have to point at a forty-five-degree angle upstream to land somewhat close to the opposite launching site. We had been informed that we would encounter a steep, angled stone wall with occasional ladders on the other side. I saw the boat that pushed off just before us turn completely around when caught in the current. Men on one side had paddled too hard without enough effort on the other side. I determined that rather than blindly dig in my paddle, I would watch our movement and work hard to compensate if necessary. Not far upriver, there was a heavy bang and swoosh as a gray plume of water shot vertically fifty feet or so into the air— the buzz of shrapnel and some secondary splashes. The momentary flash of light at the base of the watery columns was a thing of malevolent beauty. The column dissipated into a fine mist that coated us in brine. In sync, we moved the craft well by keeping the bow a little upstream.

The other side of the river emerged from the mist so quickly that we were unprepared. The river's width was only about seventy yards. We could do little as we crashed into the wall, tipping enough to half-fill the boat with cold water. The current took our half-swamped boat along the wall until a ladder appeared, and several men grabbed and held on for dear life. Securing soaked weapons, we took turns at the ladder. I was near the stern, with only an engineer behind me to steer. The other engineer had passed me to follow the men as they left the boat. His purpose was to hold the boat to the ladder. He was taking paddles from some of the men who, in their excitement, were about to take them ashore.

His hands were full as I reached for the ladder, the boat swinging away from the wall. One hand on the ladder, the other holding my rifle, I tried to jump the gap, but I plunged almost totally into the shockingly cold river. Like a shot, I was out of the water, fearing I would be a piece of ice within two seconds. Legs in the water, my eyes were level with the shoepacs of the man above me. We moved on up, and everyone lay there on flat ground a minute until the word came to move out. Surprisingly, although the water was ice cold, I did not feel nearly as bad as one would expect. Then, getting to my feet in one bound to follow along with the others, my body burst into a silvery explosion of tiny ice shards; in that short time, the water had frozen to my clothing.

Sloshing water in my shoepacs, I moved along with the others across a paved road and double railroad tracks to a large bunker sunk into the tracks, where the platoon reorganized. With 2d Platoon in the lead, Dan and I provided the point. We lost no time moving along the base of a cliff that faded into the mist above, and then we followed a trail and began ascending. The climb was an exhausting one—some four hundred feet to the top of Hocker Hill. Yet, it was the best thing that could have happened to me in my soaked condition. All the winter clothing I wore was saturated, but my body heat from the exertion of the climb helped me maintain a status quo between shaking flesh and acutely uncomfortable soaked clothes. It took two days for the clothes to change from alternately freezing and sodden to permanently damp. The immersion did, however, drown or freeze most of my fleas. We fought bugs as well as Germans. While moving along, I checked my blanket roll that contained the mortar shell tube with my drawings rolled inside. During my brief immersion, it had bobbed on the water's surface, and the artwork remained dry.

As we climbed the trail, I kept visual distance from the rear of the company ahead of us. More and more, we were emerging from fog that continued to blanket the earth below. Dawn was turning to day. Intermittent rifle fire from small arms and mortar fire echoed from hill to hill. Sniper fire occasionally popped and cracked. Carrying parties, too exhausted to lift their heads, passed us going down—empty backboards in place. Several litter-carrying parties slowly lurched past with their wounded wrapped in blankets. Enemy prisoners carefully carried many of these burdens, temporary work on their way to POW cages. I guess I, too, would be supercareful if, in their place, I were carrying German wounded, lest I were to stumble and dump my end of the stretcher and get shot.

Single shots popped a few hundred yards ahead. When I saw the rear guard of the company to our front stop and squat, I held up my arm and Dan passed the signal back. Like everyone else, I dropped my body against the rocky cliff to rest as much as possible. After a minute or so, our platoon leader and his runner climbed up to me, wondering why we had stopped. His walkie-talkie crackled, and he spoke into it. We were joined by the platoon sergeant and platoon guide; we learned that the company in front was to move farther up the trail and that our platoon was to form combat patrols to search the cliff area for snipers. Sergeant Manly would lead one and McKay the other. Our party included McKay, Sanders, Salazar, Dan, and me.

We proceeded up the trail a ways to a couple of riflemen sitting next to a large rock. They pointed out where they thought the snipers might be. Then they moved up the trail to rejoin their company. They bent over from cover to cover because this area was where casualties from sniper fire had occurred. I saw a dead GI on the trail nearby. I hated snipers.

We spread out and chose concealment where we could use all eyes in the hunt. Manly, it was said, was an especially good rifle shot. Weeks later, I would often discover him heading out on his own to snipe at the enemy—I came to realize that he enjoyed killing them.

But in this moment, he was warning us that snipers often used scopes, so we needed to expose only our eyes from solid cover and ample concealment with twigs and weeds. Once in position, we made no movements. It was a sobering thought, believe me, that a rifleman a hundred or so yards away—familiar with the trail and the terrain features of trees and rock—searched this area with his rifle-mounted optics.

I chose a cleft choked with weeds and dry leaves, between two stones, and I removed my helmet. The knit cap had no shine, and the helmet did have some where the netting had broken. The area we searched visually was composed of craggy boulders and scrub with sudden drop-offs and a maze of possible paths. I assumed if I were a sniper choosing the best location to kill from, this part of the trail would be open enough. So I spotted three or four places at a higher elevation that appeared likely to both hide and protect the sniper. I saw no movement, nor did anyone else. The German was canny. Manly decided to play decoy to draw fire while the rest of us would try to spot a muzzle flash. Bent over, the sergeant moved down the trail a ways and then moved up the trail as though just arriving from below. The sniper would catch only brief glimpses of him on the lower rocky path.

I held my breath, heart thumping, as Manly passed behind me and approached the open area. He had guts to pull this off. Manly was of sturdy build and an inch shorter than my five feet eleven inches. I was sorely tempted to turn my gaze away and see what the sergeant was about to do. I didn't, and the loud pop and ricochet of a rifle bullet interspersed with the discharge echoed back and forth briefly. I had seen nothing and turned to see Manly crawl unhurt to McKay. Instantly, McKay, who had German binoculars, exclaimed, "I see him!" He directed everyone's eyes to a group of rocks higher than the area I had been straining my eyes on. The lieutenant, runner, and platoon sergeant moved cautiously up to us and we conferred. We decided that Manly would take his four men farther up and move toward the sniper at about the same level. He would move slowly, giving McKay and us time to take the trail higher and get above the sniper. Then the company would continue moving up to the top of Hocker Hill with a man stationed here to caution men to crawl past this point. This would serve two purposes: Most important was moving the rest of the battalion past this bottleneck and into the line on Hocker Hill. Also, their movement past this point should keep the sniper or snipers' attention focused on this part of the trail while our patrols moved closer.

McKay moved us up the trail short of the top, with Manly's squad filing off the trail and disappearing in the broken ground. Then we followed McKay, angling into the brush some fifty feet above Manly. We were on a parallel track to encircle the sniper's nest. I crawled close behind McKay—Dan and his BAR right behind Sanders and me, and Salazar bringing up the rear. While we had more than ample concealment, the same held true for any enemy in the area. Although McKay had spotted one, a whole platoon could be a hidden in these rocks.

We moved along on our bellies four or five yards and stopped to listen. There was the smell of decay. McKay angled toward a mass of foliage and stone that looked like it might be a nest, but it was not. Inside, both McKay and I could rise up and study the entire area for more than a minute. A rifle shot echoed from fairly close by—we flinched. We moved out of the other end of the shrub and almost immediately found ourselves inside a mortar position littered with smashed boxes, unfired shells, and several untidy bundles of field gray and mottled black flesh.

McKay wiggled on through the mess with me behind. The mortar appeared to be an 81mm similar to ours. The bad smell of sweet rot turned my stomach. I glanced back at Dan as he took in the scene. As I caught up to McKay, he craned his neck between rocks and checked below. He crawled on about another fifty feet, took a look, and motioned me closer; then he signaled Dan to move up.

Whispering, he said there was a German beneath us and another to the left. He would drop a grenade on the left and I should do the same below me. Pull the pin and hold, locate your target, arm the grenade, hold a second or two, and drop it. Dan and the others were to protect our rear and flanks in case other enemy soldiers were nearby.

He moved off a ways and pulled a grenade. We pulled pins and leaned over. The moment I saw the German fifteen feet below, I let go of the handle. The pop of the cap starting the four-second fuse startled the man below. Then I tossed it and drew back. After the twin detonations, I checked below to see the man, a mass of blood and smoke with his arm outstretched and handless. He had caught the grenade as it went off. His face, or where it should have been, was red pulp and indescribable. I backed away from this sight.

Someone shouted "Grenade!" and a sizzling object bounced off a rock nearby with a loud bang and a buzz of fragments. Dan's BAR fired at something up the hill. I saw sparks from his bullets hitting stone and bouncing. But only grenades could get behind these rocks. We were in a scary place. I put my best effort in launching my second grenade to immediately behind the rocks Dan was spraying. But McKay also had heaved a grenade to the same area. After the explosions, a wounded German reared up shouting *"Kamerad!"* After a second or two, Salazar fired his M1, and I saw the bullet's impact on the German's upper body drive him back and out of sight.

After the initial shock at Salazar's action, I realized he was in the right because of the situation we were in. Later, when I learned that a grenade fragment had cut Salazar's neck and removed his dog tags, I could even better understand his reaction. We hated snipers. I would lose my dog tags in a similar way several weeks later.

We fanned out and began to comb the cliffs. McKay had clued Manly in on what was happening, so he combed the area below us but turned up nothing. Climbing to the top of the hill, we reported to our platoon leader. He told us the lead company was held up ahead, and we could hear the sound of machine-gun fire and grenade explosions in the distance.

Taking advantage of the local inactivity, we dropped our gear and then ourselves beside the trail to soak in the rare sunlight; yet, the air remained cold. I was thoroughly uncomfortable in my sodden uniform. But after a while, I unrolled my blanket and wrapped myself in it. I found my artwork dry, and although my pencils had become soaked in my pockets, I did attempt sketches of the men sleeping and eating around me—I was shaking too badly and gave up the attempt.

One of the men from another squad had given me a pad of good bond paper he had looted from a farmhouse. I had pulled the white sheets off the cardboard backing and rolled the good stuff in with my finished and unfinished work in the tube; I had saved the cardboard backing and stashed it with the decorative metal plate I used for hot meals, to support the drawing surface when I had a chance to draw. By this time, it was sodden pulp as I pulled the pieces from inside my field jacket and tossed them away.

I took in the panorama of infantrymen—and every kind of weapon we employed—for hundreds of yards along the trail. The rare bursts of sunlight cast warmth of tone over the men and equipment. I was particularly struck by this new light, which picked up shapes and flickered highlights on metal helmets and mortar tubes. It was so unlike the stark black and gray I had become conditioned to over the winter. The familiar shapes and form of cold gray were transformed into dirty brown. After having been transported from our prewar world of peace and color to one of endless stress and pain cloaked in the most sinister tones of black and gray, it was unsettling and most strange to be so moved by this tiny transformation—from winter gray to winter brown. As I had grown to young manhood in a world of intense color before shipping out to the ETO, I felt sadness and anguish that I was so moved by this tiny shift from one to two in a scale of one to a civilized ten.

I got to my feet and walked a short distance off the trail where I could see the river and gray and brown countryside finally emerging from the fog. I could not see our crossing site from here; and the other crossing sites at Ayl and Staadt were out of sight beyond the bends and hills of the river valley. The hills opposite were lower than Hocker Hill, where I stood. Lifting my eyes and looking west, I could only imagine the distant shapes that might be Munzingen Ridge with Wochern just beyond, but certainly out of sight beyond the ridge. Tettingen, Campholz Woods, Monkey Wrench Woods, Sinz, and Orsholz—I let the memories begin to flood my consciousness, and then Dan was next to me pushing McKay's binoculars into my hands. We took turns picking up the faraway movement of military traffic on the roads winding over and between the hills and town of the triangle.

I do not recall our saying much. Other men along the way were taking in the view—each individual with a reel of memories indelibly stamped with his unique perception of what he had seen and felt in these weeks. Two especially young lieutenants in relatively clean uniforms stood not far away talking and looking at the river. I wondered what their jobs were.

I remembered feeling a sudden need to ask Dan to rescue my drawings in case I would get hit. I already had my parents' address printed inside and outside the tube. But before I could speak, a long volley of machine-gun fire, heavier than earlier, sent lead popping and ricocheting through our area. The ground we were standing on was higher than the trail, so everyone dived for the lowest ground available.

Orders were shouted, far and near, to dig in, although the stony earth had frustrated our earlier efforts. But my first action was to roll the artwork into the tube and then unsheathe my entrenching tool to again scoop up the earth, which was almost a physical impossibility because of the rock outcroppings everywhere. As the soft whirring sound of incoming mortars announced possible death and injury, we frantically dug. Explosions blasted up and down the trail area, and our respite in sunlight was over as the frantic cries of "Medic!" replaced the quiet introspection of only seconds before. Steel fragments and stone chips buzzed over and around us. Then I remembered a place that appeared to be out of this fire. I shouted to Dan, McKay, and the rest of the squad to follow me. Their white faces and wide-open eyes showed naked fear and the mute question, Follow you where? I threw the tube into the blanket and grabbed my shovel and rifle, but changed my mind as more automatic fire sent scattered bullets everywhere.

In between bursts, I shouted, "Let's go!" and took off dashing to our lookout point. I literally dived over the side of the hill to shelter between small boulders. There were other men crouching nearby, including more men of the platoon. Then McKay and Sanders, followed by Dan and others, came flying to join us. I do not believe a single shell struck this area all day. I do know we all dug as deep as we could, and when rock prevented us from digging deeper, we groped for stones to build up walls between hot fragments and us.

All day, walking wounded and litter-bearers struggled along the descending trail toward the river crossing. Ahead, the trail intersected the ridge road the 1st Battalion had used the morning of their landing to move down to Serrig and meet up with the 301st. Serrig was a town on the river a couple of miles north in the 301st area. But elements of the 11th Panzer, our old adversary—rested and replenished—had entered the battle and taken up positions above the cliff to the immediate right of the road. Also, hundreds of yards ahead, they were well dug in with their machine guns and mortars perfectly sited to control the road that, on the left, dropped almost straight down.

As the F Company point man moved through the area, machine guns raked their ranks, and they fell back. Each time they tried to push past this narrow point, concussion grenades were dropped from the heights above. Because of a wire mesh fence along the cliff side of the road, the grenades bounced back onto the road. These grenades could be deadly, but not as lethal as potato mashers like the one thrown at us earlier when Salazar got his neck cut. The wound was not bad and was well bandaged by Sanders and later cleaned by Fred Buckner, the medic.

I recognized the sound of one of our heavy .30-caliber machine guns, and flashed on the guys I knew in H Company's heavy weapons. Word filtered down to us about the nature of the bottleneck F Company was facing down the trail. H Company had rushed a couple of heavy machine-gun squads up the road to try and pin down the German machine gunners to allow F Company to move its riflemen through the bottleneck. But despite their best efforts, the battalion was stopped there.

So this bottleneck was completely holding up the 2d Battalion. The 1st Platoon wanted to send a patrol over the high ground to the right after dark. By dark, every man had constructed a private fortress of rock and whatever could be used to offer a degree of protection. But then we were organized into a defensive perimeter to the right of the trail to guard against a night attack from that direction. Our position on the hill and cliff was tenuous at best. If we were overwhelmed, we had precious little to fall back on with a cliff to our immediate rear and the river below.

More firing came from the bottleneck. German tracers flew overhead as we did our best to dig in. Dan and I were assigned outpost duty and unrolled phone wire out about one hundred yards, where we connected our liberated German phone (it worked better than ours) and then quietly dug a hole. We had to be alert to our patrol's reentry: One of the most difficult moments for a returning patrol is the act of being challenged and exchanging the password. Men in the forward holes, and especially those in isolated outposts, were itchy on the trigger finger. The 11th Panzer had enough English-speaking men in their ranks that they could lay out close to an American position and try to overhear the password from a returning patrol or, more likely, a relief party coming up from the MLR. So, it was important to know how many patrols were due out and in. Any extra group coming in from the dark was due for a blasting.

The 301st was slated to cross the Saar at Staadt at 0400 on 22 February (two and one-half miles north of Taben), while the 376th was to cross at Ayl (four miles farther north of Staadt). The 376th was to expand its bridgehead far enough to push German artillery back and to allow a treadway bridge to be constructed, enabling tanks to cross into the bridgehead. Then the 376th and 10th Armored would coordinate as a combat team in a drive on Trier, eight miles north where the Saar and Moselle joined. In a matter of days, the combat team—much to Hitler's disbelief and anger—would take Trier. This ancient city was the southern anchor of the German breakthrough.

The fog at Ayl was as thick as experienced upriver at

Taben. Colonel Harold H. McLune, CO of the 376th, got his two assault battalions in position on the riverbank to await the arrival of the assault boats. Several calls by McLune to 10th Armored Division Headquarters assured him the boats would arrive in time. Jump-off time was 0400, and the boats failed to show. The men waited in these exposed positions on the riverbank until well after daylight without the means to cross. Before the fog began showing signs of lifting, McLune ordered the engineers to bring up smoke generators to screen the crossing site when the fog lifted. However, as the fog began lifting late morning, he ordered the troops back one mile to Ayl, where they dispersed throughout buildings.

Just before noon, a small number of assault craft arrived— not nearly enough to successfully transport a regiment and its supply until a bridge could be put in place. During the afternoon, Gen. George S. Patton, Third Army Commander, arrived at 10th Armored Headquarters, upset that the Ayl crossing had not begun. Phone lines suddenly buzzed throughout the area, and at 1625 Colonel McLune was ordered to "cross at once!" Those three words sent hundreds of riflemen out in daylight, an hour or so before dark and fog could screen them from the enemy.

Engineers started up the smoke generators, and a mild breeze carried thick, white smoke across the passage. The leading rifle companies streamed forward to the river while the enemy began harassing the area with artillery, mortars, and searching fire from automatic weapons. Up until then, the smoke denied the Germans observation. However, the intense fire from the automatic weapons found more and more of the riflemen, engineers, and smoke generators. One by one, the generators were put out of action and the smoke soon drifted away with the breeze.

German observers from the opposite bank and the hills above could then register weapons, bringing heavy and accurate artillery, mortar, and machine-gun fire directly on the American positions. The lead companies of the two assaulting battalions were especially deluged with this rain of hot steel and lead. Casualties mounted terribly in mere minutes—company officers and many men were killed and wounded almost immediately. It is a pity that Patton, who so loved this sort of war, was not on the riverbank to share the excitement of the action he had initiated.

As even more enemy guns zeroed in and the volume of fire increased, the gates of hell truly were opened, giving the men a clear and absolute view. One look at this carnage convinced Colonel McLune to order the survivors back to Ayl. More casualties occurred as engineers left their foxholes in desperate attempts to restart the smoke generators. Most smoke makers were riddled with holes and rendered useless. The small number of boats were completely destroyed where they sat near the water, and the crossing operation was stopped as darkness and fog began to set in.

The incredibly brave medics and litter-bearers distinguished themselves once again, as they moved through the twilight. They separated the shattered and smoking dead bodies from those soon to die and those to be patched together and carried from this place. The voices of men calling out were lost in the mist and broken earth.

Back in Ayl, the 10th Armored Headquarters called McLune and asked him how soon he could resume crossing activities. The colonel replied, "One hour after I receive sufficient boats."

Anyone can understand the terrible disadvantage of a river crossing that faces such hilly terrain in daylight. Yet, hours earlier the 302d had succeeded a few miles south only because of the fog and dark. Until their dying day, when two or more veterans of the 94th Infantry Division gather, they will continue to ask each other, "When 'Ole Blood and Guts' said 'Cross at once!' why couldn't he have said instead, 'Cross just after dark'?—a difference of a couple of hours."

It is true that the longer we waited to cross, the more enemy reinforcements could move up to our front. However, this former eighteen-year-old private first class now seventy-five years old and piecing together this ancient chain of events, never was a decision-making general. But what happened at Ayl and Staadt—coupled with other incidents and decisions that Patton made throughout our war—provided further evidence of unnecessary casualties. To be fair, though, evidence also seems to indicate that at other times his tactics tended to minimize casualties.

At 2130 hours on 22 February, the second boat shipment arrived at Ayl. Fog again cut observation to almost zero, and things looked good for the crossing operation to continue. The boats were unloaded and half went to each assaulting battalion.

As jump-off time neared, the reorganized assaulting units once again moved from Ayl along the open plain one-half mile to the river. The company most hurt in the earlier attempt to cross was L Company, which was replaced with I Company of the 3d Battalion. C Company led 1st Battalion to the crossing site east of town, while 3d Battalion positioned itself on the river just northeast to the left of 1st Battalion.

With the men and boats in place, the soldiers crouched there silently, undoubtedly thinking about the hell of only hours before. The stench of cordite permeated the area. The ground, torn by shellfire, caused more than one ankle to cave, especially hauling one-thousand-pound assault boats over that terrain. Sound carried well in fog, and with slung rifle butts occasionally thumping into plywood boats, no doubt German listening posts, less than a hundred yards away, were clued in to American intentions.

Men of opposing culture and belief on both sides of the stream passed mutual moments of relative quiet and listened to the rumble of battle miles to the south. There the 1st Battalion, 302d, having achieved their bridgehead early the morning before, were clearing out bunkers and pillboxes along the river road. Meanwhile, the bulk of their companies kept abreast of them hundreds of feet higher on the ridges and hills. At Staadt, in between the 376th and 302d crossings, the 301st also was late getting men to the other side and preparing to assault Serrig, a town on the east riverbank. German automatic fire and shelling could not be directed accurately at what they could not see. Casualties occurred, but without the fog they would have been much worse.

On the east bank, the Americans watched the muzzle flashes up ahead in the fog and timed their rushes between machine-gun bursts. Keeping contact with squads on the left and right was tough in the low visibility, as the riflemen systematically reduced bunkers and pillboxes.

Colonel McLune headed for the river in his jeep to cross to the east bank with his radioman and driver, but a heavy mortar barrage forced them to the ditch for cover. McLune was hit in both legs and then another fragment caught him in the chest. His executive officer took over the 376th while McLune was evacuated. It was 1st Battalion's turn to move from Ayl and cross at the southern site.

B Company managed to cross over on 23 February; but then, incoming fire gradually eliminated all the remaining boats at the southern crossing site. And Company A was being hit hard by shellfire while waiting its turn to head for the boats.

The amount of shellfire causing casualties, coupled with the lack of boats, resulted in 1st Battalion moving to the north launching site, arriving at about 0500 hours. Guided by flashlights that the enemy could not see in the fog, available boats pulled in to transport A Company to the east bank.

Meanwhile, 2d Battalion on the east side advanced to the town of Ockfen and drove the Germans out. A strong counterattack of sixteen tanks and infantry began blasting the town to rubble, however, and 2d Battalion—being without armor—withdrew to a hill to the north of town to organize a new attack. A coordinated attack of 2d Battalion and artillery drove the German tanks and infantry out of Ockfen once again. All three battalions of the 376th were then across and gradually expanding their bridgehead. Soon the gutsy engineers would get the vehicle-carrying treadway bridge in place. The 10th Armored tanks crossed and, with the 376th Regiment, swung north not only to seize the important city of Trier on the 2d of March, but also to capture a bridge intact over the Moselle—no small task. The Moselle and Saar Rivers joined just north of Ayl.

Meanwhile, at the Staadt crossing site, the 3d Battalion, 301st, discovered that plans for crossing the river at 0400 hours had hit a snag. At 0500 hours, they heard the sound of a motor convoy approaching Kastel, where the battalion waited for the boats to arrive. The truck convoy turned out to be a 302d Battalion motor train, however—it had taken the wrong road for Taben. A monumental traffic jam in narrow cobblestone streets required each vehicle to back around and head in the direction from which it had come. As daylight slowly approached, the troops' nervousness and exasperation grew. Then the situation was further complicated by the late arrival of the engineer's boat convoy trying to snake around the 302d trucks. One of the boat trailers overturned in the ditch trying to squeeze past.

It was 0615 hours on 21 February by the time the troops were on the road following the boat convoy a mile to the Staadt crossing site. Companies I and K were supposed to cross side by side, but the loss of boats on the overturned trailer caused a shortage of the craft. It was decided to cross one company at a time, I Company first. However, in carrying their boats the last few yards to the river, the enemy was alerted and machine-gun fire began knocking plywood from the boats as the men hit the dirt.

As the firing trailed off, the men reached the river and began crossing while divisional artillery began prearranged fire across the river. Heavy weapons from Companies H and M's 81mm mortars added their support. Their heavy machine guns had been set up along the road paralleling the river, and they employed overhead fire, their tracers streaming over the heads of the men paddling their assault craft. Firing blindly into the fog, they hoped to keep the enemy down until the riflemen could paddle their way over the stream and gain a foothold on the other bank.

Before 0800 hours, I Company was across. The men had to regroup after the strong current scattered the boats along the river edge. Groping through the fog, they encountered two extensive entanglements of barbed wire at the riverbank; and despite heavy machine-gun fire and the ever present danger of mines, they used wire cutters and got through. Bangalore torpedoes had been brought along, but could not be employed because the wire was too close to the river, endangering the riflemen. As the riflemen forced the entanglements and obstacles, the engineer boatmen headed back to Staadt to pick up the second wave. The current was too swift for the undermanned boats, though, and a number were swept downriver in the fog. Machine guns were heard, and these boats were never seen again.

The small boat-size groups of men isolated in the heavy fog moved north and south along the riverbank. Many sharp firefights suddenly erupted as they surprised enemy outposts and machine-gun bunkers. These squads slowly joined forces with the rest of their company.

Captain Donovan of Company I and about fifteen men discovered a minefield and marked it with toilet paper, which stood out better in the gloom than engineers' tape. Then they pushed into the first houses in the town of Serrig. For the most part, the GIs held what they had, as the German defenders began calling in reinforcements.

Across the river in Staadt, the boat situation had become serious. Of sixteen boats employed in the first wave, only six returned. Worse, they were short of paddles. Many had been carried ashore by the troops inexperienced in boat handling. Urgently, Captain Horner of the 319th Engineers sent a detail to salvage what they could from the overturned trailer up in Kastel. He further requested outboard motors and boats to speed up the operation. These were then hurried to Staadt.

The Germans could not see the foggy crossing site at Staadt; nonetheless, they consistently used automatic fire, spraying lead throughout the area. Meanwhile, German snipers bypassed the day before in the woods of the west bank began harassing the steep road between Kastel and Staadt. An L Company patrol, sent to eliminate them, did so.

Around 0930 hours, German artillery and mortar fire began landing on Staadt as the sun began clearing out the fog.

German observation and accuracy improved considerably. The fire increased, and more men and boats were hit. Company B, 81st Chemical Mortar Battalion, dropped white phosphorus shells across the river to somewhat screen the American activity from German eyes. Smoke pots were brought forward and ignited.

Enemy shellfire increased to a barrage, and Company K had insufficient boats left to cross the entire company in one wave. At 1140 hours, Capt. Bill Warren, K Company CO, put his 1st and 3d rifle platoons in the remaining boats, and they pushed off for the east side. They had instructions to find Captain Donovan at the blown bridge site. At that time, a terrific artillery concentration sank two of the boats, and fragments punctured several others, inflicting casualties. The outboard motors arrived at noon, when only one of the original assault boats remained in one piece.

The storm boats and their twenty-two-horsepower motors were hastily assembled—a complicated task because the motors had never been serviced. The noise of outboard motors brought more fire from across the river. Engineer casualties were so heavy that inexperienced men had to operate the new boats. Meanwhile, more assault boats arrived. Obviously, if more infantry would fail to cross and consolidate the small gains on the east side, the enemy would have the opportunity to push them back into the river.

By 1455 hours, Capt. Bill Warren, embarked the remainder of his platoons and crossed over. Lieutenant Colonel William A. McNulty, CO of 3d Battalion, his executive officer, radio operators, and runners crossed with Captain Warren. Joining Captain Donovan, they approached the few buildings taken in Serrig with sufficient rifle strength to begin pushing the enemy from the town. But to begin eliminating machine guns that controlled the streets, Lieutenant Colonel McNulty decided to lift the smokescreen. This was done—giving the infantrymen their first good look at the defenses of the main Siegfried line, the second fortress line of the Siegfried they faced. The word was passed down the ranks; and K Company, 301st Regiment, began moving against the houses, barns, and disguised pillboxes. They discovered that many of the forts were constructed to resemble houses: The battle-tested GIs learned to duck when they heard the creak of metal, which usually meant rusty steel doors were opening in these "houses" to allow machine gunners to fire.

Unfortunately, as the smokescreen lifted as requested, the Germans again had excellent observation of the crossing site. Machine guns and a 20mm gun on high ground east of Serrig ripped away at the men, boats, and vehicles around the crossing site. Artillery and mortars added to the hell, as all boat activity again shut down.

Once more, night and fog would prove the least dangerous way to build up our forces on the east side. Fortunately, while the 301st spent the day in dozens of isolated firefights and began corralling a large number of prisoners, the 302d was closing in from the hills to the southeast of Serrig.

Companies A and B, 302d, moved from their bridgehead across from Taben's launching site and climbed around the four-hundred-foot cliff to Hocker Hill. Then, pushing their way north over the hills, they descended toward Serrig from the east, completing a pincers movement composed of 3d Battalion, 301st, from Serrig, and 1st Battalion, 302d, from Hocker Hill. As the 302d troops were descending the hill, about one hundred German troops were spotted in the valley, marching on Serrig. Accurate fire was employed, and it virtually destroyed this German column that probably was a group of reinforcements arriving to help contain the bridgehead at Serrig.

Despite the fog, artificial smoke, and night, the Germans by then had registered their artillery and mortar fire so accurately that it was even more deadly than the automatic fire had been. As dawn of the second day, 23 February, approached, the 2d Battalion, 301st, and the 319th Engineers removed their dead and wounded and had no recourse but to continue moving men and supplies across the river any way they could devise.

Company C, 319th Engineers, replaced the decimated

Company A, and somehow they managed to stretch a rope across the river. The first boatload of men who tried pulling themselves over to the east side proved too much for this method, however. The weight of the boat and men, plus the heavy current, broke the rope—and the paddling, exhausting as it was, continued. Colonel Roy N. Hagerty, CO of the 301st Regiment, ordered the immediate deployment of faster storm boats and their outboard motors. The situation was so serious—and the pressure from higher echelons equally heavy—that Colonel Hagerty decided to take the casualties that the loud sound of the motors would bring. Certainly the casualties resulting from the slower method of paddling currently underway necessitated trying something different.

The storm boats moved the first two platoons of Company G across the river before the enemy reacted. But then the shelling resumed with an intensity that made the prior day's concentrations seem light. Throughout the remaining hours of darkness and early morning, 2d Battalion and the engineers suffered extremely heavy losses, and crossing operations again came to a standstill.

Lieutenant Colonel Francis H. Dohs, CO of 2d Battalion, came forward to personally supervise the operation. Men of his battalion rushed to the boats; and as they pushed off into the stream, a tremendous concentration of shellfire hit the launching site. Men and boats were blown into the air. In minutes, the extremely heavy casualties and loss of all the boats once again completely shut down crossing operations.

Lieutenant Colonel Dohs was killed instantly as a shell burst next to him. Captain Sinclair of F Company was hit and died soon after. Captain Flannigan, Battalion S-3 (operations officer), was knocked out by a concussion and had to be evacuated. On the beach, many dead, wounded, and dying riflemen and engineers lay next to men not yet hit. The pounding finally slowed to harassing fire, as the medics and those still able to walk moved to the injured.

Approximately two hundred seventy-five assault boats

were used in the entire operation. At the end of several days, twenty-seven were still in operation.

Major Brumley, S-3 of 2d Battalion, took over after the loss of Lieutenant Colonel Dohs. As he arrived in Staadt, he learned that a few additional boats had been obtained. About midday, a boat safely crossed to the 3d Battalion with a cargo of desperately needed batteries for radios, flashlights, and bazookas, as well as much-needed medical supplies and blankets.

With the successful crossing of this boat, Major Brumley decided to attempt the crossing of the rest of the 2d Battalion, 301st Regiment. But before this attempt began, orders arrived to move the remnants of the battalion back to Freudenburg, some two and one-half miles west. It was to become division reserve. Leaving Staadt, the men were shelled on the hilly road to Kastel. Sometime later, the 2d Battalion would cross at Taben whose cliffs on the east bank had given adequate protection during the 302d's crossing.

By dark of the second day, for the most part incoming fire had stopped at the abandoned crossing site. German artillery was focusing on other targets, and the 301st used this area to resupply their forces across the river during the time of dark and fog. They used motorboats—only the one boat of medical supplies, mentioned earlier, had made it across previously. Liaison planes had dropped ammo, and the soldiers had found food on German bodies and fairly ample supplies located in pillboxes and houses. By 1930 hours, all wounded were evacuated from the east side; resupply was then moving across steadily.

Early on 24 February, the third day, Capt. Bill Warren's K Company moved down the hill from Schloss Saarfels. This beautiful castle surrounded by vineyards had fifty thousand bottles of champagne in its cellars. Some of K Company's men spotted German soldiers at an opening in the hillside. After attacking, they discovered this was the rear entrance to the area's fire-direction center for the entire Serrig area. Fifty-four men and three officers were taken from the pillbox—which helped greatly to take much of the heat off the advancing American rifle companies.

On the morning of the second day, 23 February, our 2d Battalion, 302d, was struggling up the trails of Hocker Hill; and the 1st and 2d Battalions of the 301st (having given up the Staadt crossing site) were closing in on our Taben site— a much safer trip over. The cliffs looming near the water's edge were steep enough that the Germans could not easily direct shellfire at the crossing site. They had to content themselves with shelling the roads leading to it and the town of Taben itself.

Company B, 301st Regiment, temporarily put aside their rifles to help the engineers construct a footbridge near the boat crossing, and by 1730 hours, it was completed. Men could cross with dry feet.

Because the 1st Battalion, 301st, was in the 302d's sector, they were attached to our regiment and proceeded up Hocker Hill to relieve the 3d Battalion, 302d, after dark. This same evening, the 5th Ranger Battalion that was holding the west bank of the Saar to our south was relieved by the 3d Battalion, 101st Regiment, of the 26th Division. The Rangers crossed the footbridge in the dark and climbed the heights to Hocker Hill where they were to begin an interesting mission: They were to pass through our 302d lines and head a little east of north on a ten-degree compass bearing. Moving through the enemies' rear some three miles, they were to establish a roadblock on an important road complex. They were to impede German troop movement there until relieved by the 94th advance. (Incidentally, the 26th was our sister division from Massachusetts, our home state.)

During the entire crossing operation, American artillery was seriously hampered by the intricate and broken pattern of the American advance through such hilly terrain. The U.S. artillery spotters with frontline units would be receiving incoming fire and request counterbattery fire, which had to be refused because another American unit was moving around the enemy rear where the shells inadvertently might fall. Often, the German batteries would fire a mission or two and then move before counterbattery fire could be brought over effectively. In the first days of the bridgehead, the American batteries were placed in the hills well to the west of the Saar. The line rifle companies depended heavily on their 60mm and 81mm mortars for support. So, for some days, the Germans had the advantage of medium and heavy artillery on call at all times. American liaison planes, used as artillery spotters, began locating and helping to eliminate the German batteries as the days went by.

The truckloads of American dead going west carried the mute evidence of shrapnel-riddled and burned bodies. German small-arms fire did its part, but much less than their shellfire did. Some drowned soldiers of the regiments were carried miles past Trier and toward the North Sea. I cannot help but think that the heavy loads of ammo and equipment put many on the river's bottom where they remain today: I found no monument to them on the riverbank in April 1997; if there be none erected, then let these words stand in recognition of what they were willing to do and what they gave.

Those remnants of Companies F and G of 2d Battalion, 301st, were re-formed into one company under Captain Steiner, and for the rest of the operation in the hills, it was known as Captain Steiner's Company. It did not have close to two hundred men as a full-strength rifle company had—at best, it was closer to seventy. When sufficient replacements could be brought in, the designation of Captain Steiner's Company would revert to the conventional army TO (table of organization), F and G Companies, 301st Regiment. They would split up and form the veteran nucleus of companies rising from the ashes.

6

Fighting in the Hills

We finished digging the outpost, which was slow work due to the presence of stones that had to be silently found and removed in such an exposed place. I crouched in the fetal position at my end of the outpost, unable to move because Dan was on his knees pressing against my legs—jammed into his end of the hole. We learned to dig deep holes with the smallest possible opening to lessen the chance of unwanted hardware zipping in. Better to have discomfort than separation of body parts.

But I did as little moving as possible anyway since my bath in the river: I shook with the wet and cold of the February night wind on top of this hill, and what was becoming an added threat was chafing in my crotch and rear end caused by wet clothes. It had begun just below the crotch (from one leg rubbing the other as I walked), and the abrasion was spreading to my shoulders under the harness strap. The cartridge belt—with eighty rounds of M1 ammo, shovel, bayonet, canteen, and first-aid pouch—caused even more chafing on my hips. All I could really do was grit my teeth until we were relieved. But the way things turned out, no relief came until dawn of 24 February.

The night dragged on. Boredom set in, and my lively imagination suggested crafty movements that were not really there—a shape of a man would be resolved into a tree or rock as dawn slowly approached. I determined not to check the luminous dial of my self-winding watch. I played a variety of mental time games during nights. Like this, for instance: I would check the time and not allow another check until I mentally estimated one hour had passed. Then a glance at the watch showed how close or far off I was. And when this game became stale, I had others about as exciting as my high school algebra was. But the most creative mental exercise of all was visualizing how to draw on paper something of my perceptions of war.

I toyed with the unlikely idea that I had found a "home in the army." This thought followed my realization that I no longer subtracted the hours between Stateside and the ETO. I used to picture family and friends back in Teaneck carrying on normal lives at the same moment I was trying to deal with my current situation. At this point, it was pretty much a matter of getting through all the dramatic left hooks and low blows coming at us on a daily and nightly basis. Home life became more difficult to remember and picture in my mind's eye; those memories were fading into the abstract. War destroyed more than flesh and cities—it eroded sweet memory in still functioning flesh.

I could see the direction this was taking me but I could not see the destination, and that was scary. I didn't think Manly, Salazar, or Langley had arrived there either, but the killing virus certainly had infected them. The faces of German prisoners fascinated me, especially those of the 11th Panzer. Other than their youngest and oldest replacements, it was easy to peer into the tormented ravines under the eyes and see the winters of mud and snow lived through at the Russian front. My God, what they had seen and done while many of us still were in school. All the same, I felt no sympathy for them and experienced considerable satisfaction in helping reduce their ranks. Dan seemed to use his weapon in a disciplined way—holding up his rate of fire when the enemy displayed tendencies to surrender.

I remembered a story I had once heard my father relate to my mother that put something of a human face on our "traditional enemy, the Germans." Henri Carstens was an infantryman in the German trenches during World War I. After the armistice, he became a chemist and, along with his wife, emigrated to the United States. He found a position in my father's office at the Edgewater, New Jersey, plant of Archer Daniels Midland Company. Over the years, the Carstens and their son became good friends of ours. When Henri discovered that my father's division had been opposite his own unit during that war, an Armistice Day would not pass without Henri coming into my father's office and shedding tears. His son was serving in the U.S. Army somewhere.

Sometime before midnight, we became aware of movement to our front. Our own patrol had returned an hour before, so we were reasonably sure Germans were sneaking around. They went to ground some fifty or sixty feet away, and the occasional low sounds soldiers cause let us know they remained there. After a long time passed, we decided they were probably goofing off. We passed the night with weapons in hand, hardly daring to breathe. Earlier when the familiar whispered "pish, pish" (an almost-silent sound to alert the man on the other end of the phone line) was heard on our open line, Dan had pulled his blanket over his head and the phone. He whispered as briefly as possible our situation, and it was decided to hold up our relief. Even though the men relieving us would arrive directly at our hole by following the phone wire, their movement might well complicate things. We had no idea whether we had two or two hundred of the enemy out there.

If a large force were out there awaiting the signal to attack, our job was to warn the foxhole line one hundred yards to the rear and then try to run out to the platoon ahead of the attackers—a doubtful effort. In a couple of weeks, we would lose an outpost of four men in a similar situation of infiltrating SS troopers.

I prayed they would just fade into the night and not be there with the first morning light. The usual mist slowly thickened and drifted through the broken trees around us. Toward dawn, drops of moisture began dripping from the branches, making little plopping sounds on the ground. Periods of time passed so quietly I began to hope whatever had been out there finally slipped away. The light of dawn arrives later in foggy conditions; and when it did, we heard men stirring about. A figure rose from the mist—a dark silhouette stood there. Then we heard the sound of urine splattering while several other figures rose from the mist adjusting equipment and exchanging comments in muted tones.

For our part, we readjusted our position, released safeties, and tried to control wildly beating hearts. I recall muscles cramping from tension and inactivity. Then the BAR, pumping out rounds, suddenly shattered the stillness. I had my M1 sights on the urinating soldier and felt the rifle kick my shoulder. Aside from one fleeting figure off to the right, the rest of the Germans dropped into the mist. There was no mistaking the impact of my round on the enemy soldier who was blown down while relieving himself. Dan pulled himself to his feet to fire a long burst into the ground-clinging mist, dropped his weapon, and grabbed a grenade from our dirt shelf. Pulling the pin, he froze a moment and looked at me as though asking for my concurrence. He tossed it, and I followed with another before his detonated. Ducking low to avoid fragments, I saw Dan shoving in a full magazine. The initial screams from wounded men degenerated to moans, and then we had to consider pleas of supplication, which we ignored as Dan spoke into the phone to confirm that we remained with the living. He dropped the phone into its black leather case and said our relief would be showing up in a few minutes.

I was calming down, but the moaning and crying was working on me. Wounded men sometimes were perfectly capable of pulling a trigger, and neither of us had any intention of moving through the fog bent on rescue. Two guys from the 3d Squad showed up, and we pointed out where the Germans were. We were exhausted stumbling back to the MLR, where the squads obviously were busy getting their equipment together. We were moving out—there would be no rest. I had had only snatches of sleep in days. Reequipped with rations and grenades, our company jumped off as soon as we had enough light to move with some precision and coordination.

We moved forward and somewhat to the right—I suppose to outflank the bottleneck. We picked up the two 3d Squad men who had relieved us, encountering little resistance as we swept the area and moved beyond the bottleneck hidden from view on our left.

The company maneuvered its way somewhat to the left to clear a ridge protruding down from the hill. Machine-gun and rifle fire caught us in the open and cut down several men before we could find any cover. The enemy, as usual, had chosen their ground well. We could not continue our attack, nor could we move against the machine guns—we could not even locate them. I, at least, never spotted any smoke or muzzle flash. It was Salazar and I who had to crawl to a wounded man and drag him to a less-exposed place. Blasts of machine-gun fire harassed us continuously with several near misses.

After some minutes of fruitless firing and ducking, we got the word to start moving back. This we did, dragging our wounded with us. Then we had to contend with mortar shells. Out of practical range of the machine guns, we were ordered to dig in. The 2d Platoon formed a perimeter to the right of the company, facing an orchard and vineyard that gently sloped down to our front. We were designated as support of the battalion's right flank. The platoon to our left was digging in close enough to us, but out of sight, and this caused a serious communication breakdown before daylight that I believe was no one's fault.

The wounded were evacuated, and we passed the day staying out of sight and digging deeper. Meanwhile, my chafing problems had become so serious that I experienced pain with every movement. I was afraid that if I were evacuated, I would miss out on important action that would leave a big hole in the continuity of my pictorial history. I feared I would be stuck in a "repple depple" (replacement depot) and placed in a different unit. By then, my feelings of comradeship and G Company identity had become more important than my family relationship. The closeness, trust, and loyalty that had grown among Dan, McKay, Salazar, and me—all of us really—seemed increasingly more real to me than my Stateside memory.

There were men who could not be trusted, who complained about everything. Yet, the fact that so many were enduring day after miserable day of horrendous conditions led me to understand the few who broke or ran away. Over time I was less judgmental and more understanding of those few who cracked or ran. I had learned there was an extremely thin line between staying or running, and between complaining or keeping your mouth shut.

I doubt whether one in three men survived those months with normal health. Most everyone had colds and often mild-to-serious diarrhea. Men unable to control the noise of coughing or sneezing could not be used for outpost or patrol work. Most diarrhea symptoms, while energy robbing, would not get a man out of the line; only severe cases would be sent to the rear. Severe colds were sent back. And, of course, trench foot and frozen limbs accounted for most of the men evacuated, although most of them returned.

Fred Buckner, our platoon medic, arranged my raincoat and German rain cape to cover me in my foxhole so he could rearrange my clothing and get some of his miracle Vaseline rubbed into my raw skin. In a few days, I improved considerably.

I cannot recall a day or night without rain or drizzle. Living in mud and holes, we constantly had to bail water. My wet clothes progressed to damp dry, and my icy dip in the Saar River finally was behind me. Although the late February cold was less than what we had in January, the temperatures were still plenty cold; March and April remained cold, although less so. Some days in late March encouraged me to believe spring was possible.

Some of the sketches I did never found their way into the protective mortar tube—too wet and muddy. One was a sketch of a rifleman I had seen, and I decided it was the most successful I did—no background, just the figure holding his

M1 and bayonet at the ready. I liked the action, but even more, I liked the way the nine-pound weight of the weapon was expressed in how it affected the man's holding it. The paper became soaking wet after I ducked lower in my hole in reaction to a series of mortar shells that hit close by. Rainwater had collected in my rain cape, running down to my lap and, of course, the sketch. I was dismayed and thoroughly pissed off. I could not put this into the mortar tube without disastrous results to the other work. And it would never dry in the rain. The solution was to get the Coleman squad stove into my hole, pump pressure into the tank, and light it. In twenty minutes, the sketch dried, although it never looked the same. After the war in Czechoslovakia, I copied it the best I could onto a small canvas, and I painted it in oil—I still have that painting. By the way, the Coleman squad stove, a single burner, was truly a great addition to our equipment. Fill its tank with gas bummed from a five-gallon Jerry can and that thing would burn with a blue flame—you could heat a ration or a cup of Nescafé or a helmet of melted snow to clean up a little. We were supergrateful to Mr. Coleman, rest his soul.

About this time, replacements arrived—one was a new second lieutenant for our platoon. A couple of our veteran men returned from the hospital. I think one was Rupp, who became one of my favorite buddies. Second lieutenants rarely survived long, which reminded me of a long succession of dogs in my younger years. Due to being hit by a bus, blindness, or being killed by a large dog, they never stayed around long. Usually, they were around just long enough to establish closeness. And so it was with our junior officers.

We lost the most recent one and also our platoon sergeant before dawn. The usual miserable night of lousy weather, bitching men, mortar fire, and German patrols probing all along the lines resulted in no sleep. I recognized I was not the only one whose shaking from the cold apparently had begun to be something more sinister. I noticed that the shaking in my hands was more than the cold; it had a nervous sort of vibration. I felt, too, a tic on the side of my mouth that came and went. The cuticles around my fingernails were stripped to the point of bleeding—loose skin would drive me nuts if I did not remove my gloves and pull it off. And, if I had an itch to scratch on an eyebrow, I felt compelled to apply like pressure to the other eyebrow; this principle seemed to apply to any part of my body that needed a scratch—because although its matching member did not request like treatment, I gave it anyway. My state reminded me of when I was six years old and walking to school with my sister one day: She instructed me to avoid stepping on the cracks in the sidewalk. Not only did I take her advice to heart, trusting some esoteric knowledge that sisters five years older had, but I found it was hard to quit forty years later. The same was true with the neurotic need to strip off loose hangnails.

I discussed my nervous problem with other guys, and we compared our tics and twitches. The only comfort I received was the knowledge I was not alone in this. A good night's sleep in a warm place would delay—but not stop—the inevitable decay of the nervous system known as battle fatigue. When the syndrome spread to an area somewhere behind the eyes and you gazed at the man next to you as though he were across a field, you had the thousand-yard stare. At that point, rest off the line was mandatory, although not necessarily granted. I felt I had to work through my nerves and was confident that if so many dogfaces on the lines had kept their heads since D day, a recent arrival like me could do the same. I accepted that my sense of invulnerability was severely shaken. I had seen men I considered more able and intelligent than I suddenly blown away, and these experiences eventually altered my thinking. For a time, I considered my drawing ability, and the need to create a pictorial record of what I saw, as a sort of mystical passport toward survival. I realized this wishful thinking was but a veneer—a mask over my fears. Later, a series of light wounds had me considering whether *(a)* fate was gradually twisting the screw deeper and deeper toward oblivion, or *(b)* the hot metal, in only grazing me, was like an official stamping of my passport guaranteeing my survival trip was ongoing.

A lot of activity went on during that night, especially to our left and out in front. I was gratified to hear tanks—ours—way off in the distance. Sometime later, we would learn that the 10th Armored Division, crossing at Taben and moving along the river road to Serrig, put several tanks on the upper road to help squeeze out the bottleneck: Those were the tanks I heard. Apparently, the Germans in the bottleneck heard the same thing and, rather than be caught between our F and G Companies and the armor and infantry approaching their road, slipped away in the dark and fog.

Next morning, 25 February, G and F Companies moved to the bottleneck—F on the road and G on the heights above. But G inadvertently left our second platoon, the 2d Battalion's right-flank guard, behind and isolated in no-man's-land. I like to think our new platoon leader and sergeant, who crawled to G Company CP, were returning with Captain Griffin's order to move forward on the company right. Unfortunately, I never saw them again; both were hit as they returned. In all the smoke and confusion that followed, I never learned whether they had been killed, or wounded and later captured. Our squad leaders were in charge again.

Not long after, the enemy discovered our isolation before we did and moved to cut off our escape. German commands were heard, along with their movement to our left rear. Shouted warnings and rifle fire from the left focused attention there. Potato mashers flew in from where our neighboring platoon had been the day before. Explosions and exclamations of pain followed. I saw Fred Buckner dash from his hole to make his way to the wounded. Men of the 3d Squad were shouting and responding with grenades. My squad on the right of the line was too far to lob grenades. We could see figures moving through the vineyard and trees, heading toward our rear; and McKay had our squad of six men quickly follow him to the rear, shouting to the platoon to fall back. Machine pistols fired at us, their bullets whistling past. We fired awkwardly to our right while running, which was a waste of ammo. Most of us then kneeled and sent aimed fire at the fleeting figures, but mostly at the tangled web of bare-vine foliage. Then came the snap and crackle of heavy machine-gun fire from the east. Bullets snapped past with the unmistakable thud of a bullet in flesh and a lone grunt. Fired on from two sides, we hit the dirt hard. McKay had us crawling toward any available cover. The whole area was rock outcropping like the riverside of Hocker Hill. I wiggled past the dead man—a replacement—to the rocks. McKay, gasping for air, called for covering fire so the rest of the platoon could continue moving to the rear—between us and the German infiltration in the vineyard. I expended several clips of ammo into the tangled foliage some fifty yards away. We continued receiving automatic fire, but less of it. The ground fell away to the rear and was much too open in the direction we had been heading. Our best bet was the vineyard the enemy soldiers occupied because it led to the cliff where we had started out the day before.

Shouts went back and forth between McKay, Langley, and Manly. They agreed we had to break through the vineyard. The situation was absolutely critical, as minutes separated us from capture and worse. The squads of Manly and Langley crawled and crouched their way to the underbrush from where burp-gun and machine-pistol fire was whistling and ricocheting around us. We continued saturating the vineyard, as our guys readied to move into the brush. This sustained rifle and BAR fire was some of the most concentrated I had experienced and helped control my borderline panic. My hearing quickly dropped to zero again. Nevertheless, fear again transformed into that exhilaration unknown to me before combat. The firepower of the semiautomatic rifle and the BAR was awesome. Although I focused on keeping my aimed fire low to not overshoot Germans in the prone position, I saw the array of American grenades tossed into the vineyard. And, as the explosions tossed smoke and debris in all directions, McKay had us up and dashing to the vineyard to the left of the other squads, while they also went into the vines and trees.

I carried with me a conviction that I would die here before I would drop my weapon and put my arms up. The thought of surrender was more chilling to me than death. All that mattered was the intent to cause the most horror and pain possible to Germans in the last seconds before my lights went out. I think we all felt the same. I could not pull the trigger of that red-hot rifle fast enough; pausing to shove in a fresh clip, I burned my gloveless right hand in the process. And then we were skirmishers in among the bare vines, and I was aware of dead and wounded men in field gray. Without ever a thought of self-control, I fired into every German I saw, wounded or not. A shape rose directly in my path—a face white with terror, gasping words that I could not or chose not to hear or understand. No adjectives can describe the alien pleasure of driving my rifle butt into that hated face under that hated helmet. Then on the ground, that face crumbled under repeated beatings of my rifle butt. I was aware of being on the edge of a red-black void that replaced my sight for a second of time. It was not the only time in my life that extreme anger literally caused me to see that dirty red.

I moved on jerkily like a figure made of wood. We reached the edge of the vineyard and paused there. Squad leaders shouted words I could not hear. Scattered foxholes beckoned like open arms receiving us out of the small-arms fire flickering through the brush. Events were happening much too fast to fall into any order yet, and my only thought was to satisfy a thirst so deep I was choking from it.

I lay alone in a hole with a bloody empty rifle and pulled my canteen to my mouth. Little water remained but I had just enough sense to leave a little. My throat and lungs were so hot and dry that the cold water burned going down. I was only calm enough to rise up and look around while reloading by rote. I called Dan's name, but if he replied, I could not hear him. I saw Roberts and Siegel still unhit. I remember that oily gray smoke drifted around us then, cutting down visibility. Tracers or shelling had started a fire somewhere upwind. It encouraged me to think we could use the smoke to help conceal us while searching for our lines. But, somewhere out there in the smoke, Germans shouted commands so loud and insistent even I could hear them. Then a hail of small-arms fire again grew in volume. I pulled my head and rifle down, however nothing was hitting close to me. I took a quick look several times before seeing misty forms moving in the smoke.

I shouted, "They're coming!" I guess the sound of my voice gave me away. Muzzle flashes emerged from a burp gun, and bullets threw up dirt. A figure moved toward me in the gloom as a hissing potato masher dropped to the earth no more than four feet to the right. If I dropped down in the hole to avoid the blast, the burp gun could have me for breakfast. I inclined my head for the helmet to absorb the fragments, but a shock of concussion and a loss of feeling in my right hand rendered me powerless to use my trigger finger. Without thinking, I reversed my hand around the rifle, and a useable thumb somehow worked the trigger several times. I saw the approaching storm trooper flung back into the smoke. Using my thumb, I fired at whatever seemed to move out there. I felt the concussion of my weapon, but again could hear nothing. I saw men's mouths move—tense faces turned in my direction, and because everyone was rising from the ground, I went with them. I realized I was deaf again. My right hand was sticky with blood, and it did not shock me to see my blood was black. I had a vicious ringing in my head. We moved through the smoke and passed bodies that may have been wounded, or may have been dead. I could not tell—or care—as my only thought was to move with whomever of my unit could still move. I slowly and painfully worked a clip of ammo into the open breech of my rifle. Later I could examine my shrapnel-broken finger and admire the dent in my helmet that further unraveled the netting. But that was sometime later when we found ourselves moving through the bottleneck area and through a group of GIs.

We found that our company had moved through here in the direction of Serrig many hours earlier. In fact, the company had never stopped—it advanced with the rest of 2d Battalion toward Serrig. And, in protecting the flank of the entire battalion, the orders to move with the company had died with our platoon leader and sergeant.

We collapsed on the ground and tried to figure out who was missing, as Buckner tended to our wounds. I remember one tall guy, a recent replacement, who Buckner used tweezers on to pull several wood splinters from deep in his face and throat. His rifle had been blown from his hands, and he was weaponless. Besides the men lost the day before—dead and wounded—we had lost three more in the last hour. I knew one was hit and died near me in the initial breakout move.

Sanders spoke loudly in my ear and showed me the fresh dent in my trusty helmet. Apparently, the same grenade had penetrated his deltoid muscle, but superficially. He carefully removed his jacket and sweater, and Buckner cut through the cloth around the wound, using the same tweezers to pull out the fragment. When my turn came, no fragment was discovered in my trigger finger, but there was a deep dent in my rifle next to the trigger guard. My finger was swollen to twice normal size and the bone was broken. A small fragment had entered the back of my hand. He treated it with sulfa powder and carefully put a loose bandage around it, but he allowed the other fingers their free movement. The finger felt exactly the same way as when a football hit and jammed it years earlier—painful. The medic suggested I use a splint when the swelling subsided: We never did that. It healed slowly, and I think the swelling acted as a splint. Today, it is normal although slightly larger in diameter than its counterpart on the other hand. Buckner cracked up in Schomerich a week or so later, and we received a replacement medic.

We bummed rations from some company's supply dump, and our weaponless giant picked up an M1 rifle as we helped ourselves to munitions. My hearing returned with full daylight and I suddenly picked up sounds of battle down the road. The road through the bottleneck led to Serrig down on the riverbank. The battalion had gone that way, but apparently the enemy had reoccupied a pillbox at the road junction. Again, they were kicked out, but a third strong German counterattack retook the fort.

Unable to walk that road to Serrig then because the enemy

controlled it again, we descended the trail we had climbed days before. We moved with heavy truck and tank traffic along the river highway to Serrig, where Captain Griffin was visibly overjoyed to see his lost platoon come striding down the road. We were installed in a house and instantly fell asleep—despite our aches and pains. I had never felt such complete exhaustion.

Our tough first sergeant with a Polish name awakened us unceremoniously before noon, and we were ordered to join the company, which was dug in on a hill east of Serrig, about a mile and a quarter distant. Hot food was still unavailable, so Dan offered to search out K rations, because I desperately needed time to use some of Dr. Buckner's magic body cream on my raw hips and crotch. We had managed a sock change and a quick wash at a well. My hand was washed, treated with sulfa powder again, and rebandaged. There was no way to get a glove on it, so Buckner cut the glove's trigger finger off at the knuckle and worked it onto my hand with the swollen white finger sticking out. I knew I would have to pull it off to manipulate ammo clips and the like.

An H Company ammunition-carrying party knew where G was dug in, and most all of us in 2d Platoon had to tote ammo and ration cases to the forward CP. Our 2d Platoon was made company reserve, and we dug in downslope from the foxhole line. But we had dug only one-half foot or so when we were ordered forward to follow the other platoons. They filtered through the woods and downhill to cross the open floor of the valley. Sporadic and inaccurate mortar fire sprouted here and there, doing no damage that I could see. Our three squads of eighteen or so men filtered out of the trees in three Indian files well to the rear. We crossed the open valley and began up the hill of field and woods.

Small-arms fire suddenly erupted from the trees to our front. A large force of German infantry came running down through the trees and fields directly at us—definitely a staggering sight to see. The hair on the back of my neck rose and the sensation fit well with that high excitement and sense of exhilaration tingling my nerve ends once again. Manly or

McKay, or both of them, shouted to fix bayonets. I had had the bayonet fixed at other times but never used it, although it did appear likely that a World War I style of hand-to-hand combat was about to break over and around us. The image of cold steel plunging into my gut was especially scary. The forward echelons of 1st and 3d Platoons were firing from standing and kneeling positions at the Germans. Their nearest group was no more than one hundred yards from our forward guys when the anticlimactic shriek of artillery shells began descending everywhere. The brief flash and instant eruption of black and gray smoke exploded powerfully around us. I knew from the sound of the arriving shells that G Company and the Germans were caught in an American barrage. Instantly, every soldier in that valley was hugging the ground as the buzz of fragments cut through the stink and smoke. A tree branch landed on my legs. I saw the German troopers break for the rear. The small-arms fire had completely stopped everywhere. The forward American line was doing its best to work to the rear with their own shellfire falling around them. Both attacks, the German spoiling attack and ours, were in retreat. Somewhere, artillery observers were adjusting the shelling to the slopes of the hill to our front where the Germans were retreating.

Our troops were reorganizing back into their alignment and again advanced onto the top of the ridge. We passed through men being cared for by the medics, and farther on passed German dead and wounded. I looked at them curiously, realizing how much we had been on the verge of some truly close-in fighting. I saw a German clutching his jackboot and rocking back and forth moaning. His severed lower leg protruded blackly from the boot. Another man lay just beyond; he removed his helmet to retrieve from it a rolled page of newsprint, from which he took out a pinch of tobacco that he put in a pipe. His hands were bloody and shaky, and his unfocused eyes stared through me. His bayonet-mounted Mauser rifle was stuck in the earth. I glanced back to see Fred Buckner kneel next to him. Some of the Germans, covered in mud and looking not unlike us, appeared unhurt and held their arms high in surrender.

Again we received some mortar fire that did not slow our progress as we angled left along the ridgetop. We followed a trail with flank guards and scouts out heading north. Short of the town of Irsch, we descended through woods to dig in along a stream. Our recent replacement, the exceptionally tall guy with a long jaw, was delegated to carry everyone's canteens to be filled at the stream.

I suppose it was because we had had the luxury of a few hours' sleep that morning under a roof that we were chosen to mount a prisoner patrol. Sergeant Enright became our platoon leader to replace the two we lost fewer than twenty-four hours before. So, Enright named Langley to lead the prisoner patrol, which would consist of five men. Langley wanted McKay, but Enright would not risk another squad leader. Sergeant Enright settled on the older, experienced Private First Class Cuzak; Remich, recently back from the hospital; Frenchy, a BAR man; and myself. No M1s were to be carried on this night patrol—we would travel light. Frenchy chose a Thompson gun, as did Langley; while Cuzak and Remich chose carbines. I borrowed a grease gun because of earlier experience with it. Moreover, I could switch magazines with my good left hand and easily handle the bolt and trigger despite my bandaged finger. I traded my cartridge belt for the magazine holders and strap, plus three double magazines reversed and taped together. With some difficulty, I removed the morphine syringe from my rifle butt and, because it appeared frozen, decided to keep it useable in my OD shirt pocket, where it would receive my body heat. We left our helmets and rifles in our holes and tried to relax until 2000 hours. We had no idea where the enemy lines were and had even less knowledge of the terrain we would be moving through.

Before dark, Langley told me that I would lead off as point man. We waded the stream to sneak a look around: From the trees and underbrush, we could see farm animals scattered here and there over the winter-bleak pastureland. A large ridge loomed in the background. And although we realized the Germans probably were not planting many mines these days, the fact that the animals were browsing with all four legs still in place indicated the general direction we would go. For the rest of the evening, I stayed alert to any thuds that might have been a mine set off by a cow.

The afternoon and evening were not quiet. All over the bridgehead, we heard continuous small-arms fire and shell-fire. On our left, our lines extended about two and one-half miles to the Saar. To the right, our lines wound through the valleys and hills maybe four or five miles to Hocker Hill, where we had been the night before. The sounds seemed to indicate constant attack and counterattack up and down the line. Small-arms fire broke out less after dark, and the sounds of shells took on the rhythm of harassing fire on resupply columns and interrupted the other guys' sleep as much as possible.

At 2000 hours, we moved out in single file with Langley behind me, followed by Cuzak, Remich, and Frenchy watching the rear. For the first couple hundred yards, I stopped several times to study the landscape we had crossed so we could find our way back. We passed several large animals just standing around here and there. I avoided any animal confrontation that might alarm them and alert enemy patrols.

The muddy ground was then rising and firmer as we traversed a road and went up to the base of the ridge. We squatted, and I conferred with Langley whether to head uphill or patrol along the lower ground. Langley whispered that we should stay off the ridge slope and move along the base to the right until we could set up a blocking position on a trail that a German patrol might use. Keeping quiet, I felt a static blocking position might result in nothing. Amid the stands of trees and underbrush followed by open areas, I chose any route offering the most concealment—often stopping to smell the air and listen with my recovering hearing. Langley knew of my on-again, off-again hearing dilemma and joined me in the shadows so we could combine our senses. We moved on.

The night was overcast and dark. We began getting more trees than open areas, and then found ourselves inside an incredibly dark forest of pines. Staying close, I passed the word back to step on the blackest places on the ground, which were velvetlike moss that grew in patches everywhere. Being careful where we placed our feet allowed almost total silence during movement.

We had been promised that no shellfire would hit the area of our patrol, unless necessary of course. If a large force of enemy were identified heading for our stream, I would expect them to be shelled, and I figured *the devil take the hindmost*. However, there was shelling about a quarter mile ahead of us. If we did not encounter Germans in the next hundred yards, I knew we would turn back.

I stumbled onto muddy wheel ruts; it seemed to be a track running from the road to a farm because I could smell manure. I made out the shape of buildings with the ridge mass just beyond. I backed out of the sucking mud, and Langley decided to check out the buildings. I retraced our steps to circle around and approach them from the rear.

Doing so, I saw no light at the house, and the outbuildings appeared deserted. The going was slow due to sucking sounds caused by the mud. The reverberations from two outbuildings were typical farm-animal noises, but we checked them anyway and then moved to the house, hugging the back wall. An upper and lower window and one door faced us. Although the windows were closed, I smelled food cooking, and a moment later I heard a woman's voice. Langley whispered to Frenchy to follow him into the house, and told me that if things went badly, I should move out and lead Cuzak and Remich back to our lines.

I had heard stories about Langley's sniping episodes and his obsession with killing Germans. He was a good and steady squad leader, but I worried he might barge in on a farm family with his itchy finger. Cuzak and Remich were spread out along the back wall. I was not sure Langley had heard the woman, so I diplomatically asked, "Did you hear a woman's voice?" I wanted Frenchy to be aware of this, too. Langley grunted affirmatively and tried the door. He shoved it open, and lamplight spilled out to the mud as he and Frenchy rushed in.

There was not a sound—no female screams or barking dog. I peeked in and saw a big German soldier frozen in place sitting at a table, his mouth hanging open. A middle-aged woman, looking as though she were seeing ghosts, was by the stove. Langley jerked his tommy gun up, and the man came to his feet. He was a captain. Frenchy moved around the table to a door to shake down the rest of the house.

The officer said in bad English that no other soldiers were there. Langley pointed to the man's sidearm and relieved him of a Luger and the extra nine-round magazine in the holster. Frenchy returned and got the officer to put on his overcoat and long-billed cap. The food smelled incredibly tempting, and I was hoping against hope we would share in it, but Langley was right to move us out of there immediately before the captain's men or a patrol showed up. We got our prisoner's hands tied behind his back and made sure he understood that his life was tied to his cooperation. Before leaving, I glanced at several frameless photographs on the wall.

We had been out almost two hours when we shut the door on the old woman and made tracks for our lines. The German was behind Langley, with Cuzak covering him with the carbine. Otherwise, the order of march was the same. I thought of the three photos on the kitchen wall. I had seen several like them in homes. Apparently, the German army had a policy of sending a photo of a dead soldier's grave to his family.

Without incident, we escorted the big officer to our lines and turned him over to Captain Griffin, who complimented us on the night's work. It was almost midnight when we stumbled into our respective holes. Dan was not there because he was out on a carrying party. But, as usual, he had done his housekeeping, and the bottom of the hole was cov-

ered with broken branches. Nonetheless, I had to bail out
inches of rainwater before settling down with a shelter half
and rain cape tented over me.

The drizzle had turned to sleet and was quietly slapping
the mud all around me. I had returned the unfired grease gun
and had my trusty M1 muzzle covered under my cape. I carried two German blankets (the same ones) plus a shelter half
around my tube of drawings. All of this I utilized the best
way I could.

Right as I settled in, I was scared out of my wits by something, or someone, splashing through the muck. Looking up,
I saw a large dog, a German shepherd, looking down at me. I
could make out a harness of some sort and decided this was
a German army guard dog gone astray—perhaps a deserter.
He made low whining sounds. I knew the animal was probably hungry, and I dug out some hardtack, which he took
from my hand without hesitation. Rising up, I whispered
some soothing sounds and petted his neck. Steam rose from
his body, and I could feel his warmth under the wet coat of
fur. I had no trouble coaxing the dog into my hole and arranging our bodies for mutual warmth under the shelter half.
No words can express how touched I was by his immediate
compliance. So, depending on men in nearby holes to take
turns on guard, I actually spent a cold February night of
sleet and drizzle completely warm and relatively dry. The
dog and I slept while the German officer probably sat in a
jeep under guard on his way to G-2 (intelligence) interrogation.

Dan showed up just before light of 26 February to discover
I was not alone. After the shock wore off, he made disparag-
ing remarks about what happens the moment he turns his
back. We rolled up my blankets and tube in the shelter half
and foraged for food to give the dog. The other men thought
we should keep the dog with us and take turns feeding and
sleeping with the animal. But the dog soon wandered off.

I never saw the dog again, but I thought of him often, because he had left a few live mementos with me—but I would
not have traded those itchy fleas and that one warm night of

canine company for anything. How many nights had he provided security and warmth for an 11th Panzer corporal ducking American artillery fire? Far from upbraiding me as an enemy, his universal sense of comradeship included anyone exuding positive vibrations.

7

Wounded

All of 26 February, we remained where we were. A variety of brief firefights broke out during the day up and down the line. But that evening I paid a heavy price for the first hot meal since the other side of the Saar River on 20 February.

We took turns carrying two or three sets of mess kits back up the hill to the road; a jeep had brought up large containers of hot food and coffee. I stood in a line of a few men moving toward the open containers where a mess sergeant was doling out the chow. The men would have the mess kits filled, snap on the top to preserve some warmth, and head back to the foxhole line—there, hungry men waited. I carried mess kits for both Dan and McKay.

Now, my own mess kit was in my pack in G Company storage, wherever that was. In place of my official GI mess kit, I carried an eight-inch circular tray made of silver. I had carried this since I liberated it from a house somewhere. Highly decorated with antique scrolls, it was about to receive another GI hot meal. The only place I could carry it was inside my sweater—the cartridge belt prevented it from slipping down. I planned to fill and close the two mess kits, pull my silver tray out, eat quickly, and then get back to the squad so McKay and Dan could eat.

The small-arms fire was distant, and no one paid real attention to it until we heard the sudden hissing sound of a tumbling—something that impacted so quickly there was no time for it to register on anyone's mind. I not only heard it, but also was the recipient of its impact, which drove me backward to the mud. My lungs ceased to function—I could not breathe. I realized I had been hit, as men around me began fumbling with my clothing and equipment. The wound was painfully hot, and I felt a sticky, wet substance there. Then I was pushed to a sitting position; and, gasping for breath, I slowly began to take in large, painful gulps of air. I recognized our aid man, Buckner, whose exclamation of surprise plunged my survival hopes to their lowest level. From between me and my cartridge belt, he pulled out a bent and broken bullet and held it in front of my eyes. When that failed to get his point across, he next held up my silver tray, and I finally got the point. Two inches from its edge was an oblong puncture.

Six or eight men must have been gathered around all talking at once about a million-dollar wound. Fred told me that my sternum—the tough cartilage holding the ribs together over the heart—stopped the bullet. The mess sergeant held up my bandolier for everyone to see. They responded with exclamations of "Holy shit!" and other similar expressions. It was a spent bullet that had tumbled end over end, passing over the man in front of me and then cutting into my bandolier—scattering rifle ammo and penetrating through my clothing, tray, and flesh. I looked down at my heaving chest to examine a pink jagged hole. As Buckner was cleaning the hole of blood, applying sulfa powder, and probing around before he taped a bandage in place, I could actually see the sternum, gray in color and unmovable under the shifting skin.

I was lifted up and placed on the jeep's passenger seat, and Buckner rearranged my clothing. He wrote something on a tag, which he fastened to my jacket. Someone put my rifle between my legs, and Buckner cleaned mud from the mess kits. I managed to gasp that they were for McKay and Dan. Buckner then filled them and headed down the hill. Someone brought me some food. After a few minutes, I dug out my spoon and slowly put the food where it would do the most good. That meal was the most significant of my young life. I shall never forget the celebration of taste sensation I experienced in the meal I came so close to missing.

The mess sergeant fastened the tops of the big food containers, climbed into the driver's seat, and started the engine. I slipped the mess kit into my jacket, dropped my feet to the ground, and tried my legs. I could stand almost erect—just short of renewed pain. I shouldered my M1, and finding it easier not to use my voice, I merely winked at him and nodded in the direction he had to go.

The mist was rising from below the hill, and the day had almost faded as I made my way back toward the trees. I flashed on the telegram my folks would not receive. I left the road and the movement of men along it and carefully picked my way down through the trees. Breathing was painful as I drew the cold air into my lungs and exhaled. I felt nausea, but not enough to vomit; I felt the familiar gurgle in my gut, however. Leaving my rifle against a tree, I pulled down my GI pants, squatted, and let the foulness shoot downhill. The nausea left me, and I groped for the autumn-leaf-colored toilet paper always carefully stored in an upper pocket for these occasions.

I remained for some time with my ass bared to the wet wind. And, from deep inside the introspection of all introspections, the witness nearest my soul quietly held me in emotionless suspension. All physical and mental activity momentarily was shut off. Later, I was impelled to painfully shake with a laughter devoid of humor. Then the shaking crossed the spectrum, and I cried: I cried for happiness, and I cried for sadness; I did not have the foggiest idea what was going on with me, but I went with it and trusted it.

And the moment I asked myself why I did not use this ticket to the rear, I flashed on the blanket roll next to Dan in our two-man hole. I could not lose those drawings or the lure of even better drawings to come. The part of me that yearned to get out of this misery was insistent; it made me feel stupid as I pulled up my pants and returned to the guys who fleshed out the artwork and made it important.

I knew the squad would hear of my close call, but in the dark only Dan was aware of my return. He silently let me slide into the muddy hole and helped me unroll blankets and the shelter half and settle in for the night. I guess Dan was speechless at my appearance. Finally, he managed, "A million-dollar wound and here you are." I thought about this but did not reply, because I did not know what to say.

The next morning, word was passed along that there was hot breakfast on the hill. Dan returned through the mud and mist with oatmeal and a load of hotcakes unceremoniously dumped on top. It was marvelous.

Twenty-seven February passed with minor shelling, and I think we may have gotten by without losing anyone. Patrols went out that night, and we stayed put. I managed to arrange the shelter half in a sloping roof over the foxhole. I worked a lot of pictures and sketched in a few so I would not forget the ideas and memories that raced through my mind. My banged-up hand prevented me from finishing a drawing, but I could sketch in two-thirds of the idea. Staying put for the day was a positive, because my chest was sore and breathing was painful.

The medical tag then resided in the upper-left pocket of my combat jacket, with D bars of fortified chocolate from K rations. The deformed slug sat there, too. Whether it was a German .31-caliber or American .30-caliber no one could tell. Because it came from the east, we figured most likely it was German. One debate in the squad had me surviving in better condition if I had still been carrying the war drawings in my sweater instead of in the mortar tube. Frankly, I almost wished I had carried the silver tray and the artwork in my sweater. That would have prevented the flesh wound, but it would have cut off or punctured a lot of paper and graphite images.

Finding myself short on rifle ammo due to the loss of my bandolier on the hill road above, I did not try to duck a carrying party that afternoon to the rear for rations and ammo. The trails used to navigate the hill were, by then, so messed up by constant rain, sleet, and the movement of men that they were next to impossible to climb. Descending could not be accomplished with a dry bottom. Men chanced blazing new paths beyond the white tape that, so far, had not resulted in setting off Schü or Bouncing Betty mines. The Bouncing Betty had contact wires protruding just above ground level. When tripped, they shot vertically three feet or so before exploding in testicle-shredding devastation.

Some enterprising men had strung rope from tree to tree in the most difficult part of the climb. This gave us a steady grip although the rope was slippery. The white tape, for the most part, had faded into the color of mud and was useless. At the road, I looked for my silver tray armor and failed to turn it up.

Provided with backboards, we had crates of grenades and rifle ammo strapped onto us. Cardboard boxes contained K rations, and there were metal boxes filled with machine-gun ammo, about five boxes to each man assigned to tote them.

The sooner we could get off the road, the better, because the trucks and whining jeep motors could very well carry to the enemy ears less than a mile away. German artillery plotters would have no trouble figuring out which road to shell in a farm area of few roads.

Brief conversations between officers around the jeep were picked up and, as usual, passed from man to man. Our main topic of conversation was "What next? When do we jump off?" Conversation mostly centered on possible towns ahead and a few hours under a roof. And, of course, relief-time off the line, in reserve. Under a roof, or in a cellar and off the line, was synonymous with heaven.

Ahead were farm buildings—and towns. But one of those towns, Schomerich, would haunt me and the other survivors of that ordeal the rest of our lives. Indeed the entire division and 5th Ranger Battalion would remember the Lampaden Ridge and the ten miles of small towns lined up along that ridge—each town separated by shallow valleys of field and forest.

We returned to our holes still speculating on our next move. Facing another night here next to the stream that was rapidly becoming a small river, the men were scavenging anything available to improve their living accommodations and lessen, to some degree, their misery.

After moving from hole to hole passing out rations and ammo, Dan and I pulled broken branches over to our hole to use as roof beams to hold the shelter half over our heads. It was too dark to do anything more than dig a shallow drainage ditch between the hole and the hill behind us. This may or may not have served to drain water away from us.

I had lost all sense of time by then. My former life of stability and order had revolved clockwise, day in and day out. At this point, that clockwise order of logic was standing on its head and spinning through a time and space that seemed to impel us to some inevitable doom. The watch I carried had no use other than to point out who stood guard and for how long. I could remember little sunlight in this eternity of black, wet nights that so grudgingly gave way to the gray gloom of pseudodaylight. By then, I was so removed from childhood and had evolved into something, or someone, else—I was trying to get a fix or bearing on who or what I had become. Without a doubt some kind of stoic discipline had evolved around a cocoon of a soft and vulnerable center.

By comparison, I flashed on my first week in the army and Friday scrub night. Joining the army to learn how to use weapons, I was brought up short finding out that Friday night was the GI barracks night. We were instructed to remove all footlockers and cots to the company area outside and mop and scrub the interior to a mirrorlike image. This so disgusted me that I took off for the post exchange for candy bars and a coke before the scrub fest began. Later, when I returned to the barracks, I walked into a long, quiet room that smelled of strong soap. All cots and footlockers were in perfect order, except for one vacant space—mine. I had quite a shock seeing my cot up in the rafters: The message was immediate and tough. A couple of guys helped me get the cot down to its proper place.

Next morning after inspection, when everyone but me received a weekend pass, our platoon instructor firmly and gentlemanly raked me over the coals. Those cadres who carried the campaign ribbons and scars of the early South Pacific theater taught us all they could. But they did so only when they were not chasing each other (and our Thanksgiving turkey) with bloody bayonets and giving us an inkling of the psychological effects of war that awaited us all.

My father had a good job during the Great Depression, and we were spared all the suffering so many Americans lived through. The only evidences of that disaster that reached me were the tramps at the door, looking for a handout. Once, on a Christmas Eve, my father's entire office staff and foremen gathered for the annual get-together in our recreation room. They stayed until their wives began calling, urging them home to their families.

I remember well the chiming of the bells at the front door and the poorly dressed family that entered with a huge basket of fruit for my father. We were all touched by the unfamiliar sight of a grown man and woman, speaking little English, on their knees—they were grasping my father's legs and expressing gratitude for a job he had given them even though few jobs were actually available. This sort of thing embarrassed him, but it served to open my eyes a little.

With no clear-cut day or night, only a transition from gloom to deeper tones of the same, 28 February slid in upon us sideways. The word was making the rounds to be ready to move out, as though we weren't always ready to move out.

Lots of artillery—ours—announced that things were about to happen. Sharp flashes erupted on the ridge to our front, and small-arms fire broke out to the right some distance away. The scary noise of German rockets—"Screaming Meemies"—announced their supremacy of fright power. They plunged into the hill and trees behind us with a terrible concussion. Minutes later, another six or so screamed in to tear up the stream and trees to the front, dousing us in a cascade of water, mud, and branches.

I recognized the scream down the line—I had heard it before. Watson would not or could not stomach artillery. This was the fourth or fifth time he took off during a shelling. We saw a figure flit through the trees toward the rear. And for the

life of me, I could not fault him. We were bracketed in—
shells to the rear and shells to the front. These long shells,
some nine inches in diameter, could tear up our line of foxholes. Every sinew and muscle in my body was concrete
tight. Dan and I burrowed into the water and mud, cursing
ourselves for not digging deeper—or following Watson.

Minutes passed, and the expected barrage did not come.
Hours passed, and we remained in our holes while sounds of
battle moved from the left to the left front. All indications
pointed to forward movement by our left.

We received sporadic mortar fire in the afternoon. Then,
late, we were alerted to jump off. Finally, after dark, the
word came to move out in a skirmish line. We were to wade
the stream, which was then waist deep, climb the hill, reor-
ganize, and then move out again. Maintaining order to right
and left was absolutely crucial and especially difficult in a
night attack. With our shells roaring in overhead and blasting
the hilltop, we gritted teeth to wade the icy stream. We then
moved through pastures—past dead farm animals—to the
ridge and upward through the woods, until tracers suddenly
opened up in a crossfire ricocheting through the trees. We
hugged the ground and waited for a lull.

The less effective the handheld walkie-talkie sets were, the
more the noncoms and officers shouted. Runners were dispatched to right and left: They were hoping to find a squad to
fill a gap developing between platoons, or were urging a
group to cut their way through wire or thickets because their
neighboring units were pulling ahead. The enemy was always alert to the opportunity of pushing their men into these
gaps and rolling up on our flanks with their grenades and
burp guns. They would probe for our rear and set up snipers
and machine guns to take out our reserve as it moved up following the advance. They would disrupt communications
and supply.

The apex of the crossfire lay directly to the front of our
squad. After observing that the fire was high, McKay began
moving us under it, which was especially nerve-racking due

to wildly unpredictable ricochets. Showers of sparks from rebounding tracers added to the light show.

Beyond these fixed lanes of fire, we approached the top of the hill. Flares of different colors burst above us followed by several potato mashers (a grenade that has a wooden handle) flying overhead. Someone, Salazar or the big guy, poked me on the leg and pointed to our left. In the fading light of a flare, I saw helmets thirty feet away. They certainly appeared to be Germans, but not being sure, I alerted the men nearby of possible danger on the left. We froze and waited until, moments later, unmistakable burp-gun fire and its muzzle flash burst forth there. The fire was shooting in the other direction.

I did not need to see more as I pulled a grenade's pin—clumsily because of my bandaged right hand. Several grenades joined mine in the air. Alarmed German shouts were followed by flashes I did not see with my face buried in wet leaves. The buzz of flying fragments popping into trees and German flesh caused mayhem. Hurt, outraged men screamed briefly as Thompson automatic fire from McKay sprayed the dug-in enemy soldiers, and we quickly moved up to just short of the hilltop where shouts of *"Kamerad!"* echoed in the forest.

Flares showed distorted, shifting shapes of standing men, hands held high. Behind them, others who were running through the trees to their rear triggered fire from five or six weapons, instantly joined by everyone else. Noncoms shouted "Cease fire! Cease fire!" and it died out with the eerie green light of the fading flare.

Someone shot a flare that bounced several times through branches and burst above. We cautiously advanced to a zigzag trench where one shaking man cowered in the fetal position, rocking back and forth. There were eight or ten dead or wounded Germans—the wounded pleaded for aid. Then, in the dark I heard Captain Griffin's voice, out of breath, asking who we were, and moving on. Minutes later, with realignment of units complete, we shifted to the right where the trees ended and the hill dropped off.

I assumed the two German machine gunners had taken off as we arrived at the top of the hill. Finally, an hour or so later, we were started downhill, east again, according to McKay's compass. At the bottom of the hill, we went to ground as a flare shot up. Some mortar fire—a small mortar, followed this. Its shells created smaller-than-normal flashes and made less noise—more like a grenade. The fire was shifted east, and we were able to follow it well out of harm's way. We came to a series of buildings one hundred yards ahead, and we crouched behind whatever cover we found. The platoon sergeant and other men appeared and consulted with McKay. Dan and I were sent to the left to approach the buildings from the side. A dirt road bordered by trees seemed the best approach route.

We stayed well away from the road to the farm; and off beyond the trees, we moved slowly through an apple orchard whose bare trees had branches reaching to the ground. We had been told to check out the area and to do it quickly so that we would not hold up the battalion. But Dan and I were not about to stick out our necks rushing into a bad situation—the battalion would have to wait while we did the job our way.

To all appearances, the farm seemed innocent enough. No light showed, and not a sound could be heard. The strong smell of animals and manure hung in the wet air. Then we heard the metallic clicking sound to our left, and the sound of men moving through branches that swished and snapped, which was followed by their low voices; then six or seven out-of-breath men passed across only a few yards in front of us. Their silhouettes faded toward the buildings. We were immobilized, frozen in place. I noticed Dan's hand on my arm and realized it had been there since the clicking noise. If he meant to caution and restrain me, I could only agree with his state of mind. The second man in line had a long shape on his shoulder that could have been a machine gun. If we had challenged them or opened fire, we would have had a fifty-fifty chance they would give up—or fight it out—and we had no cover. We headed back to Sergeant Enright to report that we thought the machine gun from the hill was in the larger building to the front.

Enright turned to another man in a group of figures crouched behind a fence. The man turned out to be Captain Griffin. The captain decided Dan and I should retrace our steps and set up an ambush out of the line of fire to cut off the enemy's escape route. He intended to place squads on three sides of the house and then call on the Germans to surrender.

Dan and I moved through the orchard to the spot where the men had passed us. We chose a solid-looking outhouse with openings in several directions. Once inside, we understood the reasons for all the openings. A cart with a huge barrel was mounted on top and smelled like urine. In the coming months of spring, we would often see and smell the powerful stuff being sprayed on fields as we moved east toward the Rhine River.

We set ourselves up to cover the area behind the house. In a few minutes, several squads of rifle and BAR fire throwing lead at the house interrupted the silence of the night. This strong convincer was over after each man expended a clip of eight rounds. Then a voice shouted several sentences in fluid German. That voice belonged to the red-haired man from Headquarters Platoon who did the interrogating of prisoners. Simultaneously, a flare burst directly over the house. And as it sparkled to the ground, another shot up.

The flare-illuminated area showed a group of men running from the rear of the house in our general direction. Dan's first burst dropped the entire group to the ground. Panicky cries of *"Kamerad!"* resulted from the two rounds he had fired. With the automatic switch on, it would have been difficult to fire less.

This flare died also, and in the complete darkness that followed, a machine gunner opened fire at us from the house. Dan dropped to the floor with a sharp cry, but I felt him moving. My face was stinging. The Germans then shouted as another burst of machine-gun fire peppered the wall of our outhouse. Having no idea what was going on, I popped up, fired five or six rounds at the door of the house, and ducked. More machine-gun fire hit over my head and behind me. The burst was sustained, as only a German machine gun was capable of doing. I wanted to fire the last couple of rounds, but in the eerie light of sparks and bouncing tracers, I struggled to eject them and managed to shove in a fresh clip of eight. I realized I had been calling Dan's name and he was answering. I decided I was bordering on panic.

A grenade banged outside along with a lot of firing, yelling, and high-pitched screaming. We got to our feet to see a flare bouncing from the house roof. Someone shouted, "More flares, damn it!" The yelling subsided to panicky pleas of surrender. A squad had finally arrived and had the Germans covered. The command to get up was answered by one man emerging from the house. Apparently, all the Germans on the ground had been hit. I turned to Dan, who stood beside me, and I asked where he had gotten hit. He said it was only a nick.

Just about then, we became fully aware of how bad the stink of cow piss really was—and we lost no time in exiting. The machine-gun fire had holed the big wooden cask, and the putrid liquid was splashing on the floor as well as on us. Dan had been sitting in a growing pool of piss, and my knees and elbows were wet.

Griffin quickly put some order into the situation. He dispatched several squads one hundred yards to the northeast to provide security, and he issued orders to establish some kind of integrity with those units to our north and south. He had the buildings and area cleared, and the wounded Germans attended to. The medics had their hands full, so I opened Dan's first-aid packet of sulfa powder and sprinkled it on the gash from the side of his mouth and along his cheek. Then I tied his bandage over the wound, under his chin, and over the top of his head. The best method would have been to run it through his mouth and behind his head, but he wouldn't have been able to talk. I clapped his helmet on his head, and we went looking for the squad—we said nothing yet about our close call.

Sometime later, we again found ourselves on point well in advance of the skirmish line: McKay had sent us out again instead of relieving us because—in the words he used as he held his nose—"The farther you are from the rest of us, the better." Once again isolated from the main body, we moved through woods and fields, climbed walls, smelled the damp air, listened to moisture drop from tree branches to the mud, and moved on. The only other sounds were the occasional small-arms fire that crackled in the distance to the left and right of us.

Again, I felt close to my father because this intensely dramatic movement of thousands of men sweeping for miles over this land was what he had done—one man of thousands—as they pushed to the bitter end of their war before most of us were born.

Dan and I hit the dirt a couple of times as nervous snipers pumped rounds in our general direction. They did not slow the regiment's progress much. McKay caught up to us and walked us back to the edge of a wood we had just swept. There we dug in and posted outposts to the front, arranging watches two hours on, two hours off. The left side of my face burned, probably from cement particles blown from the wall. Dan took first watch. Of all the earthy and bodily smells we put up with, as well as the stink of cordite and gun oil, nothing compared to the odor of our latest calamity.

Early morning, Dan awakened me. Our shelter halves were covered in a light snow spatter. Nighttime wet and gloom had given a couple of inches toward daytime wet gloom. It was not easy to talk with a stiffened face and cracked lips—Dan was most economical in expression due to his facial pain.

Good old McKay, always watching out for his boys, came by to say that every fourth man could carry mess kits to the rear for hot chow. Such good news perked me up, and I volunteered, wanting to get there early for really hot coffee. I pushed myself up, uncovered my rifle, and looked around for mess kits. Dan stirred, and as he placed his BAR in firing position so he could dig out his mess kit, I noticed the forward sight was missing. I pointed it out to him, and we looked closer and realized it had been blown off by a bullet; I wondered whether it was a bullet, or the sight, that had ripped his face the previous night. I brought up my observation of the firefight: that he had fired the least amount, two bullets, that he could squeeze off with the BAR on automatic—and this in the face of some six Germans heading in our direction. My good buddy studied and patted his weapon while he thought. Finally, he said quietly, "I'm just so god-awful tired, Bill. I knew I could stop the first one and could find no earthly reason to mow them all down." He looked at me a moment and concluded with, "If they'd kept coming [pause], I'd have emptied the magazine."

I looked at the trees, and out over the field where patches of new snow were melting on warming earth, and I climbed out of the hole saying, "You got the first one; then the idiot in the doorway decided to play hero. That, my friend, caused mayhem and kaput for all of his squad and—almost us, too." From what I could observe in the fractured flare light of the previous night, the German gunner came out of the house untouched, a prisoner of war.

I took a mess kit from our big guy and Salazar, who shared the hole with him, and I announced we would refer to the big guy as simply "Giant" in the future. Giant had a habit of letting his lower jaw hang loose. He spent an inordinate amount of time with his mouth open. Heading through the trees with my hands full of gently tinkling mess kits, I flashed on my earlier childhood and remembered that I had had the same problem. In fact, I flashed vividly on the memory of myself at five years of age, opening the back door of our house to enter but first turning to gaze—open-mouthed—at the sunset. And, in that precise moment a big, black wasp flew into my mouth and right down my throat. That cured me. But Giant was too old, in his early twenties, to keep that up. That's what I thought then; but I was wrong, because later on it saved his life.

8

Surrounded by the
6th SS Mountain Division

Back in a clearing, the kitchen jeep again was the center of attention—or, rather, the food and hot coffee it carried was. Captain Griffin, the first sergeant, and a runner walked past in a hurry to get somewhere. Captain Griffin spoke so the cook, the noncoms, and anyone in earshot could hear and obey: "I want five or six men at a time on this chow line. Get your food and move away. I don't want to see you men grouping up." It was always a problem—men were naturally social, but in an instant, one mortar shell dropping in could wipe out a squad.

I noticed everyone looking out toward the road the chow jeep used to get here. Farther down, in the direction of the farm buildings of the night before, I could see a convoy of six-by-six trucks unloading men. From that direction, a column was moving toward us. Because they were close enough by then—their shockingly clean helmets and overcoats so obvious—I dared to hope they were replacements for George Company. I held my breath, hoping against hope it was true. I walked over near the captain when the formalities were being observed.

We had well over sixty new men to fill out our squads to some degree: fresh, healthy legs to carry their weight; bright, clear eyes to help guard the nights. Captain Griffin immediately broke the men up into groups and separated them in case of incoming fire. Artillery fire could be heard in the dis-

tance, although after a while one became used to it and no
longer focused on it. They did focus on it, however. I knew
that for a fact. I had been there and heard that with fresh ears
only weeks before. I looked at my filthy uniform and could
not believe how completely changed I was in only weeks.
Conversely, they looked at us in the growing daylight, and it
must have caused much consternation behind those serious,
self-conscious eyes to see what their future image was to be.
Looking at them and seeing what I had been was almost too
much for me. It was as though a cleaver had slammed down
between us; I would never again be that innocent. Even if I
lived to return Stateside, I would be a ghost of who had once
walked the familiar rooms of my home.

I looked from their apprehensive faces to the veterans of
the company. I took in, not only the condition of our uniforms and equipment, but the color and texture of skin—the
broken and blue skin around mouths and the scraggly beards.
Most of all, it was the heavy baggage around the eyes.

I now know it was such moments that helped deepen whatever the poetic mentality in me was forming. But this poet
thought and visualized pictorially, not in the written word. I
felt the weight of responsibility on my shoulders to put this
all down on paper. I feared I could never do proper justice to
my love and respect for the men I served with. And at the
same time, I felt a deep something that said I could and
would.

I found myself on the chow line and was realizing there
might not be enough food for the new guys and I had better
damn well get ours while the getting was good. I filled canteens with coffee and shut lids on mess kits. The first sergeant called me before I could slip away. I was to lead some
eighteen replacements to our 2d Platoon holes. I checked to
see that they had sufficient ammo and K rations, because
they were not getting hot food this morning. They had been
told to pile their overcoats near the jeep; this done, I led them
to an area some distance behind our holes and had them
spread out. I then found Enright and told him what we had.
He took over, and I passed out the hot food. Dan and I got

into our hole while six new men were told where to dig in nearby.

One heavyset man with Italian features was paired with me—and another guy with Dan. We would do our best to acclimate and instruct them in the way things were and how we did our job. Dreadfully quickly, they would find that Stateside training could not really prepare them for what they would find here.

The sounds of artillery and mortar rounds continued off and on. Small-arms fire broke out sporadically, near and far. We speculated with hopes that our relatively easy forward progress indicated an early end of the war. But, another viewpoint held that the open terrain we were moving through was not exactly ideal for defense. This made sense. For miles all around, we could see relatively flat country and a few small hills. This was all farmland and few forests. Nowhere to the front could we see hilly terrain that could more easily be defended. Yet, we knew it was there on the horizon—and that we would come to it.

The daily sniping and ambushing slowed us down. Some miles ahead—or maybe only a few thousand yards—the main body of the enemy used the time gained by their snipers to dig deep, plant mines, string barbed wire, and zero in their artillery. About half past two in the afternoon, the powers that be shifted us out of the trees, and we formed up and moved out. McKay's compass had us heading north by northeast. The hilltops and ridges we had fought through east of the Saar were petering out. The country was gently rolling up ahead.

A glance to the right or left revealed the stirring sight of our lines of hundreds of men moving over the uneven earth, through stands of trees, over fields and streams and by isolated farm buildings. You could see them until they faded in the mist or were blotted out from view by the thickened drizzle.

In the slight valleys and depressions, the mist was left over from last night's fog. Every platoon and company moved into terrain features that differed radically from that faced by neighboring units, and each had to be scouted on its merits: Open areas that the enemy obviously would not choose to defend were swept through at a brisk walk; other, more threatening areas were entered by the point men, scouting cautiously. This caused a slowdown in that area until the scouts had checked it out. Then the scouts, as the point once again, often double-timed forward to keep their unit abreast of those units to their flanks. Point men do not relish running toward the unknown.

At other times, the flanking units actually were halted in place until the slowed unit could resume its forward progress. Walkie-talkies and larger radios, runners, or jeeps were used to keep the integrity of the regiment's movement as much in line as possible. And, within a thousand yards, we gained a lesson in deceptive topography where the seemingly level landscape gradually dipped downward, and a shallow valley with a stream and small forest appeared. None of this could be seen earlier from our foxhole position. But, before we made our gradual descent toward the wooded stream, I could see a series of small rises a couple of miles to the north and east—they appeared small, but the light of day was tricky. Often the dark overcast would lower to the hilltops, shrouding our distorted worldview, and one could only guess at the height until the cloud mass moved off.

The on-again, off-again drizzle kept us sliding through the sludge. I had heard that our G Company was on the extreme left of the battalion line, with F on our right and E farther to the right. Well to our rear, I spotted teams of H Company machine guns and an 81mm mortar crew. We kept hearing tanks—ours—but could not see them. I glimpsed the tiny figures of men off to our left as we dipped lower toward the stream. I wasn't sure, but I thought they were the 3d Battalion of our regiment.

This slope had little cover, and we were a hundred yards from the trees and underbrush-bordered stream. I could feel the tension in the men around me—that apprehension was always there while we moved through uneven and open terrain. And the tension was intense then as we recognized the ambush potential of the place.

Dogfaces on the move rarely talk much. Only the especially anxious talked, sometimes too much. They would be told laconically to "for Christ's sake, shut your mouth," and maybe they would for a while. But, generally, men saved their energy; they quietly focused on their survival, because unnecessary talk was a distraction and wasted energy. I picked up on several terse comments almost under the breath of men near me. Some noncom, maybe Langley, reminded men to maintain their intervals.

But I heard the thump of bullets in solid flesh, instantly followed by the cracks of rifles. Machine-gun tracers darted from the trees, and shouted orders sent men moving either to the mud or forward, as a ragged crackle of fire began from our weapons. Our platoon scouts were off to the left and well in advance of the skirmish line. We were either prone in the mud or slipping and sliding toward the trees, where muzzle flashes appeared. I saw one of our scouts knocked over and the other go to him. Yet, most of the firing came from the right, and we followed McKay toward the scouts. Dan was bellowing at a replacement to fire his weapon. I found Fasco, my new foxhole companion, lying behind me white-faced, and I yelled to him to follow me and shoot. We moved in fits and starts toward the trees. It was not heroic; it was truly the only thing we could do. No way could the platoons return up the muddy slope fast enough. It was obviously better to push down to the trees and get in among the cover and the Germans. We would lose less that way. The rate of fire from the trees indicated at least a couple of squads of infantry and a couple of machine guns.

Several times, bullets viciously tore up the mud around us or popped past. Then mortar shells began dropping in behind us, spraying fragments and mud in all directions. I saw McKay and several men dashing for the trees to the right, and we went left. I realized I held a de-pinned grenade in my bandaged right hand and that someone had shouted for us to use them. Without a specific target, I let fly anyway, as did others. The sharp thuds of the grenades barely preceded our final rush into the trees. I fired twice, and the empty clip clanged out as I threw myself into the prone position just inside the underbrush. I must have landed on a rock or branch—I could feel the chest wound bleeding. I struggled to shove in a fresh eight rounds. As I did so, I became aware that men were shouting to cease fire. Only gradually did the rate of fire fall off. Mortar fire continued to fall on the slope, and I sneaked a peak through the underbrush to see Germans standing up—hands held high. They were across the stream forty or fifty feet away. Certainly our grenades never carried that far. I lay there gasping for breath, my chest hurting and heart pounding.

Then bedlam took over again as we heard the rare whirring sound of descending mortar shells. Everyone—American and German—disappeared, as several detonations erupted dropping dead leaves and twigs all around. The cease-fire order had not reached the H Company's 81mm mortar in time. Germans were screaming at us a mixture of *"Kamerad!"* and God knows what else. Our mortars had set up out of sight on the flat above the slope.

Finally, quiet descended on our little valley and our men; most of those who were still able had moved into the underbrush and trees. The German soldiers were told to cross the stream to us. Some reluctantly—others anxious to please— arrived at the stream only to be caught in the open as another series of mortar shells came whirring in. They exploded in loud cracks in the treetops and the stream sending geysers of water in thin columns vertically as high as the trees. Five or six shells hit, and no more. This barrage (the Germans fired mortars too) was fired by an enemy battery far enough away that they had no idea what the situation was here.

Our CO and the red-haired interpreter dashed over the stream and conferred with the prisoners. One of the Germans—an officer—went with Griffin and the interpreter back to their machine-gun bunker. Apparently, there was a phone line to the

Guide to white tape.

Monkey-wrench woods.

Anti-tank ditch.

Attack on Sinz.

Sinz aftermath.

Frozen feet.

Campholz woods outpost.

Mural study—1996.

Trench in Campholz Woods.

Help from P-47s.

Light machine-gun post.

Road to the ridgetop.

Top of Munzingen Ridge.

SHORT ARM INSPECTION RESULTS IN MEDICAL OFFICERS SWEARING OFF CHEESE PRODUCTS PERMANENTLY, INDIGNANT MEDICS DISMISS GRUBBY RIFLEMEN, ORDERING THE C.O. TO HAVE MEN BATHE DAILY!

Short-arm inspection.

We ambush a German patrol.

Overrun on Hill 468.

Carrying Dan.

"C" Company breaks through.

Return of the patrol.

A thankful tip of the hat.

Schu mine casualty.

First scout smells trouble.

Sculpture in white marble.

Flank support.

Near miss.

Scouts dig in.

Strange events on the Rhine.

Snipers in the soap factory.

Dan.

mortars. As I understood, the German officer was told to order the mortars to cease fire.

Our platoon crossed the stream. It looked to me as though several Germans had been hit by their own fire. I do not exactly know how we fared, but at least three men were killed almost immediately, and five or six were wounded.

It appeared that Fasco had ignored my admonition to follow me and remained stuck in the mud on the slope. I propped my rifle against a tree and took his rifle from him—it had not been fired. I returned it to him and pointed out a few truisms of army life regarding firepower even when you don't see a target. The back of his uniform, although wet from drizzle, was still olive drab; but from his face to his toes, he was the color of German mud—like the rest of us.

Counting noses, we discovered Dan's new understudy was the first one hit by a sniper's bullet. He had died instantly, a large exit hole in his back—probably from the very same Mauser rifle with telescopic sight that I saw carried away on the back of a man in the third squad.

Beyond the stream area, we were spread out; we trudged up the slope, and there we re-formed. Just to our left front was a small town some four hundred yards away. And to the front, less than one mile away, sat another town—our final objective, Schomerich.

We squatted in the muck and huddled under raincoats. I had my German rain cape over me, and I looked at the gray and grim landscape. I wondered whether the sun ever shone here, and I struggled to understand how farm peasants could pass their lives in such a godforsaken place. I studied the communication wire running past us to the road just ahead of us. I saw it for some distance to the side of the farm track in the direction of the nearer town. And that is most likely where the German mortars were holed up. You could be pretty sure that where the mortar tubes were, the infantry would be between them and us. So, if we were to find ourselves out of the winter wet this night and drying off under a roof, we would have to shove the storm troopers out into their own stinking German weather.

However, it seemed the gods of war sided with the storm troopers this late afternoon as we were ordered to dig in where we were. After all, *Gott Mit Uns* (God with Us) was indelibly stamped in every German soldier's belt buckle. Apparently, the Catholic rosary, a medal of St. Christopher, and the dog tags around my neck could not measure up. Incidentally, St. Christopher on its silver chain had an inscribed message just under his likeness that read, "I am a Catholic. Call a priest." This had been my mother's parting gift, and of course I had to honor my promise to wear it. This I did, until all this neckwear was blown off me later on.

The groans and moans and the gripes and curses were low-key up and down the line as entrenching tools began moving mud from one place to another, generally just east of the deepening hole. I would never escape the vision, while digging in, that a two-man hole—six feet long by four deep by two wide—might well become my grave. I tried, but I found I could no longer control the tic on the side of my face; it embarrassed me.

Drizzle became sleet, which later turned to snow. The snow was preferable to drizzle if the temperature was freezing and we were able to remain reasonably dry. It was a toss-up between shaking all night with the freezing, or less-cold temperatures with sodden clothing and blankets and rising water in our holes.

The buildings of the town had not yet suffered any shelling. We stared longingly as the darkness rapidly hid them from view. K rations had been carried up, along with extra bandoliers of rifle ammo. Six or eight mortar rounds flashed and detonated in our area for about ten minutes, and ours answered some minutes later.

Enright and an officer showed up looking for McKay, and then our squad leader took Dan and me back down the slope a short distance. Invited under a shelter half, a flashlight-illuminated map of the area showed us where we were pinpointed near the road leading to the nearest town, called Paschal. We were to patrol between Paschal and Schomerich along a connecting road, while another patrol was to try to see what was in Paschal. Patrols had gone out every night, and our turn was up again. McKay had a bad cough, so Dan and I were to take Fasco with us on a recon. If a prisoner could be easily grabbed, it would be appreciated, but it was not a priority.

Back at my hole, Dan and I explained to Fasco how we would conduct the patrol, his first. I would lead, and he would follow a few steps behind with Dan's BAR in the rear. Fasco's teeth were chattering so badly that he had difficulty talking (which I understood perfectly, having spent about one-third of my combat time with the same affliction, common to us all). But Fasco was trying to beg off the patrol by claiming his lack of experience. If the truth were known, Dan and I would have preferred doing this alone, but the new men needed to get into the swing of things. Because events were relatively quiet in this area, it seemed a good time to break him in and see how he would perform.

Anyway, at 2200 we moved to the outpost one hundred yards beyond the foxhole line. It was just off the road. Salazar and another new guy were there for the first watches. We stayed off the road and headed east through fields bordered by windbreaks of trees. The quiet was broken only with the occasional barking of dogs from somewhere. Far away to the south, the low clouds reflected the light of big guns and detonations. The deep rumble of sound carried three or four miles. The 301st and the 5th Ranger Battalion had stirred up a hornet's nest. In less than a week, the fight would break out all along this ten-mile front and it would be devastating to all concerned.

As usual, I moved when I felt I could and squatted to smell the air when the terrain and intuition told me to. We stayed on course, passing Paschal a quarter mile to the left and took cover in underbrush near a well-used trail. Because the night was extremely dark, I squatted down on the track to run my hands over footprints in the mud. Along with horseshoe and wagon tracks, I clearly felt jackboot and hobnail shoe tracks. They were so fresh that the drizzle and snow had not yet eroded the hobnails in one set of prints.

We decided to hole up a while and watch the farm track. As the eastern sky seemed to provide a little more light than the western, we positioned ourselves just west of the track and tried to be as comfortable as possible. Sometime later, the sound of a horse-drawn wagon provided plenty of warning. A squad of German soldiers passed us, followed by two wagons with a couple of men sitting up there driving the horses. Perhaps another couple of squads followed in the rear—then nothing. They had come from the direction of Paschal and were moving in the direction of Schomerich.

We decided to move along behind them, just far enough to hear the wagons grinding through the mud. Five or six minutes later, we clearly heard men speaking—possibly their password exchange. We left the track and cautiously moved south, becoming aware of buildings ahead and to the left. The sound of motors and other noises indicated that Schomerich was occupied. If the other patrol entered Paschal and found it empty, we would back up their discovery with our own. We figured the wagon carried the mortars and ammo from Paschal. Best of all, we just might move the company into Paschal and find cover before daylight.

Having seen all we were to see, we headed west a while and then angled northwest until we could distinguish Paschal's silhouette. We found the road to our outpost and reported to Enright and the officer. The most interesting discovery I made was Fasco's extraordinary night sight—he had diverted me around a pond when I was about to fall in. He also put us on the road back to the OP during the return.

We remained in our holes the rest of the night unfortunately; and, at first light on 1 March, we moved into Paschal where a couple of snipers were routed out. We were formed up east of town and moved toward Schomerich one-half mile southeast. I was not surprised that Dan and I were again at point. Having moved around the western outskirts of Schomerich the night before, we were considered experts in local topography. Of course, the landscape looked incredibly different in the dark of the day as against the dark of the night.

We struck out along a well-used track that probably was the same one we had been on hours before. And halfway to Schomerich, I spotted my footprints where I had entered the road to examine the German boot prints. We kept moving until we were about five hundred yards from the northwest part of town. At this point, our 2d Platoon diverted to the left and the other platoons to the right of the track. While the deployment was arranging itself, mortar shells of both armies passed each other, theirs to drop behind our skirmish line, which isolated us from our reserve. Ours were bursting on and around buildings to our front.

Then we started our forward movement in rushes interspersed with squatting to fire at windows. I became aware of our tanks behind: I could see only two, but they were a comfort. They were directing their cannon fire at buildings. One hundred yards from town, our squad set up a base of fire, and we let go with all we had as the other squads closed in. I was fascinated, while reloading, to see a couple of men firing rifle grenades, and I watched the grenades' trajectory. What good they did I could not tell from that distance. The German mortar fire had crept up behind us and then abruptly quit. Probably, our guys—moving around the houses then—had forced the mortar teams back. We had heard enemy rifle fire, but I don't recall anyone getting hit. As we hurried to join the rest of the platoon who were clearing houses, I saw machine-gun tracers darting from town toward the other platoons. But that soon quit, and our mortars were dropping shells deeper in town as the shape of the assault changed.

Now in among the houses and alleys, we were assigned a series of outbuildings and houses to clear. The roar and crackle of small-arms fire turned into the occasional grenade and clatter of small arms. Schomerich was a small town, although larger than Paschal, and it did not take much time to clear the Germans out of their ratholes. We reached the other side, facing southeast, and 2d Platoon set up a perimeter inside the houses facing a hill.

Our squad was spared OP duty until the next day. Meanwhile, squads took turns digging on top of the hill, whose designation was Hill 468. The reader should keep in mind that the picture of war I paint in these paragraphs is from a snail's point of view. Only rarely did I spot heavy-mortar teams moving along behind us in the advance. And I seldom saw the artillery batteries that normally set up a mile or more to our rear (depending on size and range). If we advanced our lines a couple of miles in a day, the artillery probably could maintain their current position. Their smaller gun, the 105mm, had a plus-or-minus six-mile range.

Contact patrols, always important to the integrity of positions separated by distance, in this situation assumed super-importance. By the next day, 2 March, we realized that F Company held the next town south of us. Two miles of wooded valley separated Hentern from us. We were also separated from Lampaden, one and one-half miles to the north, by a wooded valley. This tenuous situation existed all along the division's ten-mile front. The 5th Ranger Battalion was dug in on hills on the division's southern flank, with another Massachusetts division, the 26th, south of the Rangers.

Of course, it was years after the war that my research turned up most of the tactical situations of our division. During that week in March, in that town of Schomerich, none of us dogfaces could have grasped our actual situation.

Beyond our frequent contact patrols to meet the patrols of other companies from Hentern, Lampaden, and Paschal, we knew nothing of the rest of our regiment, much less the entire division. And when the shooting began, we knew even less of what was going on fifty or more yards away. The worst of times was when we lost track of everything but our own situation. And sometimes we lost track even of that, as—on the edge of panic—we bordered on hopelessness.

The area was full of traffic and activity. A large group of German civilians were relocated to the town church cellar, which was in a small building one block from our house. And it was located on an equally small hill and appeared sort of ridiculous, like a matchbox on a pincushion.

A half-track with ammo and rations parked close to the house so that other vehicles could get by. These included six-by-sixes belonging to the engineers, who were busy establishing barbed-wire entanglements in strategic areas. Next day, we were detailed to help the engineers drive in the ringed stakes, well out in front of 2d Platoon's foxhole line up on the hill. We used extra heavy gloves to handle the sharp barbs.

By then, we had established a four-man outpost just inside Hardter Wald four hundred to five hundred yards east of our foxhole line. The woods extended from the valley south to Hentern, and across our front through the valley toward Lampaden. Our 302d Regiment and much of the 301st were digging in to what was called Lampaden Ridge—where most of these towns were situated. To the east, it dropped down to the river (which was more of a stream than a river). H Company's heavy mortars and machine-gun sections joined us. I recall an antitank 57mm cannon placed across the street from our house, trained on Hill 468. This hill gradually rose from just in front of our 2d Platoon houses.

We were put to work digging foxholes in between our house and the next. This became a trench over the next few days, as did our foxhole line on top of the hill. The longer dogfaces remained in a hole, the deeper and longer it became. Eventually part of it would be roofed and piled with earth or sandbags and it became a trench with dugouts.

Fred Buckner established his aid station in the cellar under our house. There he administered to the scrapes and wounds of the platoon's morning scrap. The injuries included the broken arm of a sixteen-year-old German soldier who could not stop crying. He had been captured that morning when one of our guys used his M1 to knock his rifle from his hands. We did not know what to do with the frightened kid. He melted the hard hearts of several men who pressed rations on the boy; but eventually, after Buckner set and bound up the broken bone, we sent him along with the other prisoners of war.

Then my turn came to have the hole in my chest and messed-up trigger finger checked out. I had so little hair on my eighteen-year-old chest that I experienced no pain as he pulled off the soiled tape and gauze. We looked in dismay at the hole, which had been no more than three-eighths of an inch in diameter to begin with. By then it was twice that and had all the aspects of an ulcer. Nor did the sternum cartilage look any better. It smelled bad. No one could differentiate between that smell and the fifty or so other odors of my body and uniform.

I had arrived with a helmet full of well water heated on our Coleman squad stove for the purpose. Our good medic cleaned up my chest and hand, applied fresh sulfa powder and bandages, and admonished me to get my ass off the line and to a hospital with clean white sheets and cute nurses. The finger had lost much of its swelling, but it still hurt like hell because I had to use it so often—it definitely limited my grenade throwing and slowed every other activity.

I could not help but notice how bad our medic looked. This Louisiana boy with the beautifully chiseled facial features could not control his eye tic and badly shaking hands. His black hair was graying over his ears, and his voice was anything but steady.

I took some ribbing from the men later, as we came and went from the well. We carried helmets of water to heat on the squad stove or the kitchen range fired up with kindling. The kidding came about because of my bright green flannel pajamas, two pairs, which I wore in place of woolen army long johns. I explained that I had never allowed myself to be captured because the enemy soldiers would laugh themselves crazy if they ever got a look at them.

Before the squad could really get into the rare clean up, the platoon sergeant called through a window for everyone to fall out to the CP for a short-arm inspection. We looked at each other in disbelief. This inspection of our rolled-back penises for venereal disease reasons was humiliating: It had not happened since before D day, and how long had it been since anyone had even seen a girl, much less gotten close to one?

Cursing and groaning, we struggled back into our filthy uniforms and moved up the cobblestones to the CP near the church. A medic's jeep was parked out front. Dan and I were at the head of the line and entered the house, where shockingly clean, pink-faced officers sat behind a table looking us over. "Okay, you men, pull 'em out and roll 'em back." The sight of our shriveled and gunky members provoked sharp intakes of breath and then verbal exclamations such as, "All right—get out. Next! Move on soldier, next!" After five or six men failed to pass muster, one of the clean-shaven group of three, a major, called a halt to the proceedings and strode out to harangue our CO about the obvious need for more-frequent showers and improved hygiene in general.

These men, so terribly important to us as surgeons in the rear-area hospitals, were way out of their element here. I personally felt utterly speechless, dismayed, and embarrassed. It took some minutes to collect my thoughts, but Dan put it into words for the rest of us: When he spoke—which was not often—he made a lot of sense. I do not remember exactly what he said, but the gist of it always stayed with me. It had to do with the fact that if our own medical officers could not get a grip on what the infantrymen faced day in and day out, how in the world would people Stateside understand us after the war?

The town was not shelled much, but from the placement of the shelling, we knew we had been zeroed in. Clearly, a German patrol with a radio was skulking about in the woods to the northeast.

With all these defensive moves going on, it appeared we would be here a while. After the weeks of constantly living in the open, we welcomed this. Before the kitchen trucks arrived, and hot food was being prepared, we had subsisted on rations for too many days.

A rumor was floating around that we were to be relieved in a matter of days. Conversations in the ranks were turning to the theme of surviving the last weeks until the war was over—it truly seemed the Germans were worn down. We saw more older men and younger boys in the prisoners taken. With the Russians and Western Allies squeezing the enemy between them, the end seemed inevitable. Wiser heads spoke of the rumors of new weapons being developed by the ever-resourceful German engineers.

I managed several hours of deep sleep in an upstairs bedroom. It felt so strange, at first, to lie down on a bed with a roof overhead. But I succumbed quickly and awoke before dark set in. Hot food was available, and I lost no time walking to where the kitchen had been set up. The same cook who had fed me when the spent slug knocked me down asked how the wound was doing, and we talked of the disastrous short-arm inspection earlier.

He asked me why I did not have my ulcerated hole checked out by the doctors. I replied laconically that the medics had been so disgusted by our filthy condition that they might have ordered me back to a hospital. I was becoming aware that my drawings had a continuity developing, and leaving the company might cause a gap—or even put an end to the series. An extremely sensible part of me wanted out of this and to be as far away from war as possible. However, the inner voice of a graphic reporter seemed firmly in charge.

McKay came by rounding up the squad. We were to relieve a squad on Hill 468. Also, we were to take turns doing contact patrols toward Hentern, south of us.

A dirt track directly in front of the house led straight up Hill 468. We arrived at the 2d Platoon position and took over to the right of the road. The dirt track continued straight to Hardter Wald some five hundred yards. The barbed wire cut across the road to the left and right.

It was dark and less cold. Gradually, and finally, the weather seemed to be heading toward spring. We settled into the holes just vacated—Dan and Fasco with me in a slit trench. Almost immediately, the platoon sergeant and McKay gave us the coordinates to patrol the area between Hentern and us. That proved routine. At the bottom of the pitch-black valley between the towns, Fasco found a rough bridge that let us cross a brook with dry feet. Fasco was proving his value to us, but he was exceedingly frightened much of the time. After checking into the F Company outpost, we returned to our slit trench and waited several hours for our turn again.

Next day, 3 March, we were relieving one squad at a time to return to town for a meal. The few hours' relaxation in our house had given me time to knock off a couple of drawings and take a nap. I was beginning to like this kind of war. I suppose it was similar to World War I, with long periods of inactivity interspersed with intense action. Certainly this terrain reminded me of photos of World War I battlefields. The difference was theirs was fought pretty much in one shell-pocked place, while our shell-pocked areas were strung out for hundreds of miles to the beaches of Normandy. The question was, How many intact fields and villages to the east remained to be beat up?

The next several days were pretty much a repeat of this day. Fighting was heavy miles south of us with the 301st and 5th Rangers. Prisoners taken there told of impending German attacks that indeed came off as described. I found it hard to believe American POWs would willingly offer information to an enemy, leading to casualties for their own side—but it was obvious the Germans were moving troops to this area.

G Company sent recon patrols east on the night of 2 March. Our turn came on the late hours of the 3d. McKay's cough was pretty much gone as he took Dan, Fasco, and me through our camouflaged passage in the wire. We paused briefly at our OP just inside Hardter Wald, to the left side of the firebreak. The firebreak was a continuation of the dirt track that ran through the Wald and on to the town. We moved one-half mile to a road that ran right to Hentern and left to Kummelerhof.

Here I took the point position with Dan behind me, then Fasco, and then McKay. One by one, we sneaked across the road to the trees on the other side. We moved perhaps a quarter mile until the east wind carried the smell of water. A short distance farther and we could hear the quiet sound of moving water. We remained there some time, lying in the dark and listening.

I would expect the Germans to have an outpost on this side

of the river far enough away from the sound of it to be able to listen for movement. I realized, of course, their OP could be one hundred yards east of the river as well. Then I felt someone tug my boot. Fasco crawled up between McKay and me to point out figures that I could not see on our left. Neither McKay nor I ever saw them, but we all heard a sound like someone tripping followed by a laugh—after that, silence. Fasco said he thought two men were there.

Deciding not to do anything about the Germans, we slowly moved forward to the darkest place I could see near the river and holed up. That same east wind brought the pungent and strong tobacco smell and occasional sounds that kept us alert. A few times, men approached the riverbank opposite us. Sounds indicated canteens were being topped off.

After hearing motor sounds several times well to the German rear, something else occurred that so touched me I have never forgotten it. It stands out with vividness in my memory perhaps because so little of my German experience really touched me sentimentally. Perhaps a lot more emotion percolated in my pressure cooker than I realized. We heard singing that night that held me spellbound. The voices, perhaps a company of German infantry, rose and fell so powerfully, and with such a beautifully devoted tenor, that I again felt the hair on my neck rise. We heard only the strident melody of marching songs; the words themselves were filtered out over one-half mile of old forest, and the sound then faded behind a hill. The silence that followed left me so sadly devastated I must have held my breath wanting so much to hear more. Gradually, in whispers and sighs, the landscape opened, and the dark roar of voices, even clearer, ended in a crescendo of "Hurrah!"—followed by a brief silence and a different song that too soon faded. But not so soon that it failed being chiseled permanently in my consciousness.

Suspended in a moment of time and space, that inner witness within a deep well of my consciousness cried tears of troubled innocence. In later years, the cinema and television documentaries would occasionally include those stirring songs and voices, and I would instantly be transported back to that night and again feel the same powerful emotion. The feeling would be deepened with the years, however—not more intense, but broadened in understanding. The unity and courage those soldiers extracted from their ancient warrior song served their leader's cause, and I understood that, huddled with my buddies in front of their lines.

That night, we did not know which units faced us except for remnants of the 416th and the 256th Divisions. But in a few days time, those of us who would survive the coming storm would not forget the 6th SS Mountain Division and the supporting units of other regiments and divisions that hit us. In the coming months, an avalanche of information would reach us about these SS troopers. Soon after the surrender, we would learn of horrendous atrocities.

Our 376th Regiment, which was detached from the 94th to form a combat team with the 10th Armored Division, returned to us on 3 March. They had been away since they broke out of the Saar bridgehead and captured Trier to the north. The 376th, at this point division reserve, replaced our 1st Battalion, 302d, which became our regiment reserve at Irsch. Some miles south of us, the 5th Rangers also became part of division reserve.

On 4 March, the 3d Platoon, reinforced with replacements, marched east from town along the main road. I watched them spread out on the ridge five hundred yards out. They filtered through the trees and along the road, disappearing from view. They would pass through the woods one-half mile and occupy the five buildings of Kummelerhof, one hundred yards or so from the Ruwer River. It was the last I would see of them for more than half a century.

Sections of our 2d Platoon's position became trenches as foxholes extended one to another. We had two of H Company's heavy .30-caliber machine guns well dug in, one near each flank. That night, four of us did OP duty in Hardter Wald. We had a phone line to the 2d Platoon in the trench. On 5 March, the company squads took turns exchanging their shoepacs for combat boots. The boots sure felt good after breaking them in, but that night we got some snow, and I thought the changeover happened a trifle early. The weather was still cold; I remembered my first night on the line and how we suffered.

We had received mail, replacements, and clean socks. I wore two pair. The mail was a blessing: My father had written a V-mail every night since I sailed. Despite all of his many activities, he never failed to write me nightly during my two years overseas. I would receive a bundle of these V-mails from him and feel for the guys who received nothing.

The day had been even darker and more overcast than usual. Toward night, the cold increased, and once again, we suffered a cold rain that became sleet and then snow. Ironically, we faced this return to winter weather without the shoepacs we had turned in that day. We were slated to relieve the four-man OP in Hardter Wald after midnight—but events changed that.

Around midnight, intense small-arms fire broke out to the left front, coming from the 3d platoon area one-half mile away in Kummelerhof. Not long after, artillery shells screamed through the clouds on their way to flash beyond the woods. An enormously tense half hour passed and the volume of fire never slackened. Our squad occupied roughly the center of the trench that straddled the dirt track to town. The platoon sergeant was nearby, often using the radio. We had a light machine-gun crew from the 4th Platoon emplaced a few yards to the right. The platoon sergeant's voice carried to me off and on. I heard him tell the outpost to "get back to the trench." That could mean only one thing: plenty of movement near them. But they never made it back.

Every man was up and at his post. The sergeant requested artillery fire on Hardter Wald, and it soon came rushing down from the black sky to crash into the trees. Everyone pulled his head down as several short rounds erupted in the field between the woods and us. Screaming Meemies, which screeched like rusty metal on metal, began blasting the area behind us, while artillery shells probed our position. With my face against the mud at the bottom of the trench, I prayed with more sincere desperation than sincere spirituality. A sustained and painful concussion replaced my fleeting hearing; and that shaken sense again ran to the rear, leaving me one perception short. In time, the shaking and heaving earth quieted. I sneezed and coughed the smoke and mud from nose and mouth. The cadence of bouncing earth switched to that of machine-gun fire—not heard, but felt. In the light of flares, I saw men getting to their feet. The platoon sergeant almost ran over me as he jostled riflemen; he was gesticulating, with his mouth working—a mime, voiceless and persistent.

On my feet again, I expected to see a German horde to the front and was surprised to see nothing, until I realized many men were firing to our left. But then machine-gun tracers from the direction of the woods grabbed my attention. I could sense movement beyond the wire and a sudden increase of muzzle flashes. Bullets began beating up the earth around us and forced us to duck. The fire was not sustained, and we could return it by briefly raising up and firing off several rounds.

The movement on our left had petered out and our focus was on the woods to the front. This situation lasted about an hour, with intermittent mortar shells dropping in. We were in a cross fire from a machine gun way off to the left whose tracers flashed well overhead, but never found the range in the dark.

We were becoming aware of the obvious—that a major attack was slowly breaking over the entire division front. The volume of noise had been increasing around us for days as the tide slowly swept over us from the south. Artillery shells were constantly crisscrossing the sky, some sounding like hopeless sighs and others like invisible freight trains revealed in a brief orange flash. Deep thuds, *crumps,* and sustained thunder echoed repeatedly through the hills and valleys, causing the ground to tremble. Larger shells in our area caused the earth to jump. Men in the prone position learned to put a few inches between them and the ground or risk getting the air knocked from their lungs in a sudden body blow.

Lampaden to the north was getting hit hard. Flares of different colors, tracers, and flashes indicated heavy action there. The low clouds reflected dirty red for miles. And the same treatment was building around Hentern, where we had done contact patrols.

Just when we had our hopes built up to the winding down of the war, this heart-sinking horror loomed over us, and I had to fight my most-recent version of *This time there is no hope—I am going to die here.*

Five or six of us were suddenly shifted down the trench to the right where we were deployed to cover that flank. A German force had revealed their presence moving up the slope and behind our wire. Flare light showed upper bodies as they ascended. When within grenade range, we were ordered to pull and throw. By the time the grenades were dropping, our weapons were kicking shoulders. The activity was intense and short-lived as Germans were blown back, away, up, and down. A small number bravely (or drunk on Schnapps) came on and were instantly cut down. The shocked and screaming grunts and groans pleased me so deeply that I no longer recognized the stranger inhabiting my uniform.

Sent back to our original positions then, I stepped on several bodies I could not see in the blackness of the trench. Some did not move, but one did. I groped for the man I thought was wounded, but an angry Fasco pushed me away. He was out of the way of immediate harm. I tried to force him to his feet, but then gave up trying—he was too heavy and resistant. Although Fasco was our certified genius of night vision, so far he was a soldierly flop, and it irritated me deeply.

I left him there and pushed past guys until I arrived at my place. Our artillery had been adjusted to the left and behind us, where the enemy movement was likely to be. Our sense of isolation was further increased by having our own shells drop between us and the rest of the company in town. Yet, after a concentration or two, the battery once again was dropping 105s on the woods to the front. We had been getting some rockets screaming in; and, although they created large and loud explosions, they never dropped too close.

I felt as though the eye of a hurricane hovered over the hill for a while. The lull lasted too short a time. Six or eight mortar shells dropped in and cries of "Medic!" rang out tersely. Someone said, "They're coming."

One could see enough movement beyond the wire entanglements that we were left with no doubt that the main attack was upon us. I can never forget the sound of so many pops and sizzles as we let fly a barrage of grenades. They flashed and blew like supersize popcorn. A moment later, burp-gun fire tore up the earth again. As we dropped our heads, potato mashers began exploding around the trench. My hearing again deserted me; and, for an indeterminate passage of time, my actions—indescribable in words—consisted of firing and reloading my M1, as I had done with the grease gun in January and with the H Company machine gun. So much lead was flying around that I exposed only my arms and rifle. Someone shoved his way through the trench thrusting grenades onto the dirt ledge in front of each man. Then I saw Dan's profile as he squeezed off short bursts from his BAR. But within seconds, the concussion and flashes died out for the most part. We were then able to direct aimed fire, like Dan did, at the wire and beyond.

Several wounded were able to leave for town, supporting someone between them. Their spare bandoliers were passed around to us. The command to cease fire and conserve ammo flew along the trench. I had gone through one bandolier and most of another. One clip had separated in my shaking hand, and I quickly dropped it to load another. Normally, I tapped a clip of eight rounds against the stock of my rifle to ensure they were evenly spaced before shoving the clip into the rifle. But in my nervous haste, I performed a bad tap and they separated. Men were bumming rounds and clips from others. I had three clips left and a single grenade.

As my hearing began to return, I heard men grumbling about the stupidity of holding out here, and I hoped we would be ordered to get out and take up the defense in town. Instead, the platoon sergeant told four of us to rush to the CP near the church for ammo and grenades. I was shaking so badly that I could not for the life of me formulate a word, not even "okay." I hated being in the trench and hated leaving it for the open field. I could hear considerable screaming and moaning from beyond the wire as more shells began hitting the woods again. Sergeant Peters, recently returned from the hospital, was in charge of Hernandez, Fasco, and me: We were told to stay on the road and enter town ready with the password, because everyone there had nervous trigger fingers.

Because of random bullets flying nearby, we crawled over the back of the trench and crawled down the slope until it was okay to walk crouched over. Peters took the lead, with me next, then Fasco, and then Hernandez.

Halfway down the slope, Peters whispered "Down!" I passed the word back and scanned the area. More fires in the woods and buildings were reflecting off the low clouds, and slowly the garish red light increased. I had crawled next to Peters and saw several figures rise from the ground fifty feet downslope. They moved toward town—stopped and moved several times as we wiggled along behind on our bellies. I could not be sure whether they were German or GI, until finally Peters called out for them to halt with hands up. We rushed them before they could react one way or another. They were two enemy infantrymen armed with machine pistols and *panzerfausts*. Quickly disarming them, we knocked their helmets to the ground, toted their weapons, and herded our prisoners to the edge of town. There Peters called out to the antitank crew that we were coming in and for "Christ's sake hold your fire!" We passed through the street between the antitank's house and ours, answering anxious questions from out of the shadows about "What in hell is happening on the hill?"

I had so little confidence in Fasco that I kept behind him afraid he would suddenly "get lost" in an alley or doorway. Beyond the common smell of frontline soldiers, I noticed the unmistakable stink of alcohol while I walked behind the prisoners. In the next couple of days, that smell would rank equally with body rot and burned powder all around this town.

The small-arms fire and mortar shells that blew roofs apart caused us to move with utmost care as we navigated the cobblestones. We delivered our prisoners to an officer who had a phone to his ear. We had not frisked them, and I proceeded to do so—tempted to liberate a small treasure of canned sardines (but I didn't). We were especially interested to discover they were troopers of the 6th SS Mountain Division. We grabbed two cases of fragmentation grenades and two boxes of bandoliers. Hernandez ran in the door with belts of .30-caliber ammo draped over his shoulders for H Company's machine guns. We told the officer what outfit we were up against, and he whistled through his teeth as he again cranked the telephone handle to pass this information upstairs.

We moved as quickly as our heavy loads permitted through town and alerted the men on the perimeter that we were going out. We slogged through the mud uphill, and I was extremely impressed with the fact that we faced the SS. I was also impressed with their canteens of sweet-smelling booze. After the war, I would know the smell well and learn to call it Schnapps—usually made from potatoes. In my tender years I had not experienced alcohol, but at the war's end that would change.

The snow had little covering ability. It had stopped for the moment; but the ground was wet, and at times we seemed to move forward one step and then lose two. We all took spills from time to time as we tried to navigate a hill that seemed to be made of invisible banana skins. Mist becoming fog did not help either.

I had grown up on a bike and never went anywhere without it. And although my legs were exceptionally strong, the army revealed my upper-body weakness. I guess I was normally strong for most activity, but I could not climb a rope. Drill sergeants tried every threat in the book to scare me up the woven hemp, but to no avail. Hauling a fifty-pound pack twenty-five miles through the sand bordering Florida roads was terrible then. Later on, though, supporting my body on near frozen and deeply calloused feet was much worse.

We neared the top of the hill, and with respect to the continuous small-arms fire overhead, crawled and pushed our crates to the trench. There we passed the word up and down the line that we were up against the SS. I was put to work carrying belts of machine-gun ammo to the H Company crew on the right of the trench; bandoliers of M1 clips and the grenades were passed along.

Men ate, or some pulled a raincoat over their heads to sneak a smoke. They peered out at the woods and tried to squeeze off rounds at a muzzle flash. We knew the Germans had gained so much respect for our artillery that they avoided attacking over open ground the way they had done weeks before. Under cover of weather and darkness, they infiltrated slowly and silently as close to our positions as possible. When they unleashed the attack, often they were too close for us to use artillery effectively. We had the unhappy choice to call it in on our own position or to employ it to seal off their reserve and supply. And the former was about to happen.

Sometime in the wee hours, with wisps of mixed sleet and snow falling through the fog, the small-arms fire from the left and from the woods petered out—and, silently, every man, including Fasco, stood facing the woods hundreds of yards away. A pause in the area lasted a while. But, for miles to the north and south, the battle was becoming even more intense. Our radio came through from the CP that all contact with the 3d Platoon in Kummelerhof was lost. They were surrounded earlier in the five houses that comprised the village. Everything the platoon sergeant could get from the radio instantly passed from group to group along the trench.

Sometime later, Screaming Meemies came roaring overhead to fall in the town and just behind us. When that rocket split the air above you could not help but look skyward, expecting to see the very heavens rent and torn.

Shortly after the rockets and artillery roared in behind us, the dim shape of the barbed wire became confused and changed in shape, and we realized the Germans were there in force and were engaged in working through the strands. The sound of bolts clicking home was followed by shouts as well as a staccato and ragged volley that instantly became a roar of small-arms fire. The immediate reply of automatic fire blinking at us from the wire drowned out hollered instructions (if there were any), the cries of the wounded, and that warrior hate cry that welled up from God knows where. The German fire died out, but the relief lasted only seconds as the next line of SS troopers moved up to fire over the bodies of dead and dying—using them as shields. I did not hear the command for "Grenades!" but I followed the movement of men near me. The wire was well within throwing distance, and I had no doubt our frags would cause havoc out there. They did. But the SS troopers kept coming—kept firing and flipping in their potato mashers. Many of our men were hit, mostly by fragments, I think. I easily recall the sudden pain of dirt shot into my left aiming eye and thinking I had been hit. If my right eye had been open, I would have been blinded for a crucial minute. To sight my M1 then, I awkwardly turned my head to use my right eye to see and aim.

In my nervous, near panic state—momentarily half-blinded—I used up too many rounds in undisciplined firing. After reloading, I used the good fingers of my half-gloved right hand to try a quick swipe to clear my left eye of dirt, but to no avail. Trying to keep my nerve, I came up and quickly but carefully popped eight rounds down the length of barbed wire to my front.

I can best judge the time of that latest attack by the fact I had used more than half of the eight-round clips in my new bandolier. In the uneven light of the battle, I saw vague forms, Germans, dash to the trench on the right. From the yelling and noise, I figured they were stopped. Then figures were moving toward us from the wire. A dying flare revealed the total chaos of bodies in every conceivable position lying on and around the wire. There were SS men vaulting and stepping over these forms. The wire no longer held them.

I cursed myself for not having placed my bayonet on my

rifle. But the thought was fleeting as easy targets groped toward us. Flares continued to illuminate the jerky movements of the attackers, as they emerged from mist and smoke to finally locate and fire on our position—only to be knocked back by .30-caliber bullets. The worst part was not in firing at men ten to forty feet away, but in the shaky panic of being caught defenseless while groping madly for a fresh clip to shove into the open breech.

To this day, I have no clear idea how many men of our 2d Platoon and H Company machine gunners were killed or too shot up to save themselves—maybe one-half.

It was inevitable that if the Germans were willing to keep pushing men into and through our wire, we would be worn down to nothing. Someone next to me was grabbing my arm to get my attention. Dan was shouting in my ear that we were being outflanked all around. The platoon sergeant had called in artillery on our position and we were to use up our grenades in a bid to break for town. The grenades already were flying out as Dan and I tossed our last. Enright was yelling something; but everywhere I looked, our guys were hauling themselves out of the rear of the trench, many were moving backward while firing at fleeting targets in front of the trench. We headed down the dirt track through the fog and smoke. Too many figures were running toward town, so most of them had to be German. In the fields on both sides of the track, men kept pace with us, and they were our enemy. In the fog, our helmets and silhouettes were similar enough that this bizarre turn of events might keep us alive for another few seconds. No one thought we would ever make it to the town we had to defend, running almost cheek by jowl with the enemy who had to kill us to get the town.

About fifty yards from the trench, the roar of our artillery salvo came screaming in, descending just overhead and behind us. The orange light of exploding shells caused a million particles of mist and snow to reflect hellfire. Whizzing shards of red-hot metal sliced into flesh and bone of German and American bodies without distinction. The shells struck in the fields among the attackers. A German, jogging along with a machine gun over his shoulders, was on a parallel course not fifteen feet to my right. I could not shoot him because other Germans were running nearby. He glanced our way and changed direction away from the track—perhaps fearing it was mined.

Heavy tracers, the sort our .50-caliber machine guns fire, emerged from the fog and crossed from the left front and a few feet over the track. Then other American firing began from town as the SS ahead of us were closing in on the houses. I did not see any of our group hit as we raced through the cross fire of American weapons. Our only choice was to get to town or die here.

Ahead, men shouted to be allowed to pass into our lines. The shape of a house appeared, and I was in. German small-arms and shellfire was intense as we followed shouted orders to man first-floor windows in our 2d Platoon houses. There was pounding on the stairs as some of the platoon manned upstairs windows.

I found that Sergeant Peters was with me in a corner room. We stood on either side of the window facing the hill. But the Germans already were milling around directly below the window. Peters pulled a pin on his last frag and waited a couple of seconds after arming it. Then, he dropped it out the window, and at the explosion, he leaned out, raking the area below with his tommy gun. I had used the last of my grenades on the hill when we were overrun, and I felt semi-naked without the familiar weight hanging from a suspender strap.

We took turns, exposing as little of ourselves as possible, in firing out the window at fleeting forms and muzzle flashes. I could barely see in the fog and smoke that the disciplined SS troopers were prone on the exposed and bald slope, putting down covering fire for their groups moving in short dashes toward us. I felt I was hitting my moving targets with almost half of my shots, but the defensive small arms was so intense that other riflemen were simultaneously striking the same one. An extraordinarily sharp explosion sounded in the room next to ours, followed by heavy cursing. It was a *pan-*

zerfaust rocket. Sergeant Peters ran to the next room and re-turned immediately with the news that every man was down. He rejoined me at the window; visibly shaken, he shouted in my ear, "Jesus, it's a fucking mess in there." With Peters at one window, I moved to the other overlooking the antitank crew's house. They were not manning their 57mm gun in po-sition next to the house but were sending out a terrific vol-ume of small-arms fire at the hill.

Our platoon runner came in with some ammo and a few grenades stripped from the dead and wounded in the next room. Then he asked me to help carry more ammo from our house next door. We left Peters and found the medic crouched on the stairs, holding his head and shaking badly. The runner got no response from Buckner and could not pull his hands away from his head. I wondered who was tending the wounded in the cellar. Sergeant Enright shouted from the head of the stairs, and I pushed past the medic and raced up to him. He cupped his hand over my ear and shouted to me, "Bring ammo and grenades!" I tried to explain that the medic was totally out of it, but Enright was heading away.

Downstairs I found Cuzak and Giant in the kitchen where I had heated water and washed so peacefully days before. Several men were defending at two small windows. The run-ner and I hesitated at the back door, because anyone outside was liable to get shot by either army. Seeing no one, we dashed across the alley and into the arms of a GI, who showed us where the ammo was stashed.

The runner filled a musette bag with fragmentation and phosphorus grenades while I hoisted a heavy box of rifle bandoliers, and we stuffed .45-caliber and carbine ammo into our pockets. As we readied to dash across the alley again, the concussion from firing was as intense as ever. But a GI appeared out of the smoke wanting the medic, and I yelled in his ear that the medic was useless and the wounded were in our cellar. He followed us, limping badly.

We distributed ammunition throughout the house. Up-stairs, Salazar and Roberts pushed mattresses against the wall as shields from fragments. I did not see Dan anywhere—I felt a sudden chill all over as the realization hit me that he was either in the cellar, the other house, or had been hit.

Buckner, the medic, was no longer on the stairs when I returned to the corner room. Nor did I see Peters, but two men had a light .30-caliber machine gun on a table at the window facing the hill. They were part of an F Company platoon that had just been rushed in to replace our besieged 3d Platoon and were most welcome. I stumbled on something going to my window facing the antitank crew's house. I bent down and discovered a body that may have been Peters. It was headless, and the upper body was mangled. The tommy gun next to him convinced me it was the three-striper. I steeled myself to remove his magazines from his belt for reloading at the first opportunity and to keep his tommy gun close by. All movement had to be done on hands and knees because of the intermittent bullets chipping away at the walls.

Our artillery had been called in closer and closer to us. It became necessary to lie prone near the wall as the screaming rounds hit no more than fifty yards from us. They were doing a masterful job, but while it was happening, I was absolutely terrified and convinced that the short rounds would decimate us. That did not happen—but it definitely put a stop to incoming small-arms fire. Carefully looking out the windows, I could not see one weapon muzzle flash. And, as the smoke thinned and drifted off, I could see only figures of SS men moving away in the direction from where they came. Likely, they would come again given the chance. From below and to the left, tracers out of the .50-caliber machine gun in the trench shot at the retreating Germans. My F Company gunners added several short bursts as well. The incoming fire had slackened to almost nothing, so 2d Platoon blazed away from both houses. I was glad to be on the lower floor—not envying the men on the upper floors, where a short round could have made things even more uncomfortable than they had been.

My hearing improved after a while. Not much enemy small-arms fire was coming our way by then. I heard Captain Griffin or someone else run into the house shouting for

Sergeant Enright. After a quick talk, he left; and Enright called me and several other men to join him in the hall. He wanted Peters, until I told him Peters was dead. We were to patrol up the hill before things got hot again and bring in all of the wounded GIs' weapons and ammo that we could carry. He put me in charge of four other men; one new man I recall was Proctor.

I went to the door and shouted to the antitank crew across the street to watch for our return from the hill. Our artillery had walked its barrage up the hill where the last shells were erupting beyond our old trench. Someone in the antitank crew shouted from a darkened window, warning me about isolated infiltrators in the area out to cause trouble. With great caution, we filed out from the protection of the house, past our half-track, and into drifting smoke and mist. I had everyone maintain about a ten-yard interval in Indian file, just enough to not lose sight of each other, wander off on a tangent, and get shot by the SS—or one of us. I was especially concerned with the clumps of dead men scattered everywhere. Certainly some of them were alive and capable of blowing some of us away. Because of the atmospheric conditions and the nature of the patrol, I had left my M1 in the house and carried Peters's tommy gun with extra magazines taped together.

The immediate area was almost deadly quiet as I zigzagged from individual bodies to groups clustered together, probing them heavily with the muzzle of my weapon. From off the road in the mist, we all heard the voice off and on uttering sounds of pain. I could understand only *"Bitte, bitte"* (Please, please). We ignored him. After about one hundred yards, we had passed so many dead men, especially on the left of the road, that a sense of deep awe took hold of me realizing that the entire hill from town to the woods must be like this. The ground was torn up everywhere from exploded shells. A couple of glows off in the mist probably were fires started on the uniforms and equipment of men. The stink of burned powder, wet earth turned upside down, and the sickening stench of blood made me almost retch. The awe I had felt moments before nose-dived into a descending vortex of depression such as I had never experienced: It frightened me worse than the physical fear of a flesh wound. Mentally, it was so powerful that I felt it could rip away my sanity. I knew it was imperative to get this patrol over and done with and get off this hill.

Moving forms materialized from the mist—a line of six or eight Germans crossed from the left and over the road to our front. From the long shapes they carried, I decided they were medics and litter-bearers. They silently blended back into the mist and we moved on past a splattering of body parts concentrically arranged around a shell hole dead center in the road. By then, the tic around my mouth included my left eye. I could no longer control it nor the shuddering of my body. Fortunately, at that moment, my attention shifted to an M34 machine gun and scattered drums of ammo. Just beyond lay the body of the gunner. As I examined the weapon (which appeared serviceable), the gunner who veered away from me when we ran down the hill earlier flashed into my mind. I stashed the gun and ammo on the road for our return trip; we did the same for other usable weapons along the way.

A little farther on, we came upon the first dead American. The artillery had thrown him around several times, taking parts of his body with each explosion. A broken M1 and a combat boot with a leg sticking out lay together in the mud.

I froze in place as a German shouted out what sounded like a warning. Sound carries a long way in mist, and I had no way to determine how close the enemy soldier was. An answering bellow or command, plus the unmistakable click of a machine-gun bolt, sent me off the road to the right, the others following. Immediately, tracers flicked past over the road. Two or three bursts and it quit. But individual rifles fired inaccurately six or eight times and ceased; then, nervously, they fired several times over a period of a few minutes at what they could not see but could imagine. I believe a wounded SS trooper had spotted us and warned them. The firing most likely came from our old trench.

We lay quiet in the mud several minutes until one of my

patrol crawled up to whisper he had found a BAR. My heart sank as I flashed on Dan. A platoon has up to six BARs. We no longer had half that number in action. I crawled over and found that the weapon lacked a front sight: We found Dan next to two dead SS troopers. Blood-soaked, he dryly croaked for water, but he was unable to drink from my canteen. We tried to lift him, and he gasped horribly in pain. For the first time, I removed the syringe of morphine I carried with me. I had been instructed months before to plunge the needle into the soft base of the thumb, and I did so. We waited for the drug to take effect. I could smell burned cloth and had no idea what had hit him. I decided it was better not to start probing.

I sat on the body of a dead German next to Dan. Proctor moved to a blasted tree nearby where other bodies lay. He whispered my name, and I reluctantly left Dan to join him. A dead American was crouched against the tree aiming his rifle across the field; his shape, so full of action, made the scene disconcerting. Proctor moved to the dead rifleman's front and grasped the rifle by the muzzle to pull it away from the corpse. But a hair-triggered nerve acted like a coiled rubber band, and completing his last deliberate act, the dead soldier jerked the trigger. I knew the bullet had struck Proctor, who let go of the rifle as it fell to the ground along with the dead man. Immobilized, I stared at Proctor, who hesitated in shocked silence a moment. I thought he was falling over, but he had actually bent down to retrieve the M1, and then he straightened up and shouldered the weapon. I grabbed whatever ammo was handy, and we returned to Dan. Whispering in Dan's ear, I told him we had to move him. Salazar and I moved him between us, and we headed for town with an assortment of weapons and ammunition slung over our shoulders. If, for some strange reason, Proctor did not know he had been hit, I was not about to tell him. We had to get Dan and the weapons to town.

A big fire in the wooded draw between Lampaden and us turned the low clouds and smoke a dirty red. Fires had broken out in the woods and buildings. Shellfire and tracers had started fires on clothing and equipment of some of the dead. Fog, smoke, and snow particles reflected hellish light everywhere I looked. Some days later, I did sketches of the battle; one was later enlarged into a painting titled *Carrying Dan In*.

Many incapacitated wounded soldiers were in the cellar then, with a medic from another platoon having taken over. Buckner, our platoon medic, had been put to work replacing rifle parts and reloading BAR and tommy-gun magazines—he was through with treating the wounded. Then I showed Proctor the blood on his uniform. The bullet had gone through a relaxed muscle, hitting nothing really important and leaving a slightly larger hole on exiting. I left him there with his mouth and eyes wide open in shock.

We had left the hill not a moment too soon: A little later more SS troopers began moving down the slope toward us. I shouted upstairs to the platoon sergeant that we were back from the hill. He sent me off to find the CO to request artillery fire on the hill again. (His walkie-talkie was not working well.)

The CP was a short distance away near the tiny church in the center of the town. Dawn was probing the fog as I bumped into a sergeant of the H Company 81mm mortars. I hurriedly requested fire on the slopes of 468 and then found the CO at the church. Many of the German townsfolk were under guard in the church cellar. I could hear hysterical crying from several women. Activity was frantic with our men running here and there, and with orders and reports being shouted back and forth. I explained to the CO that we were again under attack from Hill 468 and that the platoon sergeant wanted artillery. His head was heavily bandaged and he did not look at all well—he probably was in a lot of pain. Later, I understood he was half-blind. Our tough first sergeant grabbed me and ordered me to take the SS prisoners behind the church and shoot them and then get back to 2d Platoon. They were too much to guard at this crucial point in the battle. He looked at me and said, "Now!" Pulling myself together, I turned to the prisoners sitting on the floor and motioned them outside. They slowly shuffled to their feet. Both were in their middle or late twenties. I walked them out the door and to the left around the building where I lost no time in firing a round into the back of the man nearest me. Both men dropped instantly. I had the fleeting thought that the single round had gone through both troopers because we were moving in file. I could not tell, though, because it was too dark, so I quickly fired a round into the head of each one. As I prepared to jump to the cobblestones from the little church hill, I changed my mind and went through the pockets of the dead men. I came up with several tins of sardines, cheese, and hard biscuits that I stuffed into my pocket—then I jumped down and headed back to 2d Platoon.

Most men kept to the buildings and moved through the streets at their personal risk, with lead splattering into walls and mortar shells scattering fragments around. Our house was about a hundred yards down the winding street, and it was crucial to plot every yard of the trip. I could not possibly know whether the forms that moved in the shadows were infiltrating SS or GIs. From memory, I knew that the other side of the street had more cover of doors and alleys. Yet, I was extremely leery to leave the comparative safety of my doorway.

That safety seemed in grave doubt, however, when I felt a weapon prod my back. But I was challenged by an American voice, and I immediately responded with the password. He was a squad leader from the F Company platoon, and he, with a couple of riflemen, occupied this building. I asked what they were doing in the middle of town while their platoon was on the northeast perimeter. Laconically, they told me that they had lost several houses, and the perimeter was shrinking. This barn was being held because it controlled the intersection of several streets. We ducked back inside the large door as shells screamed in, hitting nearby. A BAR man was at the window next to the door, and a rifleman stood to the side of the barn door.

I tried to plot where the small-arms fire was coming from, but I could not make heads or tails out of it: The fire came from every direction, so I assumed we were surrounded.

Then a jeep and trailer sped past the door, its destination a complete mystery.

I had just decided to make my dash across the street when German burp-gun fire down the street made me stop. There was movement—something small running toward us. With a clatter of hooves, several goats or sheep turned the corner. More shooting and shouts were followed by movement fifty yards down the street. Amazingly, farm animals, horses, and oxen were being spooked and driven through the street. They came on, some stopping and others pushing. Behind the animals, muzzle flashes of burp guns sent the animals clattering down the street toward us in total panic. The Germans, yelling and laughing, were using the animals as a moving shield and were coming closer. The men with me cursed a blue streak as the BAR opened up.

It was one thing to bring ourselves to shoot at men, and totally another to have this situation thrust at us. I believe I tried to fire just over the animals, but in the fog and smoke, it was not militarily practical. Bullets thumped into the panicked mass that bore down on us, and the thrashing and crying animals did not entirely come to a halt at our door: Some broke for the turn to our right toward 2d Platoon.

Four or five shouting German soldiers, mostly firing into the air, moved through the kicking and wounded beasts. We cut them down immediately. Someone tossed a grenade over the horror for good measure. After the initial shock passed, one of the F Company men went outside and began firing single rounds; I assumed he was putting some of the animals and Germans out of their misery.

Several riflemen of the 1st Platoon appeared out of the dark, exchanging the password with me. All of them appeared wounded and informed us that some mortarmen and G Company men were taken prisoners and were being held in a house a couple of blocks over. Captain Griffin and the rest of Headquarters Platoon appeared out of the smoke with remnants of squads. It was obvious from the orders he was giving that more than one-half the town was lost and we were standing in the front line. The CP and church had just fallen. I took off as cautiously as possible to rejoin my platoon a block away, when suddenly several German-speaking men moved close by and squatted about ten feet away. There was plenty of noise to cover any sound of my backing away. I almost fell over something behind me. I crouched behind a two-wheeled cart loaded with manure that tipped enough for me to half bury myself in shit. The dim forms of the enemy soldiers faded, and I resumed my trip to 2d Platoon with a wildly beating heart. I moved through the rubble as I slipped between houses and outbuildings. Griffin and the first sergeant soon came up behind me and called for Sergeant Enright; they conferred with him and then left with several riflemen. I gathered they were going to attempt a counterattack to retake some buildings.

Scattered outbreaks of small-arms fire erupted from all directions as 6 March reached full daylight. But the heavy action of the dark hours had settled down to groups of men crawling through rubble and cellar windows trying for position. For the most part, G Company held only approximately ten buildings and was busy trying to create a consistent perimeter of sorts. The Germans used *panzerfausts* and automatic fire to cover their troopers, who were constantly infiltrating with potato mashers and burp guns. Sniper duels were common. The German attack from the hill had been stopped while I was at the CP. Small-arms fire from the hill continued, and it was risky to even take a quick look out the windows.

I shared my looted sardines and cheese with Giant, Fasco, and Sanders, as we all stood watch in our house. We listened to the sound of a tank a few blocks away—American—and heard a sharp exchange of gunfire and grenades.

The fog was still at its thickest in the morning gloom when a burst of firing began just across the street, where our 57mm antitank gun sat. A shouting exchange with them informed us that Germans had occupied the house next to them, which was located just across the cobblestone street from us. I judged from the lively exchange of small-arms fire that the

Germans were about to storm the antitank crew and completely control that side of the street. Sergeant Siegel called me to the foot of the stairs and told me to support the light machine gun in the corner room. I helped shift the table with the machine gun to the window over the half-track. The assistant gunner had a smashed shoulder but was doing his best to help us with his one good arm.

We could not effectively fire on the German-held house because its thick wall facing us had no windows or doors. The one-armed gunner was squatting behind his gun waiting for the SS to show themselves if they rushed out between their house and the antitank crew's house. I was torn between staying at my post and running down to the cellar to make sure Dan and the others were being looked after. But it was totally out of my hands. I hoped the morphine would screen Dan from the pain for quite a while.

The fog remained dense, and the light snow had stopped. There was a lull in the fighting where we were, although the shelling and small arms continued everywhere else. Compared to the earlier intensity, the sniping and intermittent small-arms fire seemed like a respite.

The sound of a jeep motor whining at top speed brought me back to the window. A renewed burst of automatic fire south of town sounded from the direction of the jeep's motor. It swung into view at the base of the hill and skidded around the corner between the antitank gun and us. It barely missed colliding with the half-track and came to a stop just up the street. Several men shouted at the driver: I could see it was Watson, of all people. Understanding he was in the line of fire in a shrinking perimeter, Watson put the jeep in gear and bounced over the rubble, disappearing behind a wall.

Watson had been in our squad and several times had run off when things got too hot for him. Nevertheless, he was well liked and therefore was placed into Headquarters Platoon. He had driven through the Germans in the dark some miles to the rear, loaded up the trailer with desperately needed ammo, and dashed through German fire in the fog to get it to us. I thought that was great. The guy with the huge grin was viewed as a savior. I believe he received a Bronze Star—one of few medals given to a company full of heroes. I never heard anything good from the men about medals. There was something on the dark side about such recognition for actions best pushed to the farthest corner of memory. Medals did assume some importance after V-E Day when the point system toward discharge was better understood as a method to get a man home sooner.

Someone showed up with belts of .50-caliber ammo, wanting to know where to take them. Sanders and I relieved him of his load and, leaving by the kitchen door, turned right for the trench in front of our house. Three men were slumped there behind the .50 sitting on its tripod. We dumped the ammo on the canvas beside the big weapon and exchanged whatever information and rumors seemed pertinent. We saw movement to our front, which turned out to be a horse dimly outlined in the mist. Its gait was uneven as it moved closer, snorting and sniffing itself. It stumbled along sidewise, avoiding stepping on its smoking intestines that trailed behind. The trembling animal alternately sniffed its gray flesh and whipped its head back and forth. After some moments, both Sanders and I shot the animal. I had waited some seconds to aim for a spot just under the ear, and the creature instantly dropped to the ground.

I offered a tin of sardines to the gunner before I returned to the house. He declined and revealed a musette bag with a good stock of tins. He had been crawling around the nearest dead and wounded in the dark, killing the wounded with his trench knife and hunting for pistols. He had a Luger and a P38 pistol.

I descended to the candlelit cellar, which was a madhouse of stink and repressed moaning. Wounded men were everywhere; and in the alcove under the kitchen, some of the dead were stacked. Several times, I crisscrossed the cellar trying not to step on anyone and failed to see Dan. It was too much for me to believe my buddy was stacked in the alcove. On the edge of despair, I called out his name, when someone gripped my boot. I squatted and turned on my flashlight, but I did not recognize him. He lay on his side with his legs drawn. Several seconds passed before I forced myself to conclude this was Dan—he had changed so much: He was shrunken and blue-white; his eyes could not focus well nor could he speak. I could barely control my anguish because I realized he was dying. I forced my eyes from his face and found Sergeant Enright looking at me. He looked away. Sergeant Siegel clattered down the stairs to talk to Enright and headed me to the stairs with two words, "Another attack!"

I picked my way through the wounded on the cellar floor and looked back toward Dan, but I could make out only tangled forms in the candlelight. I climbed the stairs, trying to rid my lungs of the smelly mixture of blood, excrement, and urine that had replaced the earthy fragrances of only one day before—farm smells of potatoes and other stored vegetables. Upstairs, the gut-wrenching stink of the cellar was replaced with pungent smells of expended ammo and the steadily increasing noise of small-arms fire.

Back in the corner room, the two gunners had shifted the light .30 back to the south window facing Hill 468 and were kneeling behind the gun, firing aimed bursts of four to six rounds. I took the west window facing the antitank crew's house. From the direction the gunners were firing, I knew the latest attack was approaching from the southeast rather than from our old trench. I kept my attention on the house behind the antitank crew's house, wondering whether the Germans tried to cross the five or six yards to take the crew from the rear. Some minutes later, a *panzerfaust* burst against the antitanker's house—the telltale volume of white smoke following the explosion came from the opposing house. Almost immediately, three figures quickly moved into view approaching the smoking hole in the wall. I must have fired five-plus rounds as rapidly as possible. I knew I had hit two of them, although they dropped out of my sight. The distance was only about forty feet. The third figure froze looking in my direction. He carried an M1 rifle and had an

American helmet. We both froze for a long moment. Then he dropped the weapon and raised his hands, his mouth working although he did not or could not speak. I saw he was a middle-aged civilian. I could not afford to take a prisoner, and I kept my rifle on him. A Yankee voice called from the antitank house wanting to know the score. I yelled back, "Two down!" I passionately hated seeing that GI helmet on the German's head. A single shot from the floor above knocked the man down. I wanted to shout the correction, "Make that three down," but it just did not verbalize. It occurred to me that when our OP and the church fell to the SS, they pressed some of the farmers into service. I couldn't wait to relate the incident to Dan—then I remembered him in the cellar.

Desperate men moved from house to house and crawled through rubble everywhere, on the hunt. Every GI had an urgent need to know what was happening a block away. Information and rumors were continuously exchanged. A runner from 1st Platoon passed through looking for the captain and exchanging the latest. In this way, plus through the reverberation of more intense small-arms fire, we learned that G and F Companies' platoons were being whittled down and losing ground. Our entire perimeter kept shrinking as more and more SS men infiltrated the town. We had been killing many more of them than they killed of us, but at the rate of their increased commitment, a few more hours would see them take over the town.

The rumor we cherished most stated that another company was on the way to try and break through the circle to help us push the Germans out. Our ambivalence with rumors was that we wanted to believe them, but we couldn't.

The last GI I had seen on the street was Watson when he drove the jeep behind the wall. I had absolutely no idea who else might be guarding the cobblestone street extending from the antitank crew's house up to the church in the town center. From time to time, I could hear the sounds of firing and movement in the room above me where Sergeant Siegel and another man were. The volume of lead blasting the walls was so intense that only the briefest of glances through windows and holes could be managed.

Artillery and mortar fire never slackened all morning. Every house and barn took more than a few hits. Mortars dropped into the rooftops and streets—artillery did the same, but it also blew holes in walls. The *panzerfausts* that the SS infantry used helped them blast their way through walls and enabled the use of potato masher grenades in closer combat. The *panzerfaust,* a relatively simple one-shot weapon, was incredibly effective against our thin-skinned tanks. I never fired one, but I figured they were better than our bazooka, more punch.

I snapped out of my random thoughts as movement in the side street below caught my eye. Reaching over to slap the arm of the gunner behind me, I muttered "Krauts!" Five or six of them stood around the half-track some ten feet below the level of my window. A quick glance revealed a couple of troopers half inside the tracked vehicle, starting up the motor. One had armed a potato masher, and as he drew back his arm to launch it at my window, our eyes locked. This grenade hit me on the chest and ricocheted back down. I did not catch it and return it—it had just happened too fast for reaction. But as the masher dropped toward the hood of the half-track, a hissing phosphorous grenade dropped past my window from the floor above. I shouted "Grenade!" and dived to the floor as explosion followed explosion and yellow light and great heat pushed into the room. There was no air to breathe, and the ceiling was a mass of flame that soon dissipated. I was on fire and jumped to my feet to rip off my suspenders and pull off my field jacket. The gunner with two good arms got it off me with a few good jerks. Off came my sweater, two OD shirts, and upper underwear. I knew the gunner had burned his hands jumping to my aid.

I grabbed my cartridge belt and smoking suspenders; not seeing my rifle, I found the tommy gun. The gunners grabbed their carbines, and we quickly exited the room while the fire intensified. Worried about the enemy soldiers outside, I rushed to the side door, but the heat was too great in the street. I decided we were pretty well covered by the fire on that side and went out through the kitchen and behind the house to the wall by the street. A cautious look over the wall showed what must have been men, black and burning, lying on the cobblestones. Ammo was popping and sending sparks everywhere. The half-track was one roaring inferno, and I saw no life in the street. But on the other side of the wall, someone was moving in real distress. I moved to the heavy wooden door in the wall and pulled it open. His body from the knees upward was burned black—but the jackboots were clearly discernible. Leaning against the wall, he inched his way in my direction. A shot, possibly from the antitank, knocked the blackened apparition to the cobblestones, and I returned to the shelter of the house.

I salvaged my rifle from the smoke-filled room; yet, in my panicked mind, I forgot the artwork in the blanket. In the *panzerfaust*-smashed room, I chose the least bloody upper clothing I could salvage from the three dead GIs and headed for the cellar. In the hall, Sergeant Siegel rushed past looking at my half-nude body, but he said nothing, as though he could not believe his eyes. Shaking with the cold, I headed for the cellar and searched for our former medic's bag of supplies. I confiscated the Vaseline jar while Buckner sat in the corner—babbling nonstop. I asked him to rub the oily stuff on my back and, surprisingly, he immediately complied.

With a not-too-bloody uniform on my body again, I picked my way through the wounded toward Dan, but was stopped by the muffled voice of someone whose lower face was swathed in bandages. He motioned me to the wall where he was sitting. By the sheer size of him and his cowlike eyes, I decided Giant had gotten in the way of some metal. He pulled the bandages down to reveal two neat holes, one in each cheek. His habit of letting his lower jaw hang down probably saved his life. A bullet missed his tongue and passed between his teeth. A half-inch one way or the other, and his jaw would have been blown apart. I flashed on my own childhood habit and the wasp that flew right down my throat. Then Giant held my arm, and the expression on his face made me pause: He said Cuzak was dead, and hesitating, he added that Dan was gone, too.

Looking back over the years, I believe those weeks of one combat experience after another had so inured me to that ongoing stress that I successfully buried it until the postwar years. Then, at its own pace, it resurfaced as duodenal ulcers, trench mouth, minor-but-obvious scar tissue on my back, and insistent but difficult-to-locate inner scar tissue.

Trancelike, I moved over the filth-slickened floor to Dan's body and could find no pulse on his neck. He remained, as I had found him earlier, on his side. I groped for the waterproof package where he kept his letters and my V-mail drawing. The hole in his back, probably caused by American shrapnel, had blood-soaked his entire upper body as well as the waterproof. I forgot what I whispered to him while I considered removing one of his dog tags, black with dried blood. It was pointless, with Dan and the other dead together in the cellar, to complicate things for the graves' registration unit. Cuzak's body was nearby. Minus their personalities, the dead almost never resembled the men I knew alive. A sameness pervaded in all those killed who still had faces. Some had none. Proctor seemed to be doing okay lying on his back near the stairs. I urged Giant to collect himself and rejoin the war effort.

We climbed to the second floor to report to Sergeant Siegel. There, considerable excitement and jubilation was evident: I heard tanks—ours! At a south window facing the hill, I saw several tanks and squads of infantry moving up the slope from the west. Small-arms fire from our old trench at the hilltop broke out, answered immediately by the newly arrived GIs. Joyfully, I joined men at the windows, using some Kentucky windage to empty a couple of clips at the few Germans we could see as they hightailed out of there. The actual trench could not be seen even from the tallest building in town, as it was situated just over the hillcrest. I saw GIs digging in just west of the track leading uphill where we had found Dan.

Hill 468 was ours again. This time we would keep it. But the fighting a few houses away in our ever-smaller perimeter continued as fiercely as before. The town continued to receive artillery fire as well as small-arms fire from the ridge to the east. Fire also came from a row of trees 150 yards southeast, where an unending barrage of *panzerfausts* and automatic fire originated. A strong attack had been launched earlier from that slightly elevated track and tree line and a few houses. Enough SS succeeded in getting to town that they were able to cut off and capture some mortarmen and some G Company men. These were the men later freed by our guys, although several were hit in the process, including Sergeant Enright.

At this point, the newly arrived tanks headed in our direction with squads of supporting infantry alongside. As they filed past our still-burning half-track men in the upper window shouted cheers and questions. Despite the roar of tank engines—often so loud one could see mortar shells bursting, yet not hear the detonation over the engine sounds—we finally understood they were C Company. They had broken through the trap the SS had forced around us.

We watched as the infantry peeled off along the street to shake down the houses and barns. They fought their way to the church, and I lost sight of them as they eventually pushed the SS from the town. Several more wounded GIs were discovered—prisoners and a couple of riflemen who were overrun and in hiding. A squad from C Company was attached to us in the house and in the trench near the .50-caliber machine gun. The tanks clanked their way out of town and again established positions on the hill.

Some of us left the house and took up defensive positions in the rubble near the trench. All the fog had finally dissipated although a great deal of smoke continued to generate from burning buildings and shell bursts. We hoped the SS would simply fade away to the east. For the past forty minutes or so, heavy shelling was blasting 468 without letup. If this was not revenge for getting kicked off the hill, then it appeared the foes were determined to push their infantry at us yet again. Germans did not use this much heavy ammo without some sort of plan. My location in the rubble was within thirty feet of our kitchen door in the alley, and the first shell that dropped a little closer down the hill would see me dash for the house.

I watched Salazar as he methodically zeroed in his M1. For a target, he chose a dead SS trooper propped up against a tree some three hundred yards upslope. He fired while another man used binoculars to call his shots. Finally, when the body gave a noticeable jump, he stopped clicking the sight adjustment and winked at me. So I followed the procedure, clicking and firing until there was not much left to fire at.

I almost hoped they would come at us again, because I truly hated them and wanted the pleasure of killing more. My wish was later granted as the east wind carried the sound of tracked vehicles, not ours, heading in our direction. I strongly considered retracting my wish. Voices called down from upper windows, announcing that three self-propelled guns (SPs) had been sighted emerging from the woods on the road from Kummelerhof (where the 3d Platoon had last been seen). Fifty or so infantry were fanning out on the open ridge in preparation for their assault. The SPs opened fire, their shells screaming into the buildings to our left, and then we could see them clearly as the attack advanced. Our tanks, spread out with C Company, advanced over the track; and the first round that fired from the tank closest to us blossomed orange as it hit the front of the German gun. A cheer went up: It was so beautiful to see. Then, a tremendous volley of small arms thundered from our entire perimeter. We all rose to our feet to better see our targets and give vent to exuberance only felt and enjoyed in these moments so rare in life. We cut the attack to pieces in mere seconds; it wavered and died in its infancy, as a few survivors turned and headed east—along with the surviving SP, trailing heavy smoke behind.

The unhappy sight of many C Company casualties being

carried from the hill bore testimony to the German artillery's accuracy. C Company men had not had sufficient time to dig in before the barrage dropped in. A squad or two were positioned to hold the hill—probably in our old trench—while the rest of C Company was brought into town to the relative protection of the houses.

We heard sometime later that after our 3d Platoon had lost contact with us, off and on they were in contact by 300 SCR with F Company in Hentern. The 3d Platoon had been under constant attack since around midnight and held out to around midday of 6 March.

One by one the GIs had lost four of the five houses comprising Kummelerhof. The SPs and *panzerfausts* reduced the last house until little was left of the rubble over the cellar. Almost all of the new replacements, and some of the veteran men's charred bodies, lay scattered in the debris. The survivors—out of ammunition and wounded, with only a few men left on their feet—had no choice but to surrender under threats of being grenaded in their cellar. They carried eighteen dead American soldiers from the rubble of the five houses and placed them in a line near the road. They would be marched across Germany—subsisting on roots, pig mash, dandelions, snails, and rotten potato peelings dug up from the fields along the line of march.

Sporadic shelling continued into the night. For my part, I joined the ranks of those staying close to outhouses. And because the one behind our roofless house was in shambles, we used an area below the back wall. In between diarrhea attacks, I would pull my GI pants over my frozen rear end and either vomit or have to drop the pants again. Buckner was one of the several men constantly using our impromptu latrine. Helmetless and minus his knit cap, Buckner's normally dark hair—which had been slightly graying around the ears—suddenly appeared even more salt than pepper. I guess I decided he had a dusting of powdered plaster. But a couple of days later, we all realized Buckner's hair had turned white practically overnight, certainly much whiter than it was on the evening of 6 March.

I recall that our company cooks and clerks, who had been in the thick of the action and survived, managed a hot meal of sorts. I do not recall much of it being eaten by the fifty or so men of G Company still on their feet. The casualties of the H Company heavy-weapons men, the antitank and F Company's platoons, and C Company were as severe as ours. I cannot recall any contact with the German residents, although some made their way to inspect what was left of their homes. SS prisoners were herded off somewhere. Ambulances crammed with the wounded headed to the rear, and I remember nothing else except the smoke that deepened dusk into night. That night was a combination of fitful sleep and trips to the wall while stepping over the forms of sleeping, murmuring men. The smell of cigarette smoke hung everywhere punctuated with little glowing points of light that intensified as the smoke was inhaled. I never did smoke tobacco, but I always drew my ration of cartons of Lucky Strikes or Camels for extra smokes for Dan and the others who did smoke.

Aside from the tobacco smoke, the cold air drifted in through the smashed walls, carrying the familiar smell of farm-town manure, wet fields, and occasional whiffs of absolutely clean, fresh air. But the purity of the moment was always suppressed by the ever present stink of burned powder and smoke.

The god-awful smell of the cellar began rising through the debris. I shouldered Peters's tommy gun, left the house, and stood next to the burned-out half-track, looking at the forms of the dead SS troopers lying on the cobblestones. I tried to feel something—anything. I wanted to hate them with the intensity of passion that had ruled me yesterday, but nothing came of it. I was devoid of feeling.

The shelling of our town had petered and died hours earlier. It turned out that the Germans were conserving their supply of shells and orienting their guns elsewhere, namely Lampaden.

I leaned against the half-track next to the passenger side where the form of something vaguely human sat half in, half

out. All around me, the five or six dead troopers were beginning to give off the final stench that easily covered over the
smell of fatty burned meat, cloth, leather, and alcohol. I
thought of looting their bodies.

The night was so dark and the silence so pervasive that
sudden light reflecting on the clouds overhead startled me.
Seconds later, the thunder of exploding shells in the direction of Lampaden filled the darkness with a foreboding of
further disaster. The buildings around me blocked my view
across the landscape to Lampaden. A glance at the fluores-
cent dial of my watch showed ten minutes past 0400. I had
been hearing firing far away to the northwest, and I wondered what was going on so far behind our lines.

The vague sound of shuffling footfalls from down the
street caught my attention, as a line of some eight or ten men
moved past me. They never noticed me in the dark as they
headed toward the track on Hill 468.

Twenty minutes later, a line of men stumbled past me
heading for the town center. Apparently, the men in the trench
had been relieved. But in that twenty minutes, I had under-
taken and completed a task I later wished I had never even
considered: It began with the charred remains sitting in the
half-track. Removing the death's-head SS ring was easy. It
was more difficult with the troopers lying on the cobblestones, however, because their fingers were badly swollen
and required removal by my knife. The shelling of Lampaden
grew in volume, and the flickering cloud reflections occasionally aided me in locating the correct, but swollen, hand that
sported the trophy. The last ring I collected was from the
burned man who was shot next to the door in the wall. I had
kept a careful tally and had acquired six silver rings on which,
in the dark, my fingers could trace the shape of the skull.
Then I crossed the street to the space between the antitank
house and the house next to it. As I bent to my work on the
two Germans I had killed, I heard movement through the hole
the *panzerfaust* had blasted in the wall. I muttered the password and eventually got the countersign. A voice asked what
I was doing, and I responded I was hunting pistols.

I then had eight rings. Pausing at the third body, that of the farmer, I groped about until I found the helmet and M1, which I carried across to my 2d Platoon house and placed just inside the door. I shiver with anger even now, remembering some GI's helmet and M1 being used by the enemy farmer.

I picked my way carefully through the rubble to the kitchen door where a lone sentry leaned against the wall next to the small window. I told him I was going out and would be back soon—friendly fire was something I avoided with great care. I walked between the house and the .50-caliber machine-gun trench to the bodies of the SS men Peters had killed. The ring fingers were missing. Back at the .50-caliber machine gun, I asked a soldier if he had come across any separated fingers in the area. But from the deeper shadows of the trench, the laconic voice of the gunner who had collected the stash of tinned fish from German wounded and dead answered me. A rattling tinkle of sound in the dark piqued my curiosity. He said he had already collected fifteen or twenty rings and several P38s and Lugers. And he offered me a piece of communication wire to tie together my rings if I was also in the business. He figured the pistols were worth $100 apiece in rear echelon—the rings, rare as they were, should be worth anywhere from $50 to $150 apiece. I took the wire, strung the eight rings to it, and tied it around my neck, along with my dog tags, St. Christopher medal, and rosary. Survival in combat had both progressed and regressed me. No soldier can say otherwise.

I knew the Germans were on the move in front of Lampaden because heavy small-arms fire had joined in with the artillery thunder. The fog closed in again as it did every night well before dawn. And off to the northwest, occasional firing of small arms could be dimly heard, interspersed with the thump and *crump* of artillery. The Germans were throwing everything but the kitchen sink at Lampaden. The flat, sharp sounds of our 105mm cannons in the rear signaled that plenty of American help was plastering those areas east of Lampaden. Later on, heavier U.S. artillery shells rushed far overhead to saturate the enemy east of the town. The fighting lasted all day.

Meanwhile Schomerich received little attention from the enemy. It was 7 March, and we were put to work—with handkerchiefs over our noses—lifting the dead out of the cellar. The wounded had been evacuated the evening before while so many of us huddled in misery against the garden wall, flushing memories from inflamed assholes. In my case, one opening was not enough to handle the exodus, so I employed both ends.

At no time during the removal of the dead did I look at the blackened faces of the bodies we lined up on the cobblestones. Grave-registration troops arrived, and we helped fill several six-by-sixes with the bodies—heads to the front, boots to the tailgate. And, of course, my mind flashed back to Wochern in the freezing dusk of the January day when I saw the shattered legs sticking out of the six-by-six.

I grabbed my blanket roll and found a measure of solitude in the rubble of the upstairs bedroom. My drawings had survived the fire although one of the blankets protecting them was scorched, and I had to toss it aside. After leafing through all of them, I took a sheet of reasonably clean bond paper and tried to sketch in the trench on Hill 468. Strangely, my hand's shaking subsided considerably when the scene of carrying Dan in insisted on appearing on the paper. Just after the war, this became a painting in oil over paper.

Sergeant Siegel put everybody to work policing the area for weapons, ammo, and equipment. A patrol reached Kummelerhof and found the eighteen dead GIs but no enemy activity, so a truck was sent out to bring back the bodies.

We caught one of the patrols early in the evening of 8 March, as we repeated the route we had taken four or five nights previously—which by then seemed weeks ago. We went up the hill during the afternoon because early fog provided good cover. Although we did not anticipate much enemy activity this side of the river, we knew we might encounter a patrol. Giant and Sanders went with Manly and me back up the dirt track of 468. So much artillery of both armies had chewed and regurgitated the slope and field on top that the shape of the track had all but disappeared. Everywhere we saw holes with broken clods of dirt piled every which way. Broken and smashed weapons and equipment, mixed with bits and pieces of mangled and blackened flesh, lay scattered about. Nothing had color. Everything was in muddied tones of gray ranging to black. The atmosphere was heavy and utterly depressing as we drifted dreamlike through a miasma of rot rising from the mud. We constantly altered our course up the hill around shell holes. Some bodies were complete; others were partially stripped of clothing and skin. A shell that may have been a Screaming Meemie rocket lay half buried and unexploded in mud, and several mortar shells with fins exposed were passed with care. We arrived at the trench and squatted to visit with a squad from C Company that morosely defended the battered position. They all had scarves wrapped around their faces against the odor of death that permeated everything.

With a sense of genuine awe, for the first time in daylight I looked beyond the trench at the mayhem we had caused in this place. The area between the trench and the barbed wire, seen only dimly in the mist, was strewn with fifteen or more definitely dead SS men. After some hesitation, we moved toward the wire and passed some truly puzzling deconstructions that must have been men, although only a professor of anatomy could possibly have identified what the objects were. The wire itself was broken—cut in places. Here the dead were piled behind and on top. The next attacking wave lay dead just behind, having used the first wave as cover. Our grenades had solved much of that defensive posture. And I wondered how much of this shredded flesh was caused by my own efforts. I flashed on Dan standing in the trench squeezing off aimed fire while bullets flew everywhere. His action inspired me to at least do the same. My eye still had crud in it from the dirt kicked into it that night. Here it was Sanders behind me with a BAR and Dan was gone. Over the several hundred yards to the woods, invisible in the mist, were other scattered groups of dead. Our artillery had broken many of the trees as we moved down the firebreak. Broken branches lay everywhere; our old outpost just to the left of the break was covered with broken branches. The SS made some effort to police the area as we passed a neat row of dead, rotting beside the path. I thought of the long line of our dead in the woods after Sinz.

We observed and heard nothing on this patrol, while we again crossed the road and penetrated to the river. Peering out of the trees, I could see it was actually little more than a stream.

The marching songs hung in the vapor and echoed through the still forest. We crouched there in the wet underbrush a few minutes, water dripping from our helmets. I looked at the others—they had not heard the singing. Most likely all those singers lay decomposing in the mud. They would not quit, and they were dead; and because they would not quit, Dan and a lot of good men were dead. I could never forgive them. We prudently made our way back to Schomerich by a different route. Manly had about as much stomach as the rest of us to once again set foot on that hill. Instead, we cut right and exited the woods southeast of town. A tracked vehicle appeared out of the fog and appeared to be the armored self-propelled gun. Its cannon barrel was sheared away, and it smelled so bad that I avoided the wreck and continued, passing by more dead Germans. They smelled of rot and alcohol, which was better than the area near the SP, which aggressively exuded a combination of odors beyond belief.

That evening, my superficial burns were attended to. My upper back was a mess of Vaseline and peeling skin. One of the guys did his best to clean it up and then used the last of the oily jellycream on me. Next day was the 9th of March and men of the 301st appeared out of the mist to take over our positions. The lifting fog revealed visual testimony to what had occurred here, and the questions were many.

We fell out in the street, counted noses, and joined up with the rest of the fragmented battalion near the burned-out church. One block away lay the dead animals sacrificed by the SS mountaineers in their stupid, drunken gesture of offense. *What would these farmers think of such a loss and whom would they blame?* I wondered, but try as I could to care, no emotion came through a wall of numbness that each day grew thicker and higher.

I do not recall looking back at the area where we had been for more than a week. Nor did I think of how short a line of men G Company had on the road. Because remnants of H and F along with C formed part of the spread-out column, we stretched for miles. But I knew we were at one-quarter strength.

Some distance back, we passed a battery of artillery in a field. Cannoneers worked around their guns while a group of artillerymen leaned on a stone wall by the road. One by one, most of the riflemen removed their helmets as they moved past—a sardonic kind of "Thanks." Some artillery batteries had to actively defend their guns with small arms when SS groups broke through the MLR and infiltrated to the rear.

We arrived at a long line of six-by-six trucks and hauled ourselves aboard. The convoy wound its way over much of the ground we had captured during the past weeks. We drove slowly onto a pontoon bridge over the Saar, climbed the hills, and drove on through the Saar–Moselle Triangle. In passing through the woods and fields near Orsholz, I was dismayed to see bodies lying where they had fallen in January. Most were American infantry, probably from the 301st. These men had died in the minefields about one week before I joined the 94th; and the engineers were too busy keeping us moving into Germany to be able to clear the mines so the dead could be collected, identified, and properly buried.

Fifty-two years later, after visiting with Alex Arendt and his mother and father in the Saar–Moselle Triangle, Nadia and I drove beyond our Saar River battle areas to the Lampaden Ridge. Schomerich and Kummelerhof showed little damage from our combat there, of course. We slowly drove past the church and my second platoon house and up the dirt track to where our trench had been. Barbed wire and trench were long gone with a line of young trees marking where the trench had been—a simple brick monument some eight feet high marked the place where the trench had crossed the track. A niche displayed a religious figure and an inscription in German that translates, "To the German dead of all wars." A few young fir trees stood like sentinels to the side of this construction. Out in the field between the forest and us, a tractor was plowing the field. We watched and wondered about the half century of crops fertilized by so much blood a long time ago.

9

The Drive for the Rhine

We crossed the Moselle River and went into Luxembourg. Eventually G Company's trucks pulled off the road at a group of five or six houses. The 2d Platoon was assigned to the second floor of a house reached by an outside stairway. We settled in a large attic room by spreading blankets on the rough-hewn floor and, most important, removing combat boots for the first time in many days. I was dead asleep almost instantly.

Next morning, we ate hot breakfast and plenty of it—all the coffee we could drink. Inspection of weapons and equipment was followed by requisitions. By late afternoon, those who needed fresh uniforms could have them: Finally I was rid of the OD pants that had been saturated in cow piss, manure, gun oil, blood, food, mud, and other unmentionables. A fresh shirt, field jacket, and socks fulfilled my needs. We cleaned up my hand; the swelling that had been going down a week ago was up again. The hole in my chest had increased to just under the size of a quarter; and, although it looked kind of ugly, I had no real discomfort from it except when the wound took a hit or I landed on it.

On 11 March, around three truckloads showed up carrying replacements in overcoats and shiny helmets. Captain Griffin, sporting a new trench coat and no sign of a bandage under his helmet, stood in front of his CP with the first sergeant and whichever officers and noncoms could still stand. The captain gave a little speech that I did not hear because I was waiting my turn at the outhouse next to the CP. When my turn came, I sat over the hole next to Buckner, who seemed to own his side of the two-holer. His case of the GIs could not have been more chronic—twice as bad as my own. His hair was almost snow-white by then. I questioned my memory of his dark brown hair with the graying around the ears. I had discussed this with other guys and knew this weird change had to be true.

I watched as the replacements were assigned to squads and platoons. Sergeant Siegel and Sergeant Roberts walked over to us, and I got the shock of my life when Siegel informed me I was to be acting squad leader of the 2d Squad.

Soon I was able to pull up my pants and get myself organized. "Jerry Colonna," with his big black mustache, had his top hat in place of his helmet again, and with a bottle in each hand, he was ready to party. The area was full of new men mixed with the old trying to get their bearings. Some had approached the two-holer where Buckner was babbling on and on about the horrors of combat. I headed across the road to climb the stairs to our attic where I disassembled my M1 for a first-rate cleaning—borrowing a cleaning rod and patches. Every nervous tic I had experienced at various times in the past couple of months seemed to descend on me all at once. *What in the name of God would I do with the responsibility? What could I say to them?* I decided to tell Siegel I could not do this and let him find someone else.

The clattering of many boots ascending the stairs did not help my nervous condition at all. Sitting on my blanket on the floor, I watched Siegel lead a group of pale-faced men in clean uniforms to stand around me. He swung around and left with the cryptic remark of, "Okay Foley, tell 'em what to do." I had no time to react one way or the other as a sudden eruption from my stomach burned its way upward. I had only enough time to turn my head and vomit explosively into my helmet. The retching continued with a mixture of personal embarrassment and sympathy for the new men who stood there wondering what in hell they had gotten into. Between babbling Buckner, Jerry Colonna in his top hat, and their incapacitated squad leader, their immediate future must have appeared bleak—at best.

In between retching, I caught a bleary-eyed glimpse of their faces. The worse my embarrassment became, the worse grew the nausea. At the minimum, I believe I continued this way at least a quarter hour. Those poor guys stood there unable to move in the midst of about ten bedraggled veterans of combat who were quietly sitting against the wall, listening to me, and trying to control their own physical and mental demons.

Finally, too weak to talk, I was forced to give myself another minute of recovery if I was to have any authority in my voice at all. Still not knowing what to tell them, I simply repeated what I had been told along with the other new men months before, standing on the cobbles of Wochern: "Just keep your heads and follow me."

After washing out my helmet at the well that served this hamlet, I found even more men in the attic. From the nucleus of eleven men, we had become a platoon of about thirty—ten short of full strength. I gathered my bunch into a corner to see who could do what. We had two BARs to assign. At five feet eleven inches, average height, I found I was among the tallest, which could be a setback because tall men generally make better scouts. That was why Dan and I had been chosen. Eberly was about five feet nine inches and stocky; and despite his glasses, he claimed 20/20 eyesight. He got a BAR and became my second scout. Sergeant Siegel traded Fasco for one man. It was not my idea. With things moving too fast in too small a space, Siegel was doing his best to organize the three squads equitably. Fasco was slightly taller and heavier than I was, but I still did not trust him. True, Giant was well over six feet, but I could not see him doing point as a scout.

Because of the dim light, it took a few minutes to realize that one man was a lot older than anyone else: I felt sure Merrill was no younger than forty-eight and probably older; he was stocky, five feet nine inches, and carried himself like an officer. He spoke little during the next few months and was always on the ball. And if it was difficult for me to tell these men what to do (I was actually younger than all of them), it was especially tough to give orders to Merrill. But after a day or two, I found I was pretty good at managing a squad—and especially good with the older man simply because we thought alike and he was the steadiest and most reliable man I had. Ultimately, we heard he had been an officer and something had occurred that convinced him to take a demotion to volunteer for combat. I never asked and he never opened up.

I felt much better the next day. After we test-fired our weapons and drew our allotments of ammo and rations, I advised the new men on what to carry with them and what to leave in their barracks bag for company storage.

I managed to put a couple of hours into my artwork, which interested the new men. That gave me the opportunity to ask them to be alert to finding paper and pencils I might be able to use. We had a great party that night. Bottles were produced from God knows where. Three guys provided music, imitating the Andrew Sisters, and Jerry Colonna traded his top hat for Captain Griffin's helmet. But no one got seriously drunk.

Next day, 12 March, we were issued K rations and had the usual informal inspection. We also received the latest thing in maps. They were simplified, colored sections of the front that had been copied from aerial photos. Laminated against weather and rough usage, they had a grid that made it super-easy to transmit target information to artillery firing centers. Because we were moving so fast during the coming week, we would run out of one map and new ones had to be airdropped to us.

A line of trucks showed up, and we piled aboard. The captain's jeep led off. It was the middle of a sunny, cold afternoon as we headed east. We had been briefed before leaving the rest area. The 301st on the right and our 302d on the left were to jump off over the Ruwer River with the 376th in reserve. That's all we were told. The following I gleaned from histories years later: The 26th Division was on the 94th's right flank while the 3d Cavalry Group was on our left or northern flank. The 5th Rangers were released from the 94th Division control.

As the sun was dropping to the west behind us, we rolled up to the base of a ridge I did not recognize, but it looked like a northern extension of the Lampaden Ridge, and that is what it turned out to be. We left the trucks behind, and in extended order, we moved along a dirt track winding up the ridge.

It bothered all of us that Buckner had not been replaced because he was obviously out of his mind. He would be of no help to any wounded we might have, and—out of respect to his great service in the past—we plotted an accident that hopefully would send him back. Our opportunity came during our first ten-minute break. The men fell out beside the track. Buckner removed his helmet and lay down next to a tree where Eberly had leaned his BAR. We exchanged significant glances, and although I did not see who pushed the weapon, the twenty-two-pound BAR struck Buckner on the hairline. The blow produced a bloody wound that we quickly treated with sulfa powder and a decent bandaging job. I used the moment of confusion to raid his musette bag of several morphine ampoules. I had used my last one on Dan. Men were getting to their feet farther up the track and we were falling out on the road again. I shook Buckner's hand, thanking him for his help, but he looked as though he did not hear me. A lot of guys patted him on the back as we double-timed a few yards to close the gap. I looked back at the guy sitting with his back to the tree and felt glad he was out of it.

Buckner had trained with the division or joined it when it was heading overseas. He exposed himself to enemy fire many times to patch up some GI. He had earned some time off and probably he would never see combat again. The first vehicle coming down the ridge would take him to the rear.

I figured we were about five miles north of Schomerich, and I glanced over my shoulder and squinted my eyes to see the landscape in the brilliant setting sun. We took a long break just short of the ridgetop. We were told to dig in although no one put much effort into it. We heard no artillery fire coming up, and things were quiet.

After dark—and dark it was—we moved several hundred yards east. As quiet as we were, two medium mortars hit off to the left. And that was it for the night. We dug in, wrapped blankets around ourselves, and settled in. I had arranged my eight guys to connect with the 1st Squad on our left, and we tied in with another platoon on the right. Our 3d Squad was somewhat behind us. I understood we were dug in a short distance behind the front lines manned by another regiment.

At 0300, the sky above suddenly was filled with the familiar racket of freight trains rushing along. The ground in front could not be seen in the dark, but we had been briefed that it dropped off suddenly for about two hundred feet to the narrow river and then climbed sharply to a series of hills where the Germans would be dug in. I had not been able to make out the opposing hill in the darkness where the enemy would be waiting; but when the shells began bursting on the hilltop, I judged the distance from us at about one-quarter mile. The shelling was intense with medium and heavy shells exploding in yellow orange glare.

E and F Companies led off with G in reserve. I had not been told we were in reserve; therefore I was prepared to be shot at. At early daylight our platoon moved out. E and F had jumped off earlier at dawn and already took casualties from mines and small arms. At the edge of the extremely steep hill, we encountered a group of German POWs. Where they had come from, I do not know. Most likely, another company had captured them. We immediately utilized them by herding them out in front of 1st Squad. They were started down a track that hugged the side of the hill toward Pluwig, with 1st Squad following. If there were mines, the German jackboots would locate them for us. Pluwig consisted of about three houses and a small blown bridge.

Double-timing, we were halfway down the hill when the first mortar shells detonated on the hillside. Men cried out they had been hit. I crouched against the hillside and counted noses. My squad was intact, and we continued to the bottom.

The river was shallow and about forty feet wide. Siegel was sending us across by threes, and then he went over. The blown bridge was a short distance to the left and the three houses just across the river. Siegel reached the nearest house and motioned to me. I sent Fasco and two others across; then I followed with the rest of the squad, expecting sniper fire all the way across. The water was less than knee deep. A few more mortar shells hit on the hillside, and then things became quiet as we ran in the door. The German prisoners, feet and legs still in place, were herded back up the track to the rear.

Siegel moved to a north window and pointed to the hill fifty yards away. The hill was thickly wooded and especially steep. I was to move my squad to the top and dig in. But we had to wait until a radioman joined us. The hill's height promised to provide good observation for artillery spotting, and it was supposed to be cleared of enemy troops.

The radioman carried a 300 SCR and a carbine. This radio is carried as a backpack and is capable of reaching artillery control centers. Our job was to get him up the hill safely and provide his security. As during the day before, the sun provided good visibility. The other two houses by then were occupied and the area secured. We could not make out any enemy presence at the base of the hill. Placing the radioman at the rear of my squad column, we hugged the bank of the river for the scant protection it offered, until we arrived at the blown bridge. Then, up the bank we went one at a time, and crossing the road that the bridge connected, we made it to the trees. There we formed a skirmish line; and after I asked the radioman to follow us about ten yards, we moved up through the trees. The hill was shaped like a pyramid on this side: Directly to our left, it made a sharp turn. So although our slope faced west, the other was oriented north.

As we neared the summit, I heard a shout from above, which was followed by several potato mashers crashing through the branches below us before exploding. The undergrowth was too thick for the Germans to have seen more than a couple of us. I looked downhill and saw the radioman crawling up to us white-faced, but apparently unhurt. I signaled Rupp and Eberly over and asked them what they thought of the idea that they shift around the hill to the left. Rupp, who was my assistant squad leader, nodded and suggested an extra man. I told him to coordinate movement upward with ours and to use grenades, but to keep them away from us. Kane went with them, and we began up the last forty or so feet, each man holding a grenade.

A couple more potato mashers hit well to the right and downhill. The enemy soldiers were directly above us as we clambered up just short of the top. I pulled the pin while I looked at the men spread out around me, and they followed suit. I prayed no one would hit a tree as we let 'em fly. Shouts, detonations, and cries of *"Kamerad!"* broke out as I caught a quick look at a German officer who popped up and then down. Then a different German rose up waving a white cloth. Angry exclamations sprung from the German position about thirty feet away. By then, pretty much all of us were lined up on the lip of the hill. I was, by this time, a linguistic master of four or five phrases in German. *"Kommen Sie hier!"* I shouted several times. A single shot, probably a pistol, was fired, and the white cloth disappeared. I instinctively ducked, although the shot was not aimed at us. Afraid the enemy confusion would result in more potato mashers because they knew where we were, I fired four or five rounds where I had seen the officer, and then I pulled another grenade from my suspenders. The response was immediate with the officer waving a white cloth this time. Then came several desperate cries of *"Kamerad!"* I shouted *"Raus mit du!"* (Out with you!) as heads and shoulders slowly and tentatively rose from their holes. Then, as confidence grew that they would not be shot, they began climbing out and standing on the ground. Hurley, our second BAR man, began rising to his feet, and I shouted him down to the prone position again. A little harder than I intended, I snarled at him, "Nobody told you to expose yourself." I was not about to risk someone getting shot by a shell-crazed enemy soldier hiding in his hole.

The ground and some trees were pretty well chewed up from last night's shelling, and these Germans looked pretty shaky.

Finally, five POWs stood with hands clasped behind their heads, and one stood in what appeared to be a trench, his back to me. With a quick glance to the left, I saw Rupp covering the prisoners, and to the right I saw a flat field extending more than one hundred yards, stretching somewhat less across the field to the front. The question was, Are these men alone or are there more in the trees bordering the field? I yelled to Rupp and Eberly to watch the trees, and I made sure the guys with me were doing the same. After I told Salazar to come with me, we ran to the group of prisoners, banking on the belief that the POWs would not be fired on by their own army. We jumped into the trench, where I immediately landed on a German who screamed in pain—probably hit by a grenade fragment. It was a logged-over bunker through which I could see to the other end of the trench where the officer was standing. I crawled through the dugout and got to my feet. The officer had a Luger in his right hand and was frozen in position staring at nothing. A man lay on the trench bottom not moving. I reached over and pulled the pistol from the officer's hand. It came away easily and was still warm, almost hot.

The dead man had tried to surrender and was shot for it. Then the officer—in a fit of panic—thought better of it and decided to surrender after all. The dead man appeared to be my age or younger and had an intense expression of surprise in his wide-open eyes and mouth. I pushed past the officer and prodded the young German. Getting no response, I lost all self-restraint. My M1 came up and jumped in my hands. I only dimly saw the officer collapse, because my eyesight again was almost blotted out by a dirty-red film that took over my vision for a few seconds. Perhaps the phrase "seeing red" refers exclusively to the Irish. I did not fail to avail myself of the wooden-handled Luger and its holster, plus magazines. Also, his excellent binoculars and carrying case would come in handy, although I had to wipe his blood off the case with his uniform.

Salazar was staring at me wide-eyed, and glancing at the prisoners, I saw apprehension in some and approval in others. A couple were wounded and needed quick attention. We climbed out of the trench, and with sign language persuaded several prisoners to haul the bodies out of the trench and drop them well to the rear of us. Then they carried the wounded man out. While they were doing this, I noticed that the dugout, with two firing apertures and several nearby foxholes, was oriented to the south, facing the field. We had hit them from the west on their right flank. I think they were not ready for such a move. We were lucky.

We completed searching them, and I asked Rupp to escort them down to the house. Meanwhile, the rest of the squad had occupied the trench, and the radioman set up in the dugout. But the moment the prisoners disappeared into the trees for their descent to 2d Platoon, rifle bullets split the air so close to me that I felt the air pressure. I dived for the nearest hole and found myself not in the trench, but in a foxhole more than five feet deep. I had never seen and never would see another hole so geometrically perfect. Only a German with a mania for order could have dug this. I instinctively had my boots wedged into the sides just above the dirt floor. I had heard stories of Schü mines hidden in the bottoms of such clean-cut and inviting holes—a GI jumps in and is blown out again leaving body parts behind. I heard Salazar call my name from the dugout, and I answered that I was okay. Then I asked for a nose count. Sikora was not in the trench, but he called out from nearby that he had dived into a foxhole when the sniper opened up. I knew I had made a serious mistake in standing outside after the prisoners were escorted away.

No way could I place my feet on the bottom of the hole, and they were rapidly losing circulation with their awkward posture. I had isolated myself from the squad and felt stupid and embarrassed. I called to Sikora to ask how he was doing. Then a new threat came calling, as the soft warning sound of a mortar shell added to our worries. It exploded nearby, throwing dirt and stones over me. I lost count as a barrage of shells bracketed our location much too accurately. I began to feel a genuine claustrophobic fear that I would be buried in this vertical grave—it was all I could do to prevent myself from springing to the surface and diving to the dugout. But one shell landing in the dugout trench would be devastating because the dugout was completely open on both ends.

My position was totally ridiculous—me, with my feet wedged into the sides of the hole, fearing a mine on the bottom, while shells were dropping from above. We were getting a real pasting. Although my hearing was pretty much gone, I did hear a high-pitched scream, and glancing up, I saw Sikora wildly dash over my hole. But I grabbed an ankle, and he toppled over and ended up on my head and shoulders. He was still screaming "Jesus! Jesus!" And if I had been ridiculous before, here I was "The Three Stooges" kind of ridiculous. Instantly, I could not sustain the pressure on my feet, and I thrust him off me with all my might. I grabbed my M1, pulled my weight out of the hole, and—just behind Sikora—scrambled for the dugout trench. I think the thick smoke screened us from sniper fire. We lay there exhausted and gasping for air. When the barrage suddenly stopped, another sound was heard as the scream of 88s erupted in airbursts. But the shells were all bursting in ugly black puffs over the houses and bridge area. We could not see the scene below, yet it was obvious that the bridge area was getting hit. More than likely the engineers were exposed there trying to erect a bridge for armor and supply vehicles. Sikora was shaking badly, and I was not much better. I sure could not blame a new man for reacting this way to his first real shelling. But it had not been the shelling that got him out of his hole. He blurted out that a shell buried itself in the bottom of his hole, its fins sticking out between his legs. Although it proved to be a dud, he panicked.

Periodically during the day, 88 airbursts were shifted several hundred feet from the bridge and houses to our hill. Then, as the closer shriek of "Incoming!" was heard, anyone outside the dugout had only a couple of seconds to dive into the shelter. Five or six times, fragments rained down around us. I had already learned that the majority of German airbursts exploded rather high compared to American airbursts. Our proximity fuse was deadly and timed to explode around fifteen feet above the target: We had dramatic proof of that during the day as targets presented themselves, always by German tactical blunders. And, of course, the enemy was not at all comfortable with artillery spotters in high places, which is why the hill was defended and why they expended so much hardware on us.

At times, I sat outside in the trench drawing what had been going on, including one picture of myself drawing near the dugout. The dugout was composed of two crisscrossing layers of five- to eight-inch logs, and there were two firing slits one foot long by six inches high. Earth and sandbags were piled on top. After Rupp returned from his POW escort, I sent several guys to crawl around and pull in any handy smashed logs and available material, to strengthen and enlarge our accommodations. I entertained myself several times by lifting a German helmet on a stick to draw fire from one end of the trench while someone spotted for me from a firing slit. At first, we got a hot response from several riflemen, but no automatic fire. When they got tired of being fooled with, they quit and waited for a better target, which we were determined not to offer. Merrill did, at odd times, relish popping off two or three rounds at carefully selected and likely places in the underbrush across the field.

Rupp was concerned that we were tactically in the same position as the original occupants in that we were without protection in the rear. We needed an outpost to warn us of any aggressive patrols out to get us from that open direction. As we had too many eggs in this little basket anyway, we decided to send Sikora and Eberly, with Rupp to take charge. I crawled with them the forty or so feet to our rear and selected a spot between trees that visually controlled both sides of our pyramid-like hill. Rupp kept watch while the other two dug their outpost. Feeling more secure, I headed back to the trench, passing the bodies where they were dumped. The officer's camouflage jacket was open and pulled back behind him, revealing his decorations and badges—some sort of iron-cross ribbon was displayed diagonally on his uniform.

After Schomerich's avalanche of SS rings, I seemed to have lost the collector's lust, and I left the officer to the mercy of body collectors. I bet dollars to doughnuts, however, that on that isolated hill, they were uniformed skeletons by the time some farmer climbed up there.

Early in the afternoon, I saw considerable movement way off to the left front. Several long hills, higher than ours, extended from half a mile to our left and moved several miles to the east. Wooded like all the others, they did, however, have open areas. I got Fasco and the radio operator to see what they could make of the movement. Even with my binoculars, neither Fasco nor I could make out which army they belonged to. We knew the 301st was the other prong of our attack, jumping off south of us from the Lampaden Ridge sector. These men were northeast, however, and I came really close to asking for artillery fire. About that time, we could see mortar bursts falling among these troops. We watched as they veered off to the right and then lost them as the sounds of the explosions reached us.

Not long after, I was trying to understand the numbered system inscribed within the binocular lens. I understood that the small, evenly spaced numbers going off each side of a central zero were an aid in correcting artillery or mortar fire. By superimposing the zero over the target and seeing a shell burst to one side, the system could be of some help in zeroing in on the target.

I saw movement on top of a hill several miles to the east. Fasco had Rupp's binoculars, and I called his attention to the hill I was focusing on. I admit I was pleased I had spotted both events before Mr. Super Eye did. We had the simplified terrain map—laminated and easily read—that had recently been issued. We identified which hill it was, noticed the road running over it, and reported the coordinates by radio. After studying the movement a few minutes, we determined the Germans had committed an obvious blunder in sending troops and vehicles over a hill silhouetted against the skyline. Even my brief basic training pointed out that such a move must be avoided, that movement should be made on the "military crest" just below the skyline. Apparently, P-47s and occasional Piper Cubs, spotting for the artillery, had not picked up this activity. I felt genuinely excited at this opportunity to do some serious damage to reinforcements obviously rushed to the point of attack any way they could get there.

Our radioman fed the info into his mike and explained the process to us. He was speaking to a crew—at a fire control center set up in a boxlike trailer—whose job was to compute location, distance, and wind for a variety of artillery battalions located anywhere and everywhere behind us for miles. Those batteries were composed of 105s, 155s, 240s, and 8-inch cannon. In a matter of minutes, orders would be issued to these batteries: the target info and, last but not least, when to fire. The technique was called time on target (TOT), which dictated that all the shells would hit the target at the same moment for maximum killing potential.

Everyone was pressed to the wall of the trench and staring at the hill, when the biggest concentration of artillery fire I had ever heard began flying past above. Thousands of feet overhead, those invisible ghost trains roared east, unstoppable and all-powerful. In an instant, the entire hill disappeared in a gray eruption. The volleys were repeated. Some of the batteries, I imagined, shifted their fire to the roads and towns just east and west of the target.

Many seconds passed before the deep, loud rumble of the concentration reached us. The experience shook all of us—it was awesome. I reflected on the chain of events, or at least various links, that had brought us to this: the officer's binoculars, the German blunders, the laminated map, the 300 SCR, the fire control center. Without a doubt, my eyes had caused many, many deaths. There were men lying on that road and in burning vehicles dying in terrible pain this precise moment. But on the other hand, the series of coldly logical decisions probably would save many American lives that otherwise might have been lost in the hours and days to follow. The German reinforcements were blunted, or worse. Our guys would likely encounter less opposition.

I could not take my eyes off the gray drifting smoke as the hill slowly reappeared. Large and small fires and black smoke emanated from burning vehicles. I do not recall any more shellfire or small arms hitting our area by late afternoon. After dark, Rupp showed up to say that men were coming up the hill from the house area. We immediately covered the woods that we had emerged from that morning. I was not surprised to hear McKay's voice with the countersign. McKay had been blown through a wall at Schomerich and we thought he was hit pretty badly; but here he was, bringing his squad to relieve us and easing himself into the trench. He had been treated for strains and bruises, and although the aches and pains were still there, he found his way back to 2d Platoon. I was really glad to have him back. He showed up during the afternoon with several other replacements, a lieutenant and a medic among them. This was news because most second lieutenants, when one was assigned to an infantry platoon, did not live long. As a result, most of the time sergeants had to take over. And when we did get a second lieutenant, he normally observed how things were done by the sergeants—and usually a day or so of this advanced schooling would see him ready to participate, or even take over.

McKay got his old squad back; he was replacing Sanders, who was relegated back to rifleman status. Like me, he had been assigned as acting squad leader. We got our gear together, the radioman his, and explained the local layout and situation. Before leaving, Rupp led him to the outpost, which was hard to locate in the darkness.

We arrived back at the house below the hill. Sergeant Siegel took us into a candlelit room where we could remove our gear and settle in for the night. A couple of men were squatting around our Coleman squad stove on the floor. The blond one looked up at me and offered a bite-size piece of steaming meat on a fork; it was dripping with gravy. Boy, it was delicious. I dropped my gear and introduced myself. His name was 2d Lt. Davis F. Nations, and he resembled a young, unsophisticated Errol Flynn. I liked Nations immediately. We pulled out family photos. His showed a pretty blond wife and blond children. We had had no hot food, and having subsisted on K rations, I felt grateful for that hunk of beef and took the taste with me into sleep surrounded by snoring men wrapped in blankets.

On 14 March, we were awakened unceremoniously before dawn by a shell slamming through the roof. I awoke and heard that the bridge area had been shelled for several minutes—I had slept through part of it. And the explosions occurred around the bridge located only one-half a football field away from us. Told to head for the cellar, I discovered the tiny area under the kitchen was already full of white faces peering up at the rest of us. I pulled out a breakfast K ration, the least objectionable of the three meals, and tried to shield it from dust falling from the shelling.

The bombardment paused, and 2d Platoon was quickly organized to double-time up the road a couple hundred yards, and the rest of the company followed. My squad led off with Siegel naming me scout, followed by Eberly and his BAR. The night's fog stayed thick as the signal was passed up through Eberly to move out. This was hostile territory, not yet overrun. We were to move through it several miles to the village of Schondorf, the actual front line.

The landscape rose to the left of the road and dropped to the right across wooded fields toward the river. The road wound through rising ground. Again, I felt the heavy responsibility of being the point for a company of infantry. I would have been just as happy to turn the job over to someone else, let there be no doubt about that—there is a definite degree of security to be a hundred yards back of the point. However, once I was ordered to take the point, a mixture of fear and pride set in. It would take time and experience for one of the new men to be able to step up to this job. Of course, I had no experience my first time, come to think of it.

Slowly, daylight increased, and the wet fog rolled in and out, thicker and then thinner. I glanced back often for any arm signals. I could see Eberly some forty feet behind and two or three riflemen fading in the mist. It was decidedly eerie and lonely.

Something on the road ahead caught my eye. Whatever it was, it was not moving. Cautiously, I approached several still figures on the road. I felt the hair on the back of my neck raise up as I wondered what a white marble sculpture was doing in the center of a narrow dirt road in the middle of nowhere. The nearest figure of the apparition turned out to be a frozen German infantryman lying on his back. But the figure kneeling prayerlike just beyond him was unsettling to say the least. As I passed him, I could see he was an American, his hands clasped around the barrel of his M1, its stock on the ground between his knees. His head was thrown back, helmet on the ground, eyes staring straight up. To his front, another German lay on his back. All three dead men presented an unsolvable tableau of the cause of death. The three were permanently united in a design imprinted in my consciousness. They, and their scattered equipment and weapons, were frozen marble white.

I never paused in my passage through their area because I had been ordered to keep up the cadence. I glanced back at the scene and wondered how Eberly would react to it. Another half mile beyond that haunting place, we climbed above the fog that still clung to the valleys. The shell-damaged barns and houses of Schondorf were etched against the black smoke of burning houses.

For the last mile, I was aware of the sounds of shellfire and small arms. As we marched past men and past tanks parked behind buildings, the sound intensified. But the action was taking place beyond the town and over a hill east of town. I saw Siegel, the captain, and his radioman double-timing up from behind me. Other men met them, and they all entered a house. I sat on a low wall and was joined by Eberly and others. I watched a Red Cross–marked half-track and jeeps in front of a barn where medics tended to wounded men. Down the road, several walking wounded headed to the aid station in the barn.

The captain and the others came out and were joined by the platoon leaders. The other squad leaders came up, and Siegel led us a couple of streets over to the other side of the little town. Men were dropped off one or two to a building and told to keep their eyes open. We were forming a defensive perimeter on the south end of the town. My house was next to the last on a street that turned northeast and continued on over the hill where the action was.

A three-quarter-ton truck careened by carrying 81mm mortars. I could see them setting up their tubes behind a couple of houses between the hill and me. I had three men of my squad with me and the other four next door. The upper stories of both houses were burned out and the town's inhabitants apparently had been evacuated.

We stayed put all morning and much of the afternoon. The intermittent shelling and airbursts continued without letup—which was a concern because there were no cellars and little or no cover overhead due to the rubble that remained of the roof and walls. Many walking wounded moved past during the day, and I was able to direct them to the aid station a couple of blocks away. Several times, I left my post or sent one of my squad to help carry men who seemed on the verge of collapse. I believe it was F Company that had gone over the hill that dawn and into a minefield trap, where they were systematically machine-gunned.

A hazy sun broke through the smoky atmosphere and took the edge off the chill. From my smashed window, I could see across the unpaved road and down the steep hill to a wooded valley that more than likely remained in enemy hands. Early in the afternoon, I spotted a lone figure emerge from the woods and begin climbing toward us. With my binoculars, I could easily see a large red-faced woman struggling upward. I lost sight of her in the landscape, but minutes later she reappeared, moving across the road and heading for our front door. She burst into the hallway and went back to the kitchen. I followed her there and could understand none of her out-of-breath German. One thing was especially clear— she was hugely pregnant and extremely upset. She collapsed into a chair, seemed uncomfortable, and slid to the floor—all the time using sign language to try to get across to us. I finally understood that she was in labor. A pool of water had formed under her, and even I (knowing next to nothing about such things) realized she was about to give birth. Flashing on the new medic who I had not yet seen, I headed at a dead run for the aid station. Shouting for the 2d Platoon medic of G Company, I met up with our new aid man, Joe. Briefly, I filled him in on the situation, and together we returned to the house on the double. Joe cleared the kitchen table, and we got her on top of it. I was put to work filling a large kettle with well water and balancing it on top of the squad stove. We got the wood-burning kitchen stove going and more pots of water heating. The woman never shut up for a minute; so, between her and the noise of the shelling, the tic next to my mouth became uncomfortable again.

The baby arrived before the water heated. I had covered the woman with my German army blanket and a couple of us held her down. Joe was absolutely calm through the ordeal; although he had never delivered a baby before, he knew the general principles of tying off the cord and the other procedures. As the sound of motors was heard approaching, the reddish-looking infant was spanked into emitting a loud wail of indignation at being born into such a ridiculous situation.

A line of tanks roared into view and stopped right in front of the house where my other four troopers were holed up. The driver in the lead tank, red-faced and anxious, craned his neck trying to see around the corner of my house. He moved his tank a few feet forward as a couple of 88s screamed in overhead and, thinking better of it, pulled back again. The 88s' shells probably ended up miles away. Meanwhile Siegel, Lieutenant Nations, and the runner showed up with the rest of the platoon shouting over the din of the motors for us to get ready to move out. I ran back into the house to check on the mother. She was in a corner of the kitchen with my German army blanket wrapped around her and the child. She was fairly out of it and did not notice the K ration and extra D bar of chocolate I left on the floor near her.

My squad was climbing on top of a tank, and I joined them, grasping for anything to hold on to. I had no idea where we were going. I assumed we would have to go over the hill, exposing ourselves to the same direct fire that hit F Company. Moments later, we lurched forward, exhausts blowing smoke, the hot engine warming our lower bodies while the cold air stung our faces.

We swung right—almost pulling me off to the left—and plunged down a steep and narrow dirt-track incline that dropped off to the valley where the woman had come from. There may have been ten or more tanks in the column following behind us: The entire company was mounted on these bucking monsters. You had to holler in a man's ear to be heard.

At the bottom of the hill, the track veered right a little, and we traveled about one-half mile only to stop at a fork. The powers that be consulted maps and radios. Meanwhile, we spotted a highly complicated weapon that most likely had been a 40mm multipurpose gun—either antipersonnel or antiaircraft. It was a mass of twisted metal, wheels, ammo containers, tree limbs, and human bodies, blown inside out with odd bits and pieces scattered and plastered to anything and everything around. Several of us stood there, fascinated. The haphazardly displayed anatomy reminded me of the patterns created from the flesh and hot blood that had frozen in the snow and ice of Sinz, during my baptism of fire back in January.

Shouts from the tank brought us back to mount our beasts, and we moved on. Obviously, we were moving around the enemy flank, which was some relief—though not much, because who knows what we would find down there. This was definitely not tank country. In fact, tanks always try to avoid forests and hills. Such country has too many places for anti-tank guns or *panzerfaust* teams to remain hidden until their optimum opportunity comes. Tanks are best used in open country and desert areas.

Daylight was fading; we had covered about four miles from Schondorf when the column halted, and we dismounted to enter the woods on the left. We were formed into a company line about 150 yards long and proceeded to dig in. My hole was on the extreme left and was responsible for the flank. Both Fasco and I shoveled the earth out between some trees. Meanwhile, the tanks moved up a few yards behind the foxhole line. Our lead tank was parked some twenty-five feet behind us.

I had no doubt that German patrols were off in the trees watching our every move. Tanks make a lot of noise and can be heard a long way off. But, so far all was quiet. It appeared to me that we were at the base of hills to which we had called in the TOT the day before. Of course the thought ran through my mind that if that barrage had never happened, if the Germans had been smarter in their movement, we might be in one hell of a firefight this exact moment. But we were not—and for whatever reasons, all was quiet. Later I learned that the rest of the battalion, on foot, was close behind us. At the moment, I felt we had overextended ourselves, with a company of infantry and a column of vulnerable tanks practically lost and isolated in the forest.

We settled in for the night—two hours on, two hours off. But experience with Fasco made me aware that I would likely not sleep at all. True to form, he almost never raised his head to look and listen. Instead, he stayed as low as possible in his end of the hole and made ceaseless, unintelligible conversation with himself. I kept him with me for his superior night vision and had to put up with his fears. For my part, I was cold and hungry. I had one K ration I was saving for the morning, and my last German blanket was gracing the shoulders of the new mother. Well after dark, Manly came over and said he had to put a four-man patrol together and wanted a BAR man and me as point. I decided Eberly was proving to be steady, and I got him out of his hole and met Manly and Salazar behind our tank. We were to try to locate E Company: We were supposed to have joined up here at the first checkpoint.

With Manly a few yards behind me and all staying close, we moved away from the perimeter. Although it was dark, I could usually see the shapes of trees and obstructions nearby. But the darkest shapes, as in previous night patrols, were moss. And as before, we passed the word back to step only on the black in order to avoid the crackle sound of dead leaves. After an hour, we returned, having found nothing.

Sometime later, Lieutenant Nations stirred me out of my hole; and, again with Eberly and one other man, we moved out in another direction up the wooded slopes of Hill 708. We had gone about one-half mile or so, moving slowly, cautiously. At this point, we still had not come across E Company or any other unit—American or German. Then we all heard voices. Lying still, we listened for several minutes. Nations whispered in my ear that we should get closer to find out what was there. About to move, we heard clearly a few spoken words, and they most definitely were not American. So, either this was an outpost, and MLR, or a resting patrol.

Nations decided we should return to our perimeter and relieved me at point with the fourth man. I lined up behind him, then Nations, and then Eberly. We began moving downslope. But we had not progressed ten yards when a blinding flash completely put out my lights. I could only have been unconscious less than a minute because I came into what seemed a silent dream state of flashing lights. I do not know how long it took me to realize these were tracer bullets drumming into trees, creating violent sparks and ricochets. I could feel the concussion of pounding, but minutes would pass before some hearing returned. I found I was on my back, and I began moving my arms and legs. My neck was warm and sticky—probing with my good left hand, I located a scratch on the side of my neck. But I was unnerved to discover that my dog tags, SS rings, Catholic medal, and rosary were gone. Then I discovered something warm and slippery on my chest. On the verge of panic, I groped inside my uniform for the mortal wound I thought was there. My confusion deepened, but as my head cleared a little, I found that the fourth man—never got his name—had more than likely set off a mine or booby trap that I had passed on the way up. Other than a headache, I began to gain confidence that I had suffered only a scratch.

Meanwhile, the tracers stopped searching, and I was buried in darkness—too scared to risk inadvertently moving on to other mines. I believed our point man was dead and that parts of him splattered over me. I could sense no life nearby, and knew I had to search for Nations and Eberly. Having been in line behind me, most likely they were okay and looking for me. I began groping the area with infinite care until I finally found my I.D. and the other neckwear tangled together at the base of a tree. My rifle was some twenty feet away, nearer the point of explosion. The SS-ring necklace had disappeared. I never missed that witches' charm. I had been blown a fair distance and rolled into a depression in the forest floor that gave some protection from the machine gun. Unbuckled helmets catch the force of explosions if the angle is right, and it took many anxious minutes of crawling about before locating it. The fit was unfamiliar, however, and I realized it probably belonged to our point man. Only after I found the one with netting that felt right did I let the other go.

I saw no sign of the other men, and I sat quietly for a while, trying to get my ears back in some sort of hearing mode. My dog tag tangle went into the upper-left pocket of my field jacket, where I kept my chocolate D bars. A month later, I pulled out a dried mixture of I.D. neckwear buried in a mass of chocolate and paper wrapping—all glued together by a grizzled parchmentlike material that must have been flesh from the fourth man. Whatever the point man had set off seemed more powerful than a Schü mine. It was generally understood that more than seventy pounds of weight would set one off. But by crawling over one buried a few inches in the earth, a man's weight could be distributed over a wider area and he might survive the crawl. On the other hand, exceedingly little pressure is needed to suffer the results of jiggling a Bouncing Betty's prongs hidden in leaves.

In the almost-total darkness, I began crawling downslope in the direction I could only hope was the same I had come up. I literally inched forward, gloveless, with all the digital sensitivity I could muster. The sudden touch of twigs on the forest floor caused momentary panic. I finally calmed my nerves enough to realize that the fluidity of the military situation almost precluded the organized planting of minefields here. At the part of the forest where the trees thinned out, I decided my sense of direction had put me in front of the company perimeter. But because my chancy hearing might be a serious disadvantage exchanging passwords, I opted to move well to the right and then left to the road. There, I was shocked to walk right into a group of tankers gathered next to their tank. Although I was relieved to have so easily reentered the perimeter, I intended to raise a little hell about flank security. I found our platoon CP hole and reported to Siegel. He was relieved to have me back, and before I could ask about the others, he told me Nations and Eberly had come in not two minutes before I did. Much relieved, I realized we had been traveling a parallel course on the way back. When I told him of my unchallenged return, he said he would take care of it. The lieutenant, meanwhile, was with the CO reporting on our patrol and had not heard of my return.

Before returning to my position, I groped my way to Eberly's hole to let him know I made it back. They had reacted as I did in working their way downslope. At the rear of the four-man column, he had had enough distance from the explosion that he saw me blown and rolling through the underbrush, but the immediate firing of the machine gun put a stop for some minutes to searching for me. We had been groping silently within yards of each other.

Salazar, who was in the hole with Fasco, left for his own, and I reoccupied my end. I was hurting and exhausted and needed sleep badly. Fasco was intermittently mumbling or asleep over the next hour. Finally, I lost my self-control as he emitted a snore that could be heard for quite a distance. If it had been daylight, I believe I would have seen that dirty-red film again. I started punching him on his arms and chest, and he snapped awake. I hissed in his ear threats I would never carry out, and probably could not carry out. But he was way out of his element here—I was, too, but I had adapted and he had not. Anyway, I made my point and he put his eyes to work. Sometime later, he nudged me from a stupor to whisper he had spotted movement. Rising up, I saw only the dark and foolishly whispered there was nothing out there.

I never heard the brief conversation reputed to have taken place between a GI and a German who was pretending to surrender and who then fired a *panzerfaust* or German version of our bazooka. Instead, what I clearly recall is that immediately after I put down what Fasco claimed to have seen, a rocket flashed a couple of feet over our hole and detonated on the tank behind us. Totally taken by surprise—and probably with my mouth hanging open—I took several seconds before reacting. Some of us got off some wild small-arms fire, and a rifle grenade was shot off from the hole next to us. By this time, Manly had climbed up to the tank's turret and let loose several long bursts of .50-caliber tracers, which powerfully bounced from tree to tree. Much later, some believed that the figures Fasco saw, that I could not see, made good their escape. Not true— a man groaned out there in the dark for some minutes and gradually grew quiet. I never saw him because we pulled out before dawn.

As light began to rise on 15 March, we were reassembled on the road; and, because I had been on two patrols during the night, as usual I was considered an expert in the locality. I recall leaning against the tank, which had a track blown off by the rocket attack, and eating my last K ration. I learned a member of the tank crew was burned—not too badly—by the explosion. Nations and Siegel came over, and I remember how curious it seemed when Siegel apologized but had to ask me to take the point again. When I had seen him and the lieutenant as they approached me, I cringed and wished I could turn into a tree or be something other than a soldier, because I knew what they wanted. Nevertheless, as usual, I met his gaze, covered up my fear, and answered, "It's okay, Sarge."

We left the tanks sitting there as Eberly and I moved off through the forest. Hill 708 did not have a lot of underbrush, and the way the trees were spaced revealed generations of good forestry. The occasional trails were designed in a pattern as firebreaks, and the woodsmen could reach anywhere on this great hill. It was not all that high, but its gradual slopes covered many miles and supported a variety of big trees, mostly firs.

Gradually light filtered through, and as visibility improved, the interval between men lengthened. We were too high for night mist to have formed. It was going to be a perfect late-winter's day and under other circumstances, I easily could have drifted into an idyllic frame of mind. But, for the confrontation we were marching toward, my childhood readings of *Fairy Tales of the Brothers Grimm* would have fit well that early morning in an ancient German forest. Mystery abounded in every shadowy grove of trees where enemy infantry waited—not ancient warriors and maidens.

In my frequent glances to the rear for arm-and-hand signals, I could see our platoon sergeants and Lieutenant Nations and riflemen trailing behind until I lost them in the trees. It is difficult to describe the weighty importance of the scout experience: the mixture of a responsibility way beyond my eighteen years and the almost wild sense of pride. The fear of making a mistake that would endanger my company took precedence over personal fear for my own safety.

G Company followed along in Indian file for more than a thousand yards. I knew that even though I could not see them. The added weight was E Company following along just behind G. And while tanks can give a sense of security, they also draw fire. All in all, it was better to slip through the woods silently in hopes of bumping into the enemy where they least expected it. The tanks remained behind for the time being. They would slowly find their way to us later over wider trails.

I realized that the Germans, more than likely, had men and radios posted where they could keep tabs on us. As I found myself heading toward open area and clearings, I would change direction for areas that offered more cover for us. A couple of times, I got the signal to drastically change direction, which I liked.

Just before 0700, I checked out a dirt track well chewed up by tracked vehicles. It crossed another track fifty yards to the left that I had been watching as I moved. It moved directly upslope, and tracked vehicles had gone this way, too. I began walking on the track marks, hoping they were so recent that there had not been time to plant mines. I hated snipers and canny Germans who planted mines as lovingly as farmers plant seed.

My hope was to find enough evidence of the proximity of the enemy that we would deploy into skirmish lines right and left. But the only signal I received was to keep moving on. The sky reflected on Eberly's glasses as he shrugged his shoulders, and on up the track we trudged a couple hundred yards. At this point, one set of tracks had cut off to a clearing to the right and chewed its way over stumps and dead leaves until I lost sight of it. Getting Siegel's attention seventy-five yards back, I pointed emphatically to the deviating vehicle track so he would not miss it.

By then, I could hear sounds of an axe chopping wood up ahead. And as in times past, the east wind carried the strong smell of a tobacco that Camels and Lucky Strikes would have turned up their respective noses at. The forest-softened sound of a voice somewhere ahead convinced me there was German activity close by. I trotted back past Eberly to the powers that ran things; and, because I failed to convince them that I smelled Germans, I was told to get on back up there. Belatedly, I learned not only were we looking for the enemy MLR, but also for another American unit out there somewhere.

I stood in the gloom of the trees shaking and trembling so badly that I had to repeat my message a couple of times—my voice shook too. How much of this was due to the cold, and how much to fear, I never knew. I was pooped from lack of sleep, and I could smell something bad about to happen. The cold was worse in March than it had been in January, or so it seemed at the time. So back up the track I double-timed taking Eberly and his BAR close behind me. Feeling naked on the open track, I went into the fir trees and underbrush on the right. Once more, good fortune was on my side—because remaining on the track would have exposed my right side to a well-hidden German OP. The path I took, however, thrust me suddenly in front of two Germans in the act of vacating their slit trench and disappearing through the foliage. I mean they were out of there fast. And I was out of there fast too, taking Eberly with me and waving my arm at the men below to get the hell off the track. In the blink of an eye, they were out of sight. Some were deployed to our left, but most of us went to the clearing where the tank, or whatever it was, had passed through.

After we were quickly arranged into a rough line extending a hundred yards from the track, Lieutenant Nations and his runner began chopping away with their shovels, and Nations told Eberly and me to dig in next to him. A line of men were working their shovels a hundred feet behind us at the edge of the clearing. The ground was extremely hard with stone and soil frozen like cement. I told Eberly to follow me about twenty-five feet closer to the trees, and we began digging in the broken earth of the tank track, which was easier to remove. But we never got six inches down before we were interrupted by the all-too-familiar noise of a Screaming Meemie rocket rushing in. At the same precise moment, an unheard 120mm mortar shell that had been on its way since we deployed, came dropping in. We were already pressing ourselves flat to the earth, warned by the rocket. The 120 burst behind me, and my shovel got a jagged hole in the metal blade. Other explosions, accurately placed, followed immediately. Behind me, I heard a loud moan I will take with me to the end of my life. It was as accurate a sound as a man could create if he were imitating the noise of a Screaming Meemie. I glanced back through the thick smoke and saw the runner staring at the mess that had been the neat and handsome Lieutenant Nations. The shallow shell hole was exactly where we had tried to dig next to Nations.

Against the noise of shells dropping in, a new sound of a tank engine and cannon caught all of my attention. It was firing at trees on the other side of the clearing as fast as its gunner could shove the rounds in the breech. I saw men being hit by shrapnel and other men rushing to pull wounded away. Several shouts of "Pull back! Pull back!" had most everyone grabbing equipment and the wounded moving to the trees and the track. I could see the runner's mouth moving while, wide-eyed, he seemed to implore me to do something. But in an instant, with walkie-talkie and carbine in hand, he was gone. Eberly shouted, "Come on!" and headed for the track.

On my knees in the process of grabbing shovel and rifle, I saw movement to the front. The silhouette of three men in a close group dropped to the earth thirty feet away under the fir trees. It had to be a machine-gun team. I saw their body profiles as they had their focus concentrated across the clearing where men still milled about with the wounded. The three German soldiers never picked up on my presence, and I emptied eight rounds into their midst. I passed the burned and broken thing that had been a new friend a couple of days before, and I did not stop until I heard shouts all around me at the other track I had crossed fifteen minutes earlier. I found my squad. Rupp and Sanders had been hit. Rupp had gone for treatment to the aid station, wherever that could be in this wilderness. And Sanders had a head wound that Joe, the medic, was getting ready to patch up. Rupp would return in a couple of days. My squad came out of it in pretty good shape.

Shells from our own artillery began hitting the area where the self-propelled cannon had been hidden. Our perimeter was positioned at the west side of the north-south running track. Then, the German shelling was being walked down the slope to us, and again we began chopping at the earth between trees. More than one direct fire cannon was hitting trees to spray fragments down on our heads. This was in addition to the mortars. I gave up the fruitless chipping away at roots and stone and just lay there next to a 60mm mortar of our 4th Platoon. The last thing I remembered at about 0725 was the sound of shell fragments buzzing through the air and the hollow *pock!* when it would strike a living tree.

The next thing I knew, someone was tugging at my cartridge belt. A rifleman was replacing my canteen in its canvas holder. He had been detailed to get refills from a water point somewhere. I realized I was half-covered in dirt, leaves, and a branch. I could not understand how or when this happened until a glance at my watch revealed the time as 1500. I had actually slept through a barrage and escaped the stress of experiencing the reality. I could hear tanks—ours—off to the left coming up the east-west track in the direction of the clearing where we had gotten hit. I checked on the squad and saw Sanders with his white bandage.

Siegel called me over with the other squad leaders and explained the latest poop. Nearby, the dead were lined up. Lieutenant Nations was one of them. Other troops were set to jump off with the tanks and attack up the track. Our job was to tie in on their right and provide flank protection to the hilltop and beyond, to a town on the other side of the hill. I availed myself of three K rations from boxes and found the squad had already gotten theirs.

Our skirmish line moved out over the track, and I could see the tanks to the left with riflemen scouts in front moving up the track. We went fifty yards through trees and shell-smashed branches when rapid-firing machine guns opened up, although their fire was high. Most mortar shells and direct cannon fire landed around the men and tanks that were slowly moving forward some seventy yards to our left. I watched a tall fir tree being hit every eight or ten seconds until it toppled over. Then the German gunner up the trail sighted on the next tree to use for a fragment shower.

Creeping and crawling, we passed the clearing where Nations was killed. I could see the self-propelled cannon that had fired the tree bursts. It was burned out. I angled to the left toward the track until I found the machine gunners I had shot at. Only two were lying behind the M34. A blood trail led to the third a distance away. I felt little or nothing—only a vague satisfaction.

Later, my squad and I were moving with the tank destroyers, and I anxiously watched trees ahead being shelled; I sweated it out until the tree fell before we arrived at it. It was impossible to hear or give orders. Tanks made so much motor noise you could see a mortar shell burst, yet not hear it. The lead tanks expended 90mm shells, .50-caliber and .30-caliber fire, at every suspicious clump of trees ahead. In this way, an occasional German self-propelled gun or tank was put out of action. We lost tanks, too. Once again, we experienced the smell of burning rubber, superheated metal, burned powder, and wood smoke, along with burned meat. Every so often, forward movement stopped and we would dig in. Altogether, I hit my all-time high of five good-size two-man foxholes. The digging was better the higher we went—don't ask me why.

At one point, a screaming, red-faced major arm-signaled my squad to the other side of the road. I understood we were being outflanked on the left, and indeed, we were getting small-arms fire from there. So, after we crawled around and Salazar had a bullet knock his helmet halfway around his head, suddenly an American top sergeant, with almost white hair, raised up—most bravely—some distance away. Hands raised, he approached and shouted in my ear that we were shooting at his platoon. I retorted that he had been shooting at ours. He had some wounded men from the so-called friendly fire. We reoriented him to the direction he should go and tied in to the track on his right. Then we double-timed back between the hot and stinking tanks to our place in the line. Siegel or Roberts wanted to know what in hell we were doing across the road, and I gave up trying to explain. That is the way it went the rest of the afternoon, when by twos and threes, German infantry began trotting along to our rear with hands clasped behind their long-brimmed caps.

I confess I gave a good hefty kick in the rear to one POW who stopped long enough to say he was happy to be going to the United States of America. I just wanted to hasten his trip in that direction and was not terribly pleased he would arrive there long before I would. The last place we dug in I needed to relieve myself and wanted to do it alone, so I left the three or four holes of the squad and wandered off to drop my pants and squat in the late afternoon sunlight that so peacefully filtered to the forest floor. The sounds of combat had petered down to intermittent sputterings, bangs, and pops. Then I suddenly was besieged by irritated shouts. Looking behind me, I was aware of a heavy .30-caliber machine gun staring me down—probably part of H Company. I had stupidly daydreamed myself into their field of fire. I waved and began pulling my GI pants up, when a German noncom peeked out from some fir trees. Both he and our machine gunners had me with my pants down. The noncom tried a nervous smile in those hardened lines and square angles of a face. Arms up high, he came out of the shadows followed by eight or so baggy-pants men in long-brimmed caps; they left a pile of helmets and weapons in the shadows. With one hand holding my pants up and the other trying to brandish my M1 with some authority, I herded them past the machine gunners who were left scratching their heads. The squad watched curiously as their acting squad leader marched past with his "capture" while holding up his pants.

The shooting war on Hill 708 died out toward evening. George Company formed up on the track and filed into the village—more of a hamlet, really. We were moving through the trees and then suddenly emerged in cold, damp wind on the village square. There was only one street off the track: It ran downhill both north and south. Another company had occupied the place as the Germans retreated. We took over the houses for the night, and in glancing out an east window, I could see a brick outhouse in a tiny backyard. Beyond was a precipitous drop-off of about three hundred feet, obviously Hill 708 ended here.

Having had a deep sleep all morning and part of the afternoon, I had no trouble trading off the night hours with Eberly behind a .30-caliber machine gun on a tripod, which sat on a table by a window overlooking the south road. I had found a GI overcoat in the house and was glad to have it. The house had a lot of holes, and the cold wind found all of them.

Hill 708 rose gradually from the west, leveled off, and then did this sudden drop to the east. I hoped there would be no fog down there at daylight, so I could see far to the east. Maybe I would see a war-ending rainbow on the horizon.

I stood behind the machine gun for a long time, never even seeing the road I was to cover—it was too dark. The entire night passed without my hearing a single shell or rifle shot, only the mournful hum of the wind rising and falling. At times, I could hardly stop my imagination from creating voices—individual whisperings, and then choruses. I wondered whether I would follow up on my plan to visit the families of good men who had lost everything. The one thing they had had in common was their persistent guts: Against all the deep-seated urges to be anywhere but here, they stayed with their comrades until that special light was blown out of them.

Before dawn of 16 March, McKay shuffled into the room, wrapped in blankets (as was I), and we stood together a half hour or so without a word passing between us. Then, someone from the 3d Squad relieved me at the window. Siegel needed to send out a patrol, and we were it. I woke the men to some degree of grumbling acquiescence. As usual, only Merrill was up immediately, rolling up his blanket roll and pulling on his equipment. I lit a couple of the tiny German candles we found everywhere—they were like flat white cupcakes about two inches in diameter and sat in brown paper cups. I always had a supply in my pockets. I wanted light to see whether I could catch anyone with his combat boots off, which was taboo. On the lines, we had to go many days without removing them except for an occasional change of socks or to tend to blisters. I no longer had concern for my feet. They were finally conditioned to contacting the ground on their outer edges. The calluses in the center of my flat feet continued to grow painfully deeper no matter what I did. Salazar called me Duck Feet.

We were sent north by northwest, and I used a compass because even with my good sense of direction, one tree looked like any other tree. We left the road and moved through the woods until we came to a road that followed the azimuth I had chosen. The area had been shelled, and we passed burned-out trucks. The dawn was without fog as we came out of the forest onto a bald area of 708. Much traffic had used the road. We passed a number of dead civilians who had been equipped with shovels to keep the well-rutted byway usable. The open area was choked with smashed vehicles—but mostly broken wagons and dead horses. Equipment, all kinds of military hardware, was scattered on the road and well off of it. We examined some 105mm artillery pieces with their hard, tubeless tires. Bodies and pieces of bodies were scattered throughout.

Here we were, already deep into their country. This war was, for all practical purposes, won; but, the madness still filtered down from the top. Shafts of sunlight behind us began illuminating distant hilltops. We reached a point where we could see downhill, and nothing moved anywhere—even the night wind had stopped. Yet, all around us we saw brutish testimony of terrible, hellish action and agony. More than the dead men, it was the horses—innocent and loyal—who brought tears running down my cheeks. I had not cried for Dan yet, nor for the others.

Fasco was the one who figured it out: He pointed out a village in the distance and the set of hills and ridges, and then he looked at me. The day's second dawning hit me like thunder right between the eyes. I realized the incredibly real possibility that we were standing on the bald hill where three days ago our TOT barrage had descended. The more I scanned through the binoculars the hill beyond the village and the ridge to the left, I felt Fasco was right.

Weaving our way back through the trail of wreckage, we saw something we had missed before. Two figures were sitting, unmoving, on the front seat of a Volkswagen scout car that was parked alone some distance from the road. We approached, and aside from a few shrapnel punctures, the Volkswagen seemed relatively untouched. The two helmeted soldiers, one a noncom, were coated in dirt and looked and smelled dreadfully dead. Finding no obvious wounds, I assumed concussion had instantly sucked the life out of them. One Luger pistol went to Salazar, and we all feasted on canned sardines before hitting the trail back to G Company, where we reported on the patrol.

In 2d Platoon's house, I explored the rooms on the lower floor and discovered about forty fur-lined backpacks. Most had large hunks of crude tobacco wrapped in newspaper, a few pipes, clothing, and one revolver. The weapon was dilapidated and untrustworthy, so I dismantled it and tossed it out the window toward the drop-off. Upstairs, a shattered bedroom had a six-foot hole in the east wall and a bed with naked springs, but no mattress, sat on the opposite wall. I stood at the shell hole and took in the vast panorama. Hundreds of feet below, I saw GI infantry formations moving through hedgerowed farms and buildings. Other formations milled about buildings or moved on roads. It fascinated me to have a bird's-eye point of view so totally different from all my prior combat experience—where most of what I saw was because I was in the middle of it. The men moved cautiously, pausing often, and the sound of small arms sounded only occasionally. German artillery fire seemed directed evenly between the scene below and the town around me. But only a single shell howled approximately every five minutes in our direction.

I decided to risk a nap on the springs, but first I descended to the brick outhouse behind the house, where I did my thing. Then I rolled up a GI blanket on the springs. I could not have been there long when the howl of the next shell caused me to reconsider the wisdom of choosing this place to rest. Within two seconds, I knew the shell would hit exceedingly close, and I pulled my whole body into as tiny a ball as possible. The explosion of the heavy shell was extremely loud and resulted in sustained crashing of masonry. A brick ripped my blanket and the GI pants over my right cheek. I sneezed from dust, smoke, and the sudden stink of shit. I struggled off the springs, grabbing the blanket for a quick run for the stairs. As I did so, I peered through the dusty atmosphere at shit splattered everywhere and a combination of brick, wood, roof tiles, and what might have been a broken seat from the outhouse. A quick look out the shell hole confirmed my suspicion. Unable to contain the wild laughter, I let it roar as I began a hasty descent. Below was a collection of white faces, white eyeballs, and open mouths. They thought I had gone stark raving mad. I pushed through them, trying to stop laughing. Finally, I blurted out, "We've got indoor plumbing!" Judging by the blank stares, they were now convinced that I had gone off the deep end.

Early that afternoon of 16 March, we piled into trucks and—having already broken through the enemy's defenses on Hill 708—we began the mad dash for the Rhine River, some fifty miles east.

10

Isolated on the Rhine

With Hill 708 behind us, it soon became obvious that the flat plain we were racing over provided little in the way of defensive cover for the disorganized German army. And they were not falling back in an organized retreat. We had broken through their main defenses, scattering and leaving behind much of their infantry and armor. As far as the eye could see on the dusty roads, long lines of six-by-six trucks, jeeps, three-quarter-ton weapons carriers, and armored division tanks moved eastward at flank speed. More and more German rear-echelon troops were being corralled. We began passing through the wreckage of German convoys, the result of strafing and rockets from our fighters. The P-47s roared by overhead all day long.

Our 3d Battalion had to reduce thirty-seven pillboxes southeast of Reinfeld on 16 March. Our tanks smashed through or shoved to the side every type of wagon, vehicle, or cannon listed in the German army TO. Equipment, crates, weapons, dead men, and horses were scattered about. With a sense of growing exhilaration, we raced through towns and villages where most every house had white sheets hanging from windows and balconies—it was not wash day, but capitulation day.

We ran into hard-fought as well as feeble attempts to slow us down, as groups of Hitler youth or regular army troops staged a bushwhack in a forest or town. So much was happening so fast that memory fails me with regard to the daily order of battle—although isolated incidents stand out, and the overall situation was revealed to us increasingly over the first few days of the drive for the Rhine. To the south, the Seventh Army also was breaking through and, like our Third Army, thrusting a spearhead east. Always competitive, Patton would make it a race to the Rhine. Town after town fell to the 94th and the 80th Divisions of the XX Corps. The 80th Division behind us somewhat covered our right flank. Rifle companies and tanks on the point could roll for miles uncontested and then receive punishing 88 and machine-gun fire from Volkssturm troops dug in around a roadblock. Usually, they did not hold out long. Nevertheless, our infantry and armor continued to suffer casualties. In one sector, we lost fifteen tanks to 88mm antiaircraft guns with barrels depressed to cover the roads. Instances also occurred of our fighter aircraft bombing and strafing places already occupied by our troops.

To keep the enemy off-balance and grab as much territory as possible, we had to keep moving on, day and night. Our 302d was formed into a combat team and mounted on six-by-six trucks much of the time. We would roll along truck after truck—speeding up and then crawling forward. At times, we pulled to the roadside while other troops or tanks rolled through. And, other times, near the head of the column, we would pull over and listen to the sound of combat ahead and then move on through smoking carnage.

We began leapfrogging battalions. The 1st would attack and clear a town, and then our 2d Battalion would pass through the 1st to keep jabbing the enemy off-balance. The 1st Battalion, in reserve, rested. The 3d Battalion, just to our rear, was ready to pass through us as we encountered and reduced resistance.

I recall attacking and taking prisoners in a field outside a hamlet. The tanks and vehicles of the Germans in retreat had chewed up the field. As the trucks and tanks of the 3d Battalion rolled past, we piled into the five or six houses. Three of us took a bed with our boots on, me in the middle. Fully dressed, we slept like the dead for five hours. Having had no hot food in many days, we subsisted on K and C rations. Then, before light, the trucks, covered in dew, roared up, and we were herded aboard. I rarely sat on the bench or floor, but preferred climbing aboard first to stand leaning over the cab with my M1 cradled in my arms. Although I wanted to be in position to spot any snipers or ambush, I suppose my main need was to soak into my consciousness everything I could see. I loved the cold wind in my face and never minded the dust and exhaust fumes. I took in the few faces to be seen peering from windows and tried to comprehend what the peasants were thinking about this display of might.

Farmers worked their fields, plowing and fertilizing. The all-too-familiar stink of urine from big wooden barrels, attached to small wagons and pulled by horses, stirred my memory. I recalled the night Dan and I got soaked in cow piss when the machine gun riddled the barrel over our heads and Dan's BAR had its forward sight blown off.

So, from 16 March until the 21st, we hightailed it from Reinsdorf to the Rhine. One town we roared through stands out: It had an open cobblestone area in front of a small hotel, and standing in front was a group of young women brazenly watching this invasion of their country. At the forefront was easily the most attractive girl. She was especially compelling because—with hands on hips—her eyes blazed hate with surprising intensity. If we had been Russian infantry, I do not believe she would have remained vertical for long.

We had captured a fair-size town, and another battalion moved through our ranks. We marched to a hotel across the street from a railroad station. An earlier bombing left the hotel and station reasonably intact although the tracks and railcars were totally blown up, down, and sideways. Tracks, light poles, and signals were twisted in agonizing shapes. They seemed to anticipate metal sculpture that would appear in front of office parks a half century later.

We had a good night's rest in decent beds—one for every man—despite the fact that all of the windows had been blown into the rooms. Next morning, warning shouts roused every man out of bed and into the street. Six Messerschmitt Bf 109s were circling the town about five thousand feet above. We were rushed across to the station and through a door to a cellar. But, for the same reason I liked to play lookout in a truck, I remained in the doorway, watching the German fighters. This was my first experience with enemy aircraft, and I made the most of it as two planes broke formation, peeled off, and dived directly at the station. At five thousand feet, sharp eyes could see a swarm of troop movement crossing the street. As the two planes roared closer, I made out what most likely were bombs underneath. I planned on a last-second dive for the cellar stairs immediately behind me. However, an intense burst of .50-caliber tracers flashed toward the aircraft, immediately scoring hits. I was aware of multiple .50s firing close by, and the tail of one plane and then, amazingly, the other 109 was blown away—both planes sent spinning erratically downward, pieces of aircraft falling free. The two planes had been hit identically and crashed with a series of loud explosions. I guess I was screaming with excitement, because the men in the cellar wanted to know what was happening. I gave the all clear and let them know what they had missed.

Shortly after, the trucks rolled down the street, and we were on our way out of town. Everyone scanned the skies for the other four planes, but they were nowhere to be seen while we raced to leapfrog 1st Battalion. There were trucks and jeeps way out in front and far to the rear. To the left, the fields were flat, and a low ridge to the right paralleled the straight road. And that, of course, is the direction of attack the other four planes chose. They suddenly shot into view, skimming over the ridge, their guns spitting tracers—but their aim was high, passing harmlessly over the trucks. The ridge was too close to the road for them to have time to adjust their fire. They would have had to make another pass, which would have given us time to stop, bail out, and take cover. None of that came to pass, however. No sooner had the Me-109s screamed fifty feet overhead than the air was filled with a drumroll of .50-caliber guns. Tracers slashed by from the

ridge, followed in a split second by four P-47s, empty casings falling all around us. I do not think four seconds elapsed
from the time the German tracers began this action until four
fireballs tumbled across the late-winter fields. Four P-47s
wiggled their wings as they pulled up in steep climbs over
still-rolling wreckage; then they performed a barrel roll of
victory. And they were off seeking other targets—or rescues.

No doubt we would have taken many casualties if the 109s
had had their second run at us. None of us managed a shot at
the 109s—it had happened so fast, and the action was quite
neat and clean. I wondered whether the German pilots knew
that the P-47s were on their tails and had decided, no matter
what, to go after the trucks, perhaps sacrificing themselves. It
seems likely that they were rushed into it, because while
achieving surprise from the ridge, a right-angle attack could
not score the hits that an attack along the road might achieve:
They would have been able to ride their fire along the entire
line of vehicles. I think if they had been experienced pilots—
many were not at this stage of the war—they would have
split up, tried to evade the P-47s, and perhaps half of them
could have made a strafing run or two down our road.

Later that day, after roaring through 1st Battalion and in
the vanguard of the spearhead, G Company was rolling
through a hilly town adorned by a storybook castle on a high
hill east of town. Beyond, I could make out a flat plain and
villages. The trucks were in low gear moving downhill
through the main artery when the rushing whine of artillery
shells was heard. We did not have to do much head scratching to realize that most likely a team of German radio operators was in one of those castle towers. So far, the fire the
operators were calling in was falling short, and we did not
pause on our way through town.

Once out on the open plain, we floored the gas pedal. As
we were barreling along a few minutes after leaving town,
the first shell (an 88 this time) came screaming in, but it fell
short one hundred yards. A quarter mile ahead, a few buildings and a high wall beckoned as possible protection, unless

enemy infantry were waiting there. In seconds, another 88 hit about fifty yards closer, and the captain's jeep screeched to a stop. All five trucks halted, and everyone bailed out to dive into the V-shaped slit trenches that lined most German roads. And although I usually was first man to board a truck, I was also last off. The third shell was ripping through the air, and instead of a normal jump to the road, I dived—which saved my life. At the precise moment of my jarring ground contact, the shell burst fifteen feet away, and a terrible rush of shrapnel zoomed where my body had been a quarter second before. Red-hot shards sliced through the tailgate and flattened tires: They would have ripped through me, killing me almost instantly. It was perhaps my closest shave.

Counting seconds and visualizing gunners who, having thrust another round into their long-nosed gun, were adjusting their aim a notch higher, I was up and on my way to a nearby slit trench. But as I braced to dive into it, three white-faced GIs looked up at me—no room. One wide-eyed guy shouted, "Come on in!" And I certainly did—right on top of them. A flame burst and smoke erupted as the fourth shell scrambled GM truck parts overhead. I shot out of the trench to find better accommodations in the direction of the stone wall. Most everyone used those seconds between shells to do likewise. So far, I saw no sign of dug-in Germans there, which would have put us in an interesting crossfire.

Someone on the other side of our blasted six-by-six was shouting for a medic. I had spotted a vacant slit trench on the other side of the road, but as I ran past the front end of the burning vehicle, I saw a second man down and changed course in his direction. His upper body and midsection were a mess of blood. The next shell was due at any moment. Bellowing, "Medic!" I grabbed his feet and pulled him the short distance to the trench. The shell burst farther away to the northwest and none of the other ten or twelve rounds came too close. So my moving him, dragging him, actually proved unnecessary and could not have helped his condition much. He was screaming in agony.

I kept yelling for a medic, but some of the company had

already worked their way near the wall and buildings, with the rest close behind. In the drifting smoke, I saw our platoon medic working on somebody, with a couple of riflemen aiding him. I pulled out one of the morphine ampoules I had grabbed from our former platoon medic after Schomerich, and I plunged it into the pained soldier's bloody hand and then used my bayonet to cut away his uniform. I undid his web belt and saw no ammo or weapon, but I pulled out his bandage. That was absolutely useless, however, as the cutting away of his clothes revealed a string of smoking sausages—that was my first perception, at least, but the reality quickly set in. I suppose I froze at the massive diagonal opening that overloaded my mind with the sight of just too much revealed anatomy. I retched and then recovered. Using the bandage to wipe away blood and dirt from his face, I was totally shocked to see, not a member of my platoon, but a young Black man who was especially strangely pale. He had to be our driver, which explained why he carried no ammo. I could see the tight black curls of his race under his knit cap, and my heart melted. It was the first time I had cried in many years, and I did not even try to figure out why this emotion let loose just then. He carried no weapon—he was a truck driver. I suppose the fact that he was a noncombatant was part of the emotional equation.

Having seen no Black guys in combat until then, indeed I had not even had occasion to speak to one since I was eleven. That was in 1937, and I had been walking north down the railroad tracks, taking an unusual route home from the business district on Cedar Lane. A little Black kid came down the east embankment from a run-down house that stood alone up there. He offered to fight me, but in view of his skinny little frame, I declined; and we fell into seeing who could hit a telephone pole by slinging rocks. Never saw him after that.

After a while, our driver's thrashing about quieted, and I took his hand in mine. His eyes, half-closed, held mine, and I wanted to look away but could not. I remember the tears rolling down and stopping in my beard, and I felt anger because I was powerless to stop this man from dying. Joe, the medic, came by. I explained about the morphine, and Joe reached down and took the man's hand from mine, but found no pulse and none on his neck. I was surprised because the driver still stared at me. Reaching over his body, I felt his neck, but could feel no pulse. I removed one dog tag from around his neck to turn in.

To avoid being seen by the 88's gun crew, we stayed extremely low going to the other wounded man. Joe pointed to a large piece of the truck's transmission nearby. It had struck the rifleman in the back, and the medic decided not to move him but to stay with the injured man until an ambulance could be brought up. I recognized the guy as belonging to the platoon, and I told Joe I would get to a radio to request help.

The other two men and I ran to the wall, one by one, as fast as rabbits. The shelling stopped, and we arrived without incident. The captain was on the phone trying to arrange an air strike on the 88, although no one had spotted its location. Finally, he requested an ambulance. Only one truck, ours, had been hit, and one could only hope the ambulance, bearing large red crosses, would not be fired on. We took up positions at windows inside what had been a factory.

Apparently, the 88 gun had expended its ammunition or pulled out, because the other four drivers—all Black—were sent out to bring in their trucks. By then we were a truck short and even more tightly packed in the remaining six-by-sixes. We continued east.

That may have been the night that we became lost. After dark had set in we drove on, totally blacked out, with no moonlight. It was not unusual to see Americans utilize captured German trucks and cars, so when the outline of a German truck passed us and moved out in front of the captain's jeep, no one suspected anything amiss. For whatever reason, Watson, the captain's driver, followed the German vehicle. Later, a halt was called at the entrance to a town. The retreating Germans usually removed all road signs as they moved east. It became common knowledge that these signs could be found where they had been tossed behind the nearest wall or ditch. In the first truck behind the jeep, I saw the first ser-

geant come up with a sign identifying the town. And checking a map under a shelter half, our CO discovered that we
were behind the German lines. The German truck most likely
had been manned by Germans.

This information was passed down the line of trucks. The
town was totally blacked out and quiet as a graveyard. The
only sound emanated from our idling motors. The road was
too narrow to turn our column around, so we slowly proceeded through the winding, narrow cobblestones until we
gained the plaza and shut down our motors. The captain had
about ten of us climb down, and, two by two, we were positioned at the several streets leading off from the plaza. I was
paired with Frenchy, our BAR man, and we each took a doorway near the corner of the plaza. Meanwhile, enough men
from each truck were put to work silently pushing the trucks
around until they faced the direction from which we had
come.

As quiet as we tried to be, however, we had created enough
commotion that doors began opening, and sleepily grumbling German soldiers, strapping on equipment, began
emerging from houses. Our positions offered little protection
from small arms, but as a group of eight or ten soldiers, their
hobnailed boots sounding on the cobbles, approached to
about fifty feet, we briefly opened fire. Two or three
screamed, and equipment clattered to the street. Several
shouted *"Kamerad!"* We told them to put their hands on
their heads and covered them, as the platoon sergeant ran
over with about six men to see what was going on.

The trucks were set to go, and we had seven prisoners but
no room for them. We put one on each front fender, and they
had to hold on for dear life. Motors started, and we followed
the jeep in the direction from which we had come. Slower to
accelerate than the jeep, nonetheless it did not take too long
for the column to get up to speed. We skidded around the
curves of ancient streets barely wide enough to permit passage of a truck. Perched up front over the cab, I quickly understood that the prisoner problem was being solved at every
curve in the road. We suddenly swung left on a curve, and the

German on the right fender obeyed the laws of motion and continued straight ahead. At thirty-five or forty miles an hour, his impact against a wall made an ugly sound—heard over the roaring motor. The same happened to the occupant of the opposite fender at the next violent turn. I recall the cowboylike "Yahoo!" from inside the cab at each ditching. I later learned we had lost all of the prisoners from the other trucks as well, although I imagine some managed to drop and roll out of the way.

Some miles later, we rejoined a column of divisional trucks that had pulled over to the roadside, and we sat in our trucks until light. Men left the trucks only to relieve themselves. We slept on each other's shoulders, hardly taking notice of cannon fire not far away.

At first light, the column moved on over dirt tracks until we came to a huge Panther tank lying on its side, half on the road and half in the ditch. Another convoy had run into it the night before, and in total darkness, a duel had taken place.

We forced ourselves into a sizable town and another battalion moved through us as we took over houses for a little shuteye. Water in faucets—a rare find—inspired "sponge baths" and shaving in daylight weather, which was considerably warmer. An excited Rupp burst into the house and insisted we go on a food patrol. He had found a promising-looking butcher shop a couple of blocks away: It must have looked really good because I could barely keep up with him as we dodged between half-tracks roaring eastward down the main drag. I followed him into the shop and passed a woman customer standing in front of an empty display counter. A large pink-faced butcher with fresh bloodstains on his apron stood behind the display case with his mouth hanging open. Rupp never hesitated—he strode right through a door at the back of the shop. We discovered large hunks of meat on hooks and a large woman busy at a chopping block. She had several huge sirloins ready for the skillet, and she stopped halfway through a cutting motion and froze. Large sacks of potatoes lay on the floor; I grabbed the largest, maybe forty pounds, as my partner scooped up a stack of red meat from under the woman's nose.

This backroom caper took no more than five seconds, and as we left the room, we bumped into a freshly shaven American captain in a new-looking trench coat. He halted, and so did we. Then he demanded to know what we were up to. Clearly, he was with the incredibly efficient military government assessing the needs of folk in conquered territory. I recall Rupp replying in no uncertain terms that we had a lot of hungry men who had just captured this town. We were ordered to put the food down and return to our unit, but Rupp, who had his M1 slung on his shoulder, forcefully swung the butt end of the stock into the officer's groin, doubling him over. With that, we quickly wound our way through the speeding vehicles to our house, laughing all the way. No rear-echelon captain should ever get in the way of the queen of battle, the infantry—especially when the soldiers have put their lives on the line and feel real hunger pangs. We all had enormously strong feelings about the not-too-subtle difference between the 40 percent who got shot at and the 60 percent who usually did not.

Cooking oil, salt, and utensils were enthusiastically rounded up, and the fragrance of meat cooking with onions and salt brought men running. The taste of the meat was unforgettable. I flashed to the hunk of steaming meat Lieutenant Nations had offered me the night I met him, a few nights before he was killed.

After finishing off the meal and my seeing to our equipment—I was still acting squad leader—we hung out in the street, watching the tanks and half-tracks roll by. I kept an eye out for the military government captain, because if he were to spot us, things could be awfully unpleasant. If caught, the only thing in our favor would be their problem of figuring how they could punish us. Most riflemen would welcome time out of combat and in the stockade or even a court-martial. The simple truth was that we had already been sentenced to a hellish half-life of profound stress where the longer the sentence, the greater the chance of our bodies being ripped up.

One gratifying experience, watching what I believed was the 9th Armored Division moving past our house, was seeing several men with whom I had trained in basic, such as Fisher from New Jersey, who was shouting my name and waving. He looked comfortable manning his .50-caliber machine gun on that dusty half-track. I felt a real rush of elation that he had made it this far.

On the grenade range during basic we had crouched behind a low barricade of logs to launch our fragmentation grenades. Then it was necessary to move to the open, lobbing live grenades as far as possible at a bunker. But some weeks before, when we were tossing a softball around in front of our barracks during a break, it was discovered that Fisher, for all of his masculinity, had never played ball and never learned to throw one: The drill sergeant voiced a somber prediction. And later, as five or six of us moved to the open ground to lie exposed to chance fragments, everyone urged and threatened Fisher to pull off a miracle and lob that thing beyond his capabilities. He had always awkwardly thrown the softball like a ten-year-old girl and it would fall halfway or less to the catcher. I suppose he did about the same with the grenade, but like everyone else, I tossed mine and tried crawling inside of my helmet. Later, we were told the explosive powder in those practice grenades was less than what we would be issued in combat.

That same day, we left our trucks on a dirt track in a hilly forest of pines and clambered onto tanks. We bounced along on these noisy monsters, breathing in the exhaust fumes until bullets—thankfully high—drove us off. With tank cannon, machine guns, and rifle fire, we plastered the forest and track for some minutes. Then we were organized into columns on both sides of the tanks as engineers with mine detectors joined us, and we moved ahead. Eberly and I were given the point with the engineers behind us, followed by the armor and infantry. It would have been a nice gesture to have the mine sweepers go first, but that did not happen. The detecting device was pretty good at picking up metal, but useless at locating plastic or wooden Schü mines. But, as I occasionally glanced back for arm-and-hand signals, I realized the engineers were too nervously eyeing the trees and ditches to the side and were not watching the dial whose needle would jump when detecting metal. To cap off their worthlessness, the apparatus's warning beep at the detection of metal was drowned out by the noise of the tank engines.

We moved through the area where we had been fired on, finding only empty .31-caliber cartridge cases; the gunners apparently had run off to set up farther along the track. As the trees thinned out, the tanks and riflemen would be more exposed should opposing fire open up. So we were ordered to double-time as the armor picked up speed. With the exhaust smoke, dust, and engine noise, no one could have picked up incoming small-arms fire if it had come. Fortunately, it did not. Although the tanks offered a sense of security, perhaps it would have been better to hold them back and let the rifle squads do what is traditionally more natural to their instinct and training—screen quietly ahead and bring up the armor as needed.

Fortunately, as I said, the Germans had made their point and faded into the forest either to cause trouble elsewhere or to just go home. However, to keep Patton's armor more difficult to hit, we ran. We ran for nine miles by my calculation. Not everyone made it. Some passed out, rolling into the ditch. I learned what the iron handles welded to the tank deck and sides were for—glancing back, I saw how our guys grabbed and hung on for dear life. Later I heard about one rifleman who lost his grip and fell under the tracks of the following tank. It was especially risky at the numerous curves where a tank might brake its track on one side and lurch around to its new direction. For a tired man with a white-knuckled grip on a handle, the need to dance with the tank was a high-risk necessity. I stayed away from the tanks. I suppose we halted at times and caught our breath—that seems only logical—but I remember only the double-timing and the fear of what we would run into around the next bend in the road. My light body and strong legs kept me going, barely.

Exhausted, we were halted on the outskirts of a village, where we dug in and ate our rations. Later, another unit moved through us and between the houses to the other side of town. We marched in, and the first sergeant had some German families seek other accommodations. We tumbled into beds, or on the floors, and slept. If military traffic roared through all night, I never heard it.

Everyone awoke at first light groaning about stiff legs and sore feet. I had toughened up physically all around. The rest after Schomerich had helped straighten out my digestion, and my bouts of diarrhea were nearly over. The hole in my chest was stable—that is, neither increased in size nor improved. Joe, the medic, managed a reasonably clean dressing for it about every other day. And every time my right hand seemed to improve, some awkward movement set it back. The burns on my back had healed, and dead skin was peeling off; only the back of my neck was still raw.

It bothered me that the sole drawings I had done close to that time were quick sketches. They were all outlines, really—ideas jotted down to be worked up later.

Trucks showed up, and we soon left the farm roads to find ourselves on the autobahn. So far, we pretty much had paralleled this great highway, which reached its bridge over the Rhine River just north of Manheim. We joined the mass of traffic heading east.

The sound of cannon fire drew our attention to the left, where a large number of our tanks were lined up on a ridge. Shell after shell slammed into the buildings of a fair-size town in the valley just east of the tanks. And less than one-half mile from the German-held town, our convoys were bypassing this holdout while getting no notice from the defenders. Farther east, the autobahn's central island that separated the east and west lanes was clogged with a mass of jogging POWs. Their guards sat in comfort in jeeps, keeping pace with the POWs who double-timed west. Gaps appeared in their ranks, and following prisoners had to run like hell to catch up. The central island was packed for miles with thousands of supermen.

Every time I thought the war was about over, we ran into a fight—or it ran into us. I decided not to be taken in again: It would be smarter to believe we had more combat lying in wait than to have that false sense of impending security shattered yet again.

The 376th Regiment of our division were the ones who caught it this time, as they approached the heavily industrialized city of Ludwigshafen on the southern flank of our spearhead. The city was situated on the west bank of the Rhine, just across from Manheim. The 376th, with the help of the 301st, fought fanatical German units, and both American regiments took many casualties, until they consolidated their gains on 24 March. Those German units that could do so used boats to escape across the river.

It was early afternoon of 21 March when our 2d Battalion rolled into Petersau on the bank of the Rhine. At least this is what the division's history states. My memory of events at that time places G Company in a small town at least one mile from the river. The country was absolutely flat, with farmers' fields in every direction. To the east, a tree line and some buildings marked the location of the river. The autobahn was a quarter mile to our left and, to the right, a canal and dirt road ran straight toward the river. We settled into some houses to get a few hours rest. Before dark, I was in the barn attached to the house, when a German girl—about my age—entered to feed the animals. She stood there without fear, but both of us were too timid to speak. Unfortunately, I heard my name called by the platoon sergeant, who told me to get my squad together.

We were told to patrol the road along the canal after dark and check out the group of buildings on the riverbank. We were to take over a building as an outpost and call in on the walkie-talkie. At this point, Sergeant Manly took over the squad, and I reverted to scout. My feelings were mixed because, although I felt relief, I also felt disappointed to lose the responsibility I had been pretty good at. And it would have pleased me to eventually have the added stripes that go with the job.

With extra rations, the six of us walked to the edge of town and found that H Company had a water-cooled .30-caliber machine gun sitting on the road behind sandbags. I knew the crew, and we briefed them on our mission. We stayed off the road and followed along the bank of the canal some forty feet to the right; the bank was lined with trees. Soon we began to work our way around a long stretch of bomb craters big enough to hide a tank in. There were no observable factories in the area, so a flight of bombers had apparently wasted an awful lot of hardware.

At this point, I spotted movement on the road ahead and got everyone down, as two German soldiers, apparently seeing us, hit the dirt on the road. We watched them wiggle on their hands and knees until they were out of sight. I had no intention of bringing unwanted attention on us with a canal at our backs. They may have been point for a larger unit behind them. Manly whispered a few words in the radio, and about fifteen minutes later, H Company's machine gun opened up with a six- or eight-round burst, some of their tracers flying by overhead. We moved even more cautiously because we realized there were enemy soldiers remaining on the west bank.

Once we reached the building, we could hear and smell the great river. We crossed a walkway over a lock in the canal, and we checked several buildings nearby, finding no one. Returning over the lock, we chose one building as our outpost—a restaurant bar with upper bedrooms and a walled space in the rear with picnic tables. We set up a guard rotation of three men on, three off. I was due to go on guard in a short while, so first I gave in to a desire to complete this Rhine drive as only a lowly dogface rifleman could. Alerting the others of my intention, I left by the same door we had entered and cautiously felt my way downslope toward the dike that paralleled the river.

Knowing my limitations, I am not even attempting to describe my feelings and perceptions except to say that the setting was awesome as I reached the path on top of the dike. Accustomed to moving day and night as part of a team, I enjoyed a rare moment completely alone three hundred yards from a reorganizing German army. The silence in our area was total except for the lapping and whisper of the river current. Some miles to the south, sounds of combat reached me as I felt my way down to the water's edge. Standing there, smelling the damp air, I felt the need to record the event. I could not even begin to visualize how to sketch it. But there was a way to claim it in the manner that animals create a symbol of ownership: marking their territory so others can know the boundary. More instinct than idea, I arched my urine into the Rhine as far as the trajectory would take it. I sighed with satisfaction at the culmination of a perfect ceremony. Without incident, I picked my way the fifty yards back to the house, announced my return, and took up my position outside the north window.

11

Taking Prisoners and Liberating Prisoners

I stood in bushes just under the window, and scanning the dark, I could make out what seemed to be the autobahn and its river bridge a quarter mile to the north. I could not really make out its shape in the dark, but I knew it must have been blown. Flashing on the Remagen Bridge captured virtually intact a short time earlier, I vowed to climb to the attic at first light to better view the bridge and see whether another miracle could have been pulled off. In the morning, however, I discovered that not only was the autobahn bridge gone, but it had been blown long ago by our bombers. And that explained all the huge craters in the area we moved through on the march up. Immediately to the blown bridge's south side, the enemy had erected a wooden bridge next to the rubble, and of course, the retreating German army blew that one—probably not too many hours earlier.

We debated whether we would be the chosen ones to cross another river in twelve-man assault boats. Compared to the cliffs of the Saar, the general consensus was that this would be somewhat easier because the land was so flat. Of course, every man knew river crossings rarely are pushovers.

Days later, another outfit crossed here, and it *was* a pushover. We would later cross the Rhine, too, but many miles to the north where Americans were encircling hundreds of thousands of German troops in the Ruhr Pocket.

Most days by then were at least partly sunny and warming

up, but the nights remained cold. I stood my two-hour shift out of the wind, with my back against the house. Three men slept on the floor of the room behind me; at times, I would hear snoring and an occasional cough.

We all wore rubber-soled boots, so when I heard the sound of men walking on the wooden floor with hobnailed boots, I became superalert. Almost immediately, someone leaned out the open window to gaze into the night. Flattened against the wall as I was, I became acutely aware of a hand gripping the windowsill directly over my head. I did not move a muscle as I heard muttered words in German from several men. That was followed by an exclamation of anger in English as a German stepped on a GI, waking him up, trailed by an equally terse response in German. I heard the sound of pounding boots vacating the room and heading through the kitchen out to the picnic area. It would take me too long to work my way over there, but I felt a deep-seated desire to prevent them from getting away cold.

I left the bushes until I was some yards away from the house. With the pin already out of the grenade, I heaved it over the foliage and picnic area toward the canal road. Failing me not, it banged loudly in the quiet night. Everyone was up and excited, grabbed their weapons, and manned the windows. My concern was with the other two men on guard: One had been at a front window facing the river; another was at an upstairs window facing the canal and looking over the picnic area, so he caught the heat for the lapse. Under his nose a German patrol sneaked into what they thought was an unoccupied house. I explained what I had heard and what I did with the grenade. Before I explained, they had thought the enemy soldiers were attacking with a potato masher. Finally, with Frenchy at the upstairs window with his BAR, Manly and I peeked over the wall, seeing nothing but hearing a groan and a few pain-filled German words. I opened the door, and a quick look showed me nothing at all. With everyone at windows, we waited for dawn. I did not relish the idea of going out to the canal in broad daylight without knowing whether the enemy had taken over a house just across the canal no more than thirty yards distant. The moaning was disturbing, and whoever it was knew he was heard—he alternated *"Bitte"* (Please) with "Help."

When I had just enough light in the eastern sky, and Manly was covering me over the wall, I quickly moved a few yards on the road where the wounded man lay propped up next to the picnic area wall. He had no obvious weapon. If he had made any sudden move at all, I would have shot him. I prodded him with the M1 muzzle and decided to drag him to the house. I shouldered my rifle and pulled him along (with him towing his pack). Manly and I picked him up and placed him on the picnic table next to the door. I could see a fair amount of blood on his side and on a leg. Moving him had caused him considerable pain, and he was losing a lot of blood from the leg. We cut his pant leg and arranged a tourniquet above the wound. I decided to use another of my morphine ampoules. It was about this time that I noticed the red cross on his jacket and a large one on his chest under his jacket. I searched his pack, finding basic medical items and paper bandages. I used his blanket to cover him and put something under his head for a pillow. He began to calm down by the time we had gotten his sweater and shirt pulled up to clean and bandage his side. I had to stay with him to periodically loosen the tourniquet to allow the normal circulation of blood.

He slept, and I searched him. In the growing light, I could see he was a good-looking guy, blond, and apparently normal height. He had the usual photos of family and some letters in the script typical of the Germans. Then I came across two notes in English. I showed these to the guys because they were written by wounded and captured GIs. They stated that the medic had tended to their wounds with care and that if he were ever captured, he should be treated well. This was more than enough to convince me to do all I could for our wounded prisoner. I turned up enough material in the house to place something warmer and more comfortable under the man, along with a shelter half to form a sort of sleeping bag. Manly informed the CP by radio of our prisoner and his condition. We were informed that the company Jeep would arrive after dark with hot food, and they would get the German medic to the hospital. Manly pointed out to the CP the need for a guide to walk in front of the Jeep to keep it from falling into the craters. I was able to get across to the German that he would get good medical attention before the next morning. One of our men came up with a K ration for the prisoner. And we all looked forward to the promised hot meal; the kitchen truck had finally caught up to the company in town.

Before light fully set in, and while I was tending to the medic, one of the guys spotted something in the foliage and went out while covered from the window. In the trees not far from the house, two Germans with burp guns surprised him, but fortunately they turned their weapons over to him. Our latest prisoners were conducted to the wine cellar, frisked, and locked in. In their mid-twenties, they were uncharacteristically arrogant.

After these close calls and security breakdowns, another one occurred an hour or so later in the morning. It was not that we were too few to guard the outpost: We should have been able to do so, although two men sleeping and four on duty would have been better. I did wonder, however, why only six of us were alone one mile from any support. It was potentially the same situation as when our 3d Platoon was isolated and cut off to be destroyed one-half mile ahead of Schomerich on 6 March.

With two prisoners in the wine cellar and our wounded medic to care for, we settled down in the sunlight of the picnic area. We still had our three-man rotation going, and I was due for a stint at the front window. We observed no activity across the river or around us—so it startled everyone when we heard a polite knock at the picnic-area door. Covered by the others, I opened the door. Standing there was a fantastically strange apparition, a man emaciated and filthy. He was dressed in vaguely military pants held up with rope. A campaign cap that I did not recognize topped his straggly hair, and he spoke a French that I could not understand. Because he stood in perfect view from across the river and no one else was with him, I pulled him in. Frenchy, from New Orleans, spoke the language and quickly gathered information from this exceptionally nervous man that he had been a prisoner of war since the fall of France in 1940. He had escaped two weeks before with some seventy other Frenchmen and their German guard, who had deserted and helped them move through Germany. The past night, they crossed the river through the wooden-bridge wreckage and were all hiding in bushes behind the dike. He was chosen to check out our house to see whether the Americans were indeed there.

After almost five years as a prisoner, this man could hardly begin to believe his nightmare could actually be over. We took him to the upstairs window where we could see some of his group. We did our best to signal them to remain hidden and got on the walkie-talkie to explain the situation to the CP. If the group exposed themselves trying to move to the house and the Germans had a battery set up, we could expect a heavy reaction.

Finally, Manly suggested smoke shells be dropped on the east riverbank. Frenchy wanted to go with the Frenchman to run them up to us, but Manly objected, and I agreed with Manly. We gathered at the door as the first shells passed overhead, and we observed the bursts and the way the wind affected the drift of thick smoke. Manly adjusted the fire farther north to the smashed bridges. The east wind slowly pushed the greasy-looking smoke more toward us than south. The Germans must have been thinking we were about to move boats or bridging equipment to the river. On our side of the river, we were tensed up, thinking of all those lives at stake.

The moment the corrected fire began bursting with loud pops, we got the Frenchman running to his people. Minutes later, they began appearing out of the smoke that was drifting over us. At the front window, Manly kept the CP apprised of the smoke need. As the French arrived, we herded them into the house and down to the small wine cellar. But they were in such emotional turmoil that the doorway became jammed as they threw their arms around us, crying with relief and gratitude. Outside, between the canal and our wall, they were accumulating—unable to come into our courtyard. We could not expect the smoke to completely blind the Germans, who were only three hundred and fifty yards away. The situation was out of control, and in our anxiety for their safety as well as our own, we turned to stringent measures. I found us using the butt end of our weapons to drive these men to the house. Their newfound joy suddenly turned to fear that their saviors were as beastly as the Nazis.

We finally cleared the door while more of these apparitions—many without teeth—entered to embrace us. I saw ten or twelve on makeshift crutches, supported by their comrades and struggling toward the door. Some of us rushed out into the open to give them a hand. I put my arm around one old man, and he was so underweight that I carried him with one arm up to the door. He was crying so hard that he could not talk, although he certainly tried. His feet were wrapped in gunnysacks and rope, as were many others. His uniform remnants were different—perhaps navy or air corps. As I set him down near the kitchen door, I could see his toothless mouth made him appear old, but he was actually in his late twenties. We could not get them all into the cellar, but we managed to fill the kitchen and hallway with the overflow. Frenchy moved about in a loud voice, explaining the need to push them into the house because of the danger of enemy fire and that we would have to try to move them to the west after dark. They would be fed and hospitalized.

Their immediate need was to ply Frenchy with questions about the true state of France and just what had been happening to their country the past five years. They were amazed when little by little the rest of us, through Frenchy, told them of Normandy as well as the current situation on all war fronts, including the Russian and the Pacific campaigns. The Nazis had told them little or nothing all this time. Their German guard—a man in his forties—stood apart, unsure about his situation. The French went out of their way to explain how good he had been over a long period of time, and the terrible personal risk he took on their behalf. We shared whatever food we had with them.

Still not a peep out of the Germans from across the river. If they saw something through the black and gray drifting blanket, they chose to do nothing. I suspect the smoke shells persuaded them to put their attention to digging deeper.

My German patient required more morphine and was always thirsty. He was tending his own wound and tourniquet adjustments. By early afternoon, we were totally out of rations and drinkable water.

After dark, the jeep showed up at the door. Two large GI containers were carried into the courtyard and opened on the picnic table next to my patient. I was amazed, upon opening one, to find six pairs of GI pants inside. I did not know whether to laugh or curse, until I found that, under brown paper, one-half the container was filled with spaghetti and sauce—almost hot. The second container was filled with more spaghetti. They had also delivered a container of water, which was consumed immediately. We attempted to organize a chow line of sorts, and we used everything and anything to hold portions of food—paper, helmets, mess kits, and cracked dishes were pressed into service. Men ate with their hands, but they ate. We had nothing to wash it down with, though.

The driver brought in a stretcher, and we strapped down our German medic on the hood of the jeep. We explained about the notes he carried from GIs he had helped and suggested good treatment for the German deserter. Frenchy went for the two arrogant prisoners in the wine cellar and found both of them stone-cold dead. Later, when I went in the wine cellar, my flashlight revealed what perhaps were strangulation finger marks on the neck of one definitely dead young storm trooper. His face was battered and I did not bother checking the other. We just left them there.

After more heartfelt goodbyes, the jeep was pushed back and turned around manually before it was started up. In the dark, the German medic groped for my hand, and we tried to set the proper tone of voice around words we could not understand. He never knew that the hand he gripped was the one that had wounded him. The jeep carried as many underweight Frenchmen as possible, while the rest hobbled along behind, heading on the first stretch of the road home.

At dawn, after a quiet night of two hours on, two off, I went to the canal with our canteens. I used a lot of halazone tablets to try and make the canal water less ugly. We urgently needed water, because the suffering, especially during the night, had been tough. But we paid a price for ingesting such water into our systems—diarrhea inevitably followed.

The CP radioed that the remainder of the platoon was coming up to us after dark with rations and water. I took my turn at the front window in the sunny early afternoon. The 376th Regiment and the 301st were really going through it if the noise of shelling to the south was any indication. And here all was quiet; nothing stirred across the peacefully flowing river. I sat at the table and disassembled my M1 for a good cleaning while I scanned the east bank. Later I realized I had been careless in sitting directly in front of the window. And I had been equally careless standing in the shell-holed wall of the bedroom on Hill 708. I doubt it was a coincidence that a shell had dropped into the backhouse a few minutes after I framed my body there. Good optics could have seen me, and the observer would have decided where there's one, there probably are more. He must have spoken into a phone, and his exceedingly accurate artillery put one almost in my pocket, although a brick had skinned my ass.

So here I sat putting the finishing touches on my rifle bore—I had reassembled ol' 2506819 into the last three pieces of stock-barrel and trigger assembly when the air filled with a shriek as an 88 shell burst forty feet from the window. I ducked at the shriek, and fragments slapped the hell out of the window and wall. I continued sitting there, slapping the rifle together, but I decided I could not quite finish before the next shell would hit, so I took off for the door in the wall fifteen feet behind me, where white faces peeked out at me. The shriek persuaded me to hit the floor, and my partly assembled weapon scattered into several more pieces as the shell hit either the house or immediately outside—sending more fragments whizzing into the room. Picking up all the dirty components, I joined the others in the kitchen and apologized for bringing the cannon fire on us. At least we knew Germans were over there and that they were not ready to give up—yet.

To console myself, I exchanged my GI pants for a pair that arrived with the spaghetti. And for several days I smelled like an Italian restaurant, a considerable improvement indeed.

The rest of the platoon did not show up that night: We were told they would definitely be there the next night. Instead, we were instructed to do two-man patrols to the autobahn and beyond and, after the return, a two-man patrol to the south to check buildings on the other side of the canal and beyond. No one wanted to go. Someone argued that it was pointless and asked why we should get killed this late in the game if we could avoid it. The final argument was that there were no officers up here to check on us. Frankly, I could not fault the men's thinking. But Rupp and I decided to go only because we were bored and restless with inactivity. My personal motivation was to see what was over there. Giant and Manly took the other patrol.

As the day waned, I had to turn my flashlight on so I could finish most of a drawing of the French prisoner and German medic. Before midnight, Rupp and I slipped across the back footbridge, but did not enter any of the houses. We took plenty of time moving short distances (depending on terrain) and smelling the wind from the east (rich, I thought, in the smell of a depleted army that had been by far the most advanced on the planet). Our French POWs had filled Frenchy in on the troops and equipment they avoided in their night march across Germany. I thought G-2 would also question them. Rupp and I covered a good mile, resting, goofing off, and shooting the breeze before we headed west to take a different route back, although we crossed the canal on the same footbridge. We had nothing to report except that it was eerie skirting farms absent of farmers and families.

I pulled guard in the upstairs window facing west, which overlooked our courtyard picnic area and the canal. Toward a dawn that took forever to fully materialize, I became hypnotized by the shape of a figure against the wall of a house on the other side of the canal. The more I stared, the more movement I thought I saw. For more than two hours, I hardly moved a muscle. With sore arms and fingers, I kept my rifle trained on that image. Somehow, my rational side was not getting through to my emotional side. With sufficient light, I eventually conceded that the black, hooded figure painted there had been there all along. The message in German advertised to the world at large and the German in particular, "The werewolf is alert and has his eyes on you"—or words to that effect. The so-called werewolf movement that was to take power in postwar Germany proved an empty threat of Big Brother–like thinking.

I realized I was mentally extraordinarily tired. We all were. I had seen that propaganda poster a half-dozen times during our tour of duty here. I was beginning to see things not really there. Yet the tic that had plagued and embarrassed me had, for the most part, gone away. My rather minor wounds had stabilized—no worse, no better. My flat feet with calloused centers were not healed, but I had become so conditioned to the pain that I often did not feel it. The human body is an awesome machine in making adjustments and allowances. Yet, it took years for the calluses to disappear after the war; gradually I found my feet walking the flat-footed way they had before the war—I no longer walked like a lame duck on the outer sides of those misshapen appendages.

Many years later, studying our division history, I discovered it was our 2d Battalion that made the final dash to the great river. We arrived before any other outfit in our Third or the Seventh Army. It occurred to me that my squad may have been the first of the two armies to reach the Rhine. And if that was true, I was the first man to get my boots wet in those fabled waters.

During the four days the squad was there, Manly often declared his intention to knock off some more Germans before peacetime put an end to the hunting season. He would shoulder his M1 and disappear during those times that nothing else

was happening and he was off guard duty. He was a good
squad leader and soldier, but it was disturbing to me that he
loved to snake around the bushes and attics during quiet
times to kill men not actively trying to kill us. He took great
satisfaction playing sniper. Others tried to point out to him
the danger of return fire his action could bring on the rest of
us. Manly claimed he did his enemy hunting a good distance
away from us. His sight was not telescopic, but he was a dead
shot. Telescopic sights were normally mounted only on the
World War I .03 rifle, not the M1. If Manly ever scored a hit
sniping, I never heard about it.

During the morning of our last day in the house, I was at
the front window off to the side (having finally learned my
lesson about exposing myself). About five hundred yards
south, I saw a figure approaching, walking on top of the dike.
He was in full view of any interested parties across the river.
I put my binoculars on him and saw a man in dark clothing
wearing a barge captain's cap. He moved at a normal gait,
apparently without a care in the world. I called out to everyone to check out this apparition. When he was within range,
Manly shouted, *"Kommen Sie hier!"* The stranger casually
changed his route and came up to the house, entering through
the picnic area. He and Manly were joined by some of the
other soldiers as they entered the front room. He was a well-
built man about six feet and, sporting a mustache, he carried
an air of worldly sophistication about him. I thought him to
be in his late thirties. Surprisingly, he greeted us in American
English as he removed his black pea jacket revealing a U.S.
Army captain's uniform underneath. He hung around saying
little and certainly nothing of his activities. We understood
that he was involved in undercover work and, if captured as a
spy, legally could not be executed because he had his uniform on, even though hidden. He wandered away late that afternoon following the road west along the canal. We had told
him exactly where we last saw the H Company machine gun,
but to ensure his safety, Manly radioed the CP to keep their
eyes open for him.

We received news of the Seventh Army's arrival in our

sector and that their units would be replacing us this evening. Later, troops in new uniforms and jump boots filed past the house and began digging in behind the dike. My memory is unclear on this, but I believe they told us they were the 82d Airborne Division.

After dark, the remainder of our platoon finally showed up and brought along water and rations for us. We were literally starving. Around nine new men filled out the ranks. Most everyone, except those on guard, gathered in the large candlelit room we used for sleeping and exchanged stories of their patrols in the rear for our misadventures here on the river.

I was on guard just outside the window again, and their conversation carried to me. Roberts, our platoon guide and steadiest soldier, had everyone's attention as he described his contact patrol beyond the autobahn to the adjacent unit. It was a story that brought a good laugh about getting the drop on some older German soldiers. Frenchy chimed in with an exaggerated version of my wounding a German medic by throwing a mortar shell over the house. That brought the house down. I climbed upon an empty barrel and leaned on the windowsill to explain it had been a grenade and went on to tell them of the notes the medic carried from wounded GIs.

With that explained, Roberts introduced me to the new men as 2d Platoon's point man who had a lot of guts. I was genuinely surprised and a touch embarrassed by such an unusual admittance. I cannot recall any other time when Roberts or anyone else, even Dan, expressed that degree of emotional regard about anyone. Fortunately, Siegel broke into the conversation with the unwelcome news that we had been assigned two patrols. This was greeted with groans from the veterans and silence from the new men. We were to split up and sweep two different areas not yet investigated. Some men griped that technically we had been relieved and the new guys on the block should be responsible—which was followed by more silence and staring at the floor.

After my stint at guard, I entered the room to ask when we were due to go on patrol. Roberts said to forget about it—we were not going—which was fine with me. Much later, we got word to form up on the road. And, although I did not know it, for the last time in my life I took the point, heading west away from the river. If I had still been squad leader, I would have put supersight Fasco next to me. The last thing I wanted was to stumble into one of these gigantic water-filled craters and embarrass the hell out of myself. The night was even darker than usual owing to overcast. Soon after we left the river, a drizzle began and then turned into gentle rain. The night was quiet, as everyone reversed their weapons or used condoms to keep rain from entering rifle barrels; it was 25 March.

After being challenged by the H Company machine-gun post, we passed through the town's street to a line of trucks, and then boarded and drove west through the remainder of the night.

During the past twelve days, my division had spearheaded the advance of several American divisions over one hundred miles of German territory to the Rhine River. The 94th Infantry Division encountered the elements of eighteen German divisions, and, assisted by others, destroyed more than a few of these units. The division took more than two hundred towns and, with the assistance of 12th Armored Division, captured Ludwigshafen. During this time, 13,434 POWs were captured.

12

Temporary Detachment
from Third Army

Watching artillery, infantry, and armored and bridging transport on the other side of the highway—steadily moving east—I took great pride that our 94th Division had opened the way for these units to cross the Rhine. I hoped they would soon join up with the Russians. Hours later, we arrived in the area of Baumholder, where the entire division was assembling in the area's towns to refit and rest.

A letter of sincere appreciation from Patton was circulated throughout the regiments. It was in recognition of the "splendid work of the 94th during its tour of duty" with his Third Army. We speculated on our next assignment, but after several days, and with new replacements coming in around 1 April, we ended up in cattle cars ("40 and 8's"), train after train heading generally north. We moved through Luxembourg and Bastogne, and headed to the Krefeld area, which was about 175 miles north of where we had hit the Rhine.

Riding on a "40 and 8" was a unique experience for most GIs, although some men scattered throughout the division had been forced to ride the rails in similar fashion during the depression years. Those earlier boxcars were much larger and eight-wheeled, while these European cars were only four-wheeled.

I do not recall ever traveling in one with forty men. More likely, the number was closer to thirty. Most everyone had enough personal area in which to lie down, stretch out, and let the endless clicking of wheels on rails dull them to fitful sleep. A soldier had to be extremely exhausted to remain unconscious through the days and nights of sudden jerking, jolting, stopping, and going—and the long waits in the middle of nowhere. And he would have to overcome the noise of doors being shoved open or crashing shut.

Men urinated to the wind, holding on to the doorframe with one hand, the other trying to locate and dig out a shriveled penis. Meanwhile, he positioned himself so that the outgoing product would indeed be outgoing and not incur disgusted comments from equally miserable platoon members. Team efforts had to be organized when the outgoing product was released in reverse: A man's life was in the hands of a buddy or two—grabbing his field jacket as he bared his bottom to the outside world. And woe indeed to the joker who failed to produce a true trajectory—difficult at best for the 50 percent of the troops with chronic diarrhea, who let go with bursts that would do justice (if that were possible) to a .50-caliber machine gun. The use of a helmet for potty was generally frowned upon in the close confines of a boxcar, with little water for sanitary flushing. I recall a long stopover in a rail yard that—like most of the ETO rail yards—had been bombed into hellish sculptures of twisted rails and light towers that found their way into and around locomotives and cars piled atop one another. A sufficient number of repaired rail lines allowed the minimum traffic needed to get us from one front to another and supplies to where they were supposed to go.

Sitting on a track about fifty feet from our 2d Battalion train was a supply train, not going anywhere, and a lone, freezing rear-echelon guard, with carbine slung on his shoulder. Most everyone had gotten out to stretch their legs, not moving far because one never knew when the train would begin to move out. Some of the men were in conversation with the young, clean-shaven guard, who probably was much impressed with the beat-up and laconic dogfaces of an infantry division. The crowd around him increased and was composed of the tallest men of 2d Battalion. The guard could no longer see his world outside the knot of men around him, nor observe the bucket brigade forming up between his supply train and ours. Boxes of "ten and one" (the more-varied, favorite rations of most of us) and of canned peaches began snaking across the tracks, ending up stowed away inside our cars. When our train inched forward, everyone made a dash for their car. We left the guard, hands in pockets and stamping his feet to stay warm. The place was probably near Bastogne, on the way to Krefeld, our destination.

We detrained near Krefeld 3 April and were trucked to an area of large factories and steel mills on the Rhine. Düsseldorf lay on the east side some miles south. Our platoon was billeted in two cellar rooms of a warehouse. Both rooms opened to a bombed-out open area about one hundred yards from the Rhine. We posted guards outside both rooms after dark. And, we established two outposts, OP one just above the riverbank and OP two on the fourth floor of a Krupp armaments factory. OP one was manned after dark, while OP two provided a great view across the river to the flat country of the Ruhr Pocket: In the latter days of March, the First and Ninth Armies had cut off more than 300,000 enemy troops, creating the Ruhr Pocket. The Ruhr was one of the most important industrial areas, and its capture would shorten the war.

Detached from Patton's Third Army, we were one of three divisions, along with 82d and 101st Airborne Divisions, in the so-called secret Fifteenth Army on the line, and we held the western side of the Pocket along the river.

After the guard roster was set up, another guy, Joe, and I decided to explore the maze of buildings until our turn on OP one. We carefully worked our way through tank assembly lines and storage facilities of artillery shells of all sizes. They were empty of explosive material and without fuses. We explored underground tunnels that carried cables and piping from building to building and discovered a beautiful motorcycle (but failed to start it up).

Aboveground again, we heard the sound of a light plane that suddenly appeared, flying between two tall smokestacks. One of our artillery-spotting L-5s passed over at about one hundred feet as a shell smacked near the top of a stack. We ducked into the door of the nearest building to avoid the shower of fragments, brick, and concrete. It may have been 40mm antiaircraft shells that followed the plane—which escaped.

Things were quiet again, and we discovered we were in a large shower room. The building stood on the bank of the river, several hundred yards north from where we established OP one. The water pressure was good, but cold. The next day, we got some of the guys with boiler experience to get hot water moving through the pipes. The only problem was that we could not control the revealing steam that escaped from a pipe on the roof. The idea of hot showers proved too tempting, however, as rosters were set up until nearly everyone had a shower over a two-day period. The men would dash over the open ground with towels and toilet articles—shouting and laughing—as occasional mortar shells from across the river exploded around the escaping steam on the roof. We had calculated that, short of a major barrage, the building would withstand the mortars for the time necessary to get everyone cleaned up. It was a bizarre thing to do, but almost anything seemed worth risking to bathe in hot water for ten minutes.

I want to return to an even more bizarre event that happened shortly after first discovering the shower room. In the midst of all this war production were buildings that produced and stored great blocks of green soap—row upon row of rectangular chunks of good-smelling soap, each perhaps twelve by eight by ten feet. A month later, I would recall the sight and fragrance and wonder whether any human fat was part of the green mix: not an unreasonable thought considering all we were learning daily about the Nazi scourge. After checking out the last of the buildings, all of them full of soap and empty of Germans (or so we thought), Joe and I went outside and were walking through the wreckage, when the first round of a sniper popped past and ricocheted. We hit the dirt and, despite the distorted echoes, had an idea of which debris to keep between the sniper and us.

Joe suggested I do a careful peek while he made a brief appearance. As a result, we observed a muzzle flash about seventy-five yards away from the first-floor corner window in a place we had previously looked into. The sniper's bullet passed by doing no harm. We talked things over, deciding to quickly pump half a clip each at the window and then race back to the doorway. This we did, and my love for my M1 and its semiautomatic feature increased once again. We heard no more rifle fire and decided the sniper was not any good—if he had held his fire another five seconds, he would have had us in an open area.

We lost no time in weaving our way back to the building that the sniper occupied. Entering well back from the window area, we hoped to surprise him, if he was still there. We oriented ourselves in this warehouse-size room of huge soap blocks and eventually saw a ladder against a block in the window area—and heard voices. We tried talking them into surrendering; instead we got a grenade that exploded elsewhere in the maze. We had about six fragmentation grenades between us and lobbed a couple over the ladder. The results were considerably more than expected. Apparently the blast ruptured water pipes, and the high pressure began turning the soap into froth and bubbles; and then waterfalls started slippery puddles in the aisles.

A shout of *"Kamerad!"* was heard over the rushing water sound. And a well-soaked German soldier appeared, sliding down the ladder and sputtering German as he slid down. Joe knocked the soldier's helmet off with his hand; the man was certainly in his fifties. Joe shook him down, as I ascended the ladder and peeked over in time to see a figure trying to go out the smashed window. If I had backed off to find a way out, I would surely have lost him. So, shouting to Joe, I propelled myself over the top on my stomach, and—avoiding the worst of the water—I skidded toward the window past the most unique foxhole of World War II, dug into green soap and rapidly becoming "pea soup." I spotted the German soldier running toward the area where we had been shot at; I dropped about nine feet to the ground and took off. Spotting him briefly again, I fired an unaimed shot after him, and I followed carefully from a different route than he took.

Arriving at the place I last saw him, I viewed below me a canal-like waterway about three hundred yards long that opened to the Rhine after a right turn. There were buildings on both sides of the waterway where a number of self-propelled barges were moored. The German, toting his rifle, ran down to a gangplank and into the pilothouse of a cargo barge. I had a clear shot for a good nine seconds, but did not take it. He had isolated himself, and only another bath of river water would provide an escape route for him. I worked myself around to the right through the building, ending up about fifty feet from the side of his barge. Bringing up my good German binoculars, I could see his head staring out the pilothouse window in the direction he thought a threat might come from. He could not have been more than sixteen years old; I could then see him clearly—this kid, a couple of years younger than myself. This was my best shot, and I ejected the several rounds from the M1 and shoved in a fresh eight. Was I stalling? He was a lousy shot and a poor tactician, prone to bad luck and "sudden soakings from unexpected sources." This is what the Germans were fielding by then, men too old and kids too young.

The barge hatches were open and large. I pulled two pins and lobbed one after the other into the hold of the barge. The explosions must have damaged the hull pretty well, because after an hour or two, I could no longer see the deck of the barge. It was listing to the starboard and making sucking and groaning sounds. I could not see the kid at all, and he must have become a nervous wreck. I called on him several times to come out, with no response. I worried that a fragment had hit him, but I doubted it. Then something was floating out of the half-submerged hatch. I climbed higher to see several kayaks floating out of the barge. This shocked my memory back to earlier years, when I walked near my home in Jersey.

I had come across a lifeless rabbit lying on the street, split open by a passing car. Inside were five tiny rabbits squirming about, pink and hairless. They would never survive.

Finally the German shouted *"Kamerad!"* and other words, and he emerged from the pilothouse without cartridge belt and rifle. He crossed over the gangplank, even though it was out of position due to the half-sunken barge, and made it safely to shore—although he had considerable trouble controlling the shakes. I found Joe and the German, who were both concerned for our safety. There was six-by-six truck traffic in the area, and we turned the prisoners over to the MPs.

Alone I went back to the barge and found his Mauser rifle and belt, and tossed them in the brink. I located some colorful large signal flags, cord, and paddles, and I secured the nearest kayak I could reach. It came equipped with paddle and steering pedals. With a jury-rigged mast and signal flag as a square sail, I stripped off my heavy and filthy clothing down to my waist and tossed it all into the kayak, together with my M1 and equipment. I set sail into a sunny, warm spring day with only the swish of water lapping at my boat and the sound of heavy artillery shells passing each other high overhead and going elsewhere. I was concerned only that I not drift down to the river opening, because three hundred yards across the Rhine lay the Ruhr Pocket and the German army.

It was here at the Ruhr Pocket that we received our Combat Infantry Badges (C.I.B.). This beautiful decoration—silver and blue—was designed for infantrymen who had proven their mettle in combat during the worst of times. I especially appreciated the C.I.B. because it was awarded for proficiency rather than for the killing of others.

That night, Giant and I pulled duty in OP one on the riverbank. Moonlight arose in the early hours of the morning; otherwise, the overcast night was dark. Nothing occurred during our four-hour stint apart from hearing a wooden-wheeled wagon on cobblestones across the river. We had a line to the company's other OP a couple of hundred yards south, as well as a line to the platoon and company CPs. We debated what the sounds we heard meant. I thought that the wagon either contained mines, barbed wire, or a boat for ferrying a patrol to our side. The question was, Why would they make so much unmilitary noise that could have brought mortar or machine-gun fire on them? This was the only disturbance in our area. Plenty was happening up and down the river as well as across in the Pocket. The rumble of artillery and light from fires and flares continued all night.

We sat in our hole, wrapped in blankets, and listened to the war. The night was chilly and damp, but the weather was in a warming trend. After the terrible winter of combat during which the division had performed so well, it appeared Patton had presented us with a front line of rest and recreation. I did not know it then, of course, but on this day I had fired my last shot and tossed my last grenade of World War II.

Sometime in the middle of our watch, we heard the sound of a giant shell far away to the north. I now wish I had timed its flight, because it hung up there a long time. I thought of the huge Big Bertha gun of World War I. Eventually, the shell passed from northeast to the northwest, but I never heard the great railroad gun fire and never heard the shell explode, the distances were so great. It fired only at night, sending over as many shells as it could. Years later, I read how our artillery spotters, up and down the river, did their triangulation, and G-2 checked their maps for railroad tunnels. P-47s bombed the tunnel entrances, then German crews patched the rails together again to enable the nightly exodus of the huge gun. Eventually, satisfied the gun site was zeroed in, every long-range gun the Allies possessed carefully timed a TOT and wiped out the monster.

Next day, our platoon was trucked a few miles to a lake where we were retrained on the twelve-man assault boat. We practiced stealth and boat handling with paddles, which seemed to indicate that rest time was over. That night, as soon as dark was about to fall, we darkened our faces with grease and mud and removed three boats from a truck. We carried them to the river as dark fell. There we connected inflatable life preservers around our middles.

My squad was to land on the east bank to protect the landing site while the other two squads were to infiltrate the German positions and try to grab prisoners for later interrogation on the west side. The Rhine is more than four times as wide as the Saar where we had crossed at Taben, and the current about the same—seven miles per hour. We performed well on the paddles and arrived unobserved, pulling into the sloping wall of stone. Our squad spread out and climbed to take positions on the top, where the cobbles were a flat fifty yards to the dike. Seeing that all was under control, the other squads moved through us and disappeared in the dark. I did not envy the danger they faced, but I did envy the experience of slowly and quietly locating the enemy and then making the sudden descent into their midst to snatch a couple and eliminate the rest.

We had to be back on the other side before moonrise. When we climbed into the boats, we placed our weapons next to us in the center of the craft. Mine was wet as we landed and so were my knees. I worried that the boat had a serious leak.

It was well over an hour before the other squads materialized out of the darkness. They placed a German in each of their two boats and pushed off. When they were paddling away, word passed along that our boat had floundered and we were to sit tight until the engineers could locate another. I felt that we were more likely to be captured first than rescued. Once the Germans sent a relief to discover dead men who had been knifed, and two missing, they would be on the warpath. On the other hand, the steep bank could keep us hidden even during daylight if we were not observed moving about from downriver where the bank curved.

Less than a half hour before moonrise, a boat showed up with two engineers manning the paddles. They had started out farther upstream and arrived south of us, letting the current carry them along until we spotted them. We paddled to the west bank with a touch of panic; once there, we sneaked onto the bank behind a moored barge. The 82d and 101st Airborne, as well as the 94th Infantry, had begun running a lot of patrols to the east side to draw enemy troops away from the First and Ninth Armies. Some ran into grief—shot up or captured.

Next day, Salazar and I pulled guard in OP two on the fourth floor, and several times we called artillery fire on suspected movement in and around houses across the water. The houses had roof tiles of different colors, and we began making bets. While correcting the fire missions, we wagered what tint of red, gray green, or gray would color the next shell burst. I admit we lost our heads a little expending Uncle Sam's hardware and further messing up the German countryside. Maybe, with the shooting war winding down, we were driving the point home, twisting the screw a little deeper. My father had fought them, and I did not wish a son of mine to die here someday.

Actually we were not the only ones expending ammo. Some days later, around 16 April, the surrounded Ruhr was pierced and became two pockets as resistance crumbled. That night our artillery entered the act in a serious way— twisting the screw infinitely deeper. All kinds of artillery battalions moved up directly to our rear and began a barrage to end all barrages. Hour after hour, they hurled shells into the shrinking pocket. There was no escaping the ongoing and constant clamor: Even when my hearing went, the concussion beat at my brain. It was glorious. The war ended in our area as they expended the last of their ammunition.

About 25 April, we moved south by truck and crossed the Rhine on a pontoon bridge to enter Düsseldorf. The company was billeted in apartment buildings where we remained until about 12 June.

The first thing I did was pull from the upper-left pocket of my field jacket the glob of chocolate, dog tags, rosary, St. Christopher medal, and dried flesh embalmed there. I kept the glob in a box, not knowing what to do with the remnants of a man whose name I never knew.

Some weeks before, an eight-year-old boy was taken in by one of our platoons. A rifleman managed a cut-down GI uniform for him. I never knew the orphan's nationality. He was carefully protected from the worst of combat while being well fed by men around him, who acted the roles of big-brother figures. I no longer saw him around at this point and supposed he had been turned over to the military government.

When unconditional surrender brought the war to an end in early May, I spent the day alone in my room reading *Stars and Stripes* and working on my drawings. The 94th had seen its war and successfully blasted its way through it. We deserved being spared the last days of mopping up. Nevertheless, I felt a mixture of relief, guilt, and disappointment in not being in on the actual end. There was talk of our possible transfer to the Pacific theater. But none of the rumors, nor even *our* war's end, seemed to affect me. If an emotional time bomb was ticking away deep in my head, I never knew it. I had never felt as calm. I did suspect that all was not quite right, however, because I could not actually feel my loss of comrades. The memory was intact, but the emotion appeared to be misplaced, hidden wherever the ticking was located.

13

Our War Ends in Düsseldorf

One day, Sergeant Siegel, promoted to G Company's first sergeant, ran upstairs to our squad apartment calling my name. Two men from the company were slotted for rest camp in Belgium. I immediately said yes, never asking him, Why me? Harry, from the 3d Platoon, and I stowed our gear on a six-by-six half-filled with men from other companies.

We drove over the same pontoon bridge on the Rhine and headed west. The two-hour trip, dusty and warm, was unforgettable. The farther west we drove, the evidence of postwar rebuilding became ever more noticeable. The obvious depression of German folk west of the Rhine, sorting through the ruins—separating usable brick and tile from the useless—suggested rebuilding was beginning. A few miles farther, representing weeks of combat, the sounds of sawing and hammering revealed roof beams newly restored. Several more miles of farm hamlets and villages showed roofing tiles in place with interior work—even fresh coats of paint—moving ahead. The hardworking German and Belgian people had a long history of postconflict reconstruction. I was moved by it, and felt a touch of guilt as well: After all, I was directly involved in requesting more artillery missions than necessary.

But, often in those towns and the countryside between lay the steel and aluminum ruins of the military. Tanks, barbed-wire entanglements, cannons, and smashed aircraft lay scattered on the landscape, the rust eating deeper the farther west we drove. However, the common denominator that never changed or rusted in war or peace was the shockingly blood-red poppies that appeared annually in the fields and gardens, even weaving their embrace through tank tracks and into the ruined cockpit of a broken plane. I found this aspect of non-judgmental nature especially touching because, when I was a child, the poppy had always been a paper symbol for World War I veterans. I had exchanged paper poppies for donations to the American Legion on the Fourth of July, carrying my cardboard donation cup and a large bouquet of the paper flowers.

The 94th had chosen well in their selection of a rest camp. The town of Remouchamps was situated in a storybook valley, including a river running through it. And although shells had passed overhead, the town and valley remained untouched by war other than the once-beautiful stone railway bridge; a span had been blown into the river by a retreating army. Across the river on a hilltop was the most beautiful castle I had yet seen. I knew I would make the climb to see it closer.

We detrucked at a central meeting hall, where we would take our meals staffed by army cooks. My 3d Platoon friend and I were met by a pretty Belgian girl, who knew enough English to have us accompany her to a house owned by her parents. We were given beds in one of their rooms. All the men in rest camp were assigned families who had offered shelter to men on three-day passes; everyone was kind and helpful and made our stay a rare pleasure.

The girl, about my age, was our constant companion: She showed us her town, introduced us to her friends, and even took us fishing at the river. One day, she had other things to do, so Harry and I ascended a road through the trees toward the castle. We came upon a boy of about ten years who spoke to us in especially good English. Understanding our wish to visit the castle, he said he could take us there. On the way, he pointed out a cave with an iron gate and explained that his ancestors were all buried there.

Arriving at the beautifully preserved building with a magnificent view of the valley, the boy introduced us to his father and mother. We were invited to tea and passed several hours with extremely knowledgeable people who told us much about Belgian history. The father was a prince somehow tied in with Belgian royalty. They were fascinated to learn from us what our division had accomplished. Due to the war and the difficulty of heating such a large building, they occupied only part of the castle. Next day, we hauled ourselves aboard the six-by-six and waved goodbye to those truly good people.

Back in Düsseldorf, we caught up on the back issues of *Stars and Stripes,* the army newspaper. I loved Bill Mauldin's cartoons of Willie and Joe and revered the charcoal drawings of Howard Brodie in *Yank* magazine; I wished I could do artwork as well as he. Charcoal would never have survived my war as well as pencil.

We ate our meals on the street where we gave leftovers to German kids, but not to adults. German men of all ages hung about and, with no pride at all, followed cigarette-smoking GIs—they were waiting to stoop and pick up cigarette butts to feed their habit or to sell. Often the GI ground his butt under his heel, not caring whether the German had a finger under his boot.

Soon we found ourselves again on "40 and 8's" heading for Czechoslovakia. The war had been over for weeks by then. We could relax and enjoy the beautiful sunny days as we sat in the doors of the railroad cars, admiring the scenery. Gradually, the thought that we had survived a war began taking hold, and the men became even closer now that they would no longer be losing each other to a hunk of shrapnel.

About 18 May, we arrived in Czechoslovakia, and the company took over a small two-story hotel, located alone in a valley. The nearest town was a mile away. I was made the platoon runner, but with explicit instructions from the CO, I passed the daylight hours finishing my drawings. The CO's only stipulation was that if an officer were to ask me for a drawing, I should follow through. A package arrived, one of many, from my parents and friends. But this one—along with the powdered milk and cookies—contained the art materials I had requested. I lost no time in putting these things to work.

On the roof of the hotel was an electric sign that provided a couple of days' work for me. It was large enough that at night people in town could see "G Company" in large letters. With a flip of a switch, another part of the sign illuminated two words, "Dance Tonight." Once a week, we had to flip the switch, and people and musicians would arrive for a polka party.

Another duty I had was to make maps for the company's tactics practice in the hills. I was taken to an area where I drew a topographical map covering the area where the company later would work out their field problem against imagined enemies. Runner or not, I caught guard duty on lonely country roads or to check I.D.s and passes on trains passing through. We did guard duty for several days while living in a railroad station. These checkpoints were located within a mile or so of Russian checkpoints.

Perhaps the fact that our location was so far from Le Havre and Antwerp ports was the reason that supplies were slow getting to us at times—especially food. I certainly remember the hunger we experienced. When it was serious, we set up patrols to sneak into farmers' fields at night to dig up potatoes and whatever we could find. We stole or bargained for chickens.

On one daytime excursion, Salazar and Roberts went with me to a tree-lined stream I had spotted some miles away. Farmers in the distance were tending their fields, and we felt them keeping their eyes on us. But although we did all we could to create and maintain good relations, we had to find food. At the stream, we peeked through the foliage to see several ducks floating around, and we decided to take out at least one. The reason for only doing in one was that they appeared too well fed to be wild. Giant and Salazar carried their M1s, while my sidearm was the Luger I had liberated from the German officer. I can still see little Salazar and Giant bring their rifles up and let fly .30-caliber slugs capable of tearing through a line of several men. Well, when the watery explosion subsided, a rather upset and confused bird beat its way in our direction, *unhit*. Both Salazar and Giant took several steps back in the face of the counterattack. It required three or four rounds of rapid fire from my Luger before one found flesh rather than feathers. In the distance, I saw farmers merely standing, apparently looking in our direction. I holstered the pistol as Salazar picked the bird up—alive and kicking. Things were turning rather ugly until Giant grabbed its head and he and Salazar twisted the bird in opposite directions until it gave up the ghost. A trench knife sawed our prey into three pieces that we stuffed into our helmets. We walked back toward the hotel with blood running down our faces, trying to ignore the looks from the farmers, who no doubt wondered why our helmets sat so high on our heads.

Far more interesting were our hunts in the mountains for the little white deer. These were serious, well-organized campaigns for meat. We normally carried carbines, lighter than M1 rifles and more than adequate for stopping a small deer. During one hunt, we ran into several Russian soldiers, short in stature; and after exchanging tobacco for some Vodka and examining each other's weapons, we teamed up to hunt deer. Finding and killing only one, we proceeded to skin part of it, started the fire, and celebrated our common victory over the Nazis—with them smoking Camels and us drinking Vodka. The meat was gamy, tough, and good. We split the rest with the Russians and carried ours back to the hotel.

A U.S.O. group put on a show at our company one night. The girls were lovely and wonderful. An even greater day, though, was 8 August, my nineteenth birthday. Bob Hope was putting on a show for the 94th in a valley whose geological form resembled a giant stadium. A platform stage and dressing room had been set up in the center of the bowl-shaped valley. Truck traffic was heavy on the roads and trails while they dropped off the audience. G Company was in luck, coming early to stake out the ground halfway up a hill.

I watched as the bowl gradually changed color from grass green to khaki, with little orange dots everywhere. Every man in the division had been given an orange with his meal prior to leaving for the show, so games of catch were going on all over. Then, from one corner of the bowl, a great roar of applause broke out that spread like a wave over the valley. A group of fifty or so soldiers and MPs moved toward the stage on the platform. We could barely see several jeeps at the center of the escort. I was struck by the awesome volume of verbal applause and the wide-eyed appreciation from the men around me—which could only have sprung from their deepest levels of emotion, tapped by the contrast of this sun-filled day against the awful days and nights when we had suffered the loss of thousands of our buddies. For the next several hours, I saw men laugh at Hope's jokes so hard they burst into tears. With every laugh that burst from my lips, I swept an opposite and equal sense of loss, a sadness, into a dark corner of my mind.

Before Bob Hope's entourage reached the stage, we all saw an orange dot shoot high into a mortarlike trajectory, heading most conspicuously toward the entourage. It seemed an insult, an act of vulgar irresponsibility. But then we all saw an arm suddenly appear from the center of the escort—and with a flick of a wrist, the orange reversed its course right back to where it had originated. What a roar of approval for such counterbattery fire. Of course, this was repeated six or more times throughout the show, with Hope catching and returning the oranges as though he played for an all-star baseball team.

The United States decided to present the Czechs with enough equipment to form an armored division, and in conjunction with this, a parade was held in Prague. Our company marched in a huge square that filled the street from curb to curb. I had the pleasure of marching rifle on shoulder, on the extreme right of the line. The Czech people were amazing in that they were so fresh looking, enthusiastic, and had great smiles—shouting *"Nazda!"* (which I assumed meant "Hello!") in our ears. They continually reached out to touch us as we moved past in step to our great divisional band. I could not control the huge grin on my face. After having seen the misery of displaced people and the citizens of ruined towns, this experience was truly a happy one. Although, I suppose later on the Russians took over the military weapons we had given the Czechs, and then the happy times vanished for a long time.

Sometime in August, an inspecting general paid G Company a surprise visit. After inspecting the platoons and looking for grime on kitchen pots and pans, he discovered that the 2d Platoon runner spent most of his time drawing pictures. The smell of oil paint drying on paper and canvas was hardly proper in his world of gun oil and cannon smoke. In just seconds, I found myself merely 2d Platoon runner, stripped of my company-artist title. I never found out how much flak our CO caught. But of course I continued to develop the war art whenever I could, and my drawing improved considerably at this time anyway.

Physically, I was in good shape: The tic was gone. The swelling had disappeared from my broken finger, and the bone had somehow knitted together, although it was stiff. I had to conclude that one of the small cuts on the back of that hand was the entry point of a little grenade fragment. The finger has always been a little larger than its mate on my left hand as a result of the blast. In my seventy-third year, arthritis set into my right hand, possibly because of that and from writing this book in longhand. But I continue to draw and paint. My chest wound became ulcerated by late March of 1945, but it improved by June. Eventually, it became noticeable scar tissue—still there a half century later.

By the way, we never got around to the Purple Heart. Although technically I was due two for minor wounds, and perhaps a third for the burns received in Schomerich, the carnage I had seen around me made my scratches seem small indeed. Plus, I never left for an aid station or hospital. Trench mouth was fairly common—mine lasted a few years before the VA medical treatment finally cured it for me after the war. I once saw a statistic showing that a majority of veterans who kept their nerve in combat developed stomach ulcers for a time after returning to civilian life. I kept mine for twenty years until I had it operated on in a VA hospital.

With regard to pushing the memory of negative experience to dark corners—and try as we may to hide from them, all experience absolutely will express itself in one form or another eventually—in time, I learned to objectively evaluate each war experience as it reemerged from buried memories into my life, and then to deal with it and be done with it.

Late August rolled around. Some of the men who earlier were evacuated due to wounds not serious enough for a ticket home returned to the outfit. Every man had become expert in figuring out where he stood in the point system for discharge. We earned so many points for time in the service, and more points for time overseas, as well as points for awards, and so forth. I had entertained the thought of shipping home with the division. But, soon it was apparent that low-timers faced transfer to outfits slated for occupation duty. I found it depressing to think that men who had survived combat in a close-knit line company would be thrown into other units made up of recently arrived replacements. I felt such a deep pride in what our division had been through that I could not easily accept life in the army without these fellow soldiers. When I had to face exactly that, the suddenness rocked me.

Most of the company was in the field practicing tactics that day. Those of us alerted to be packed and ready for transfer had been ready for days. So, one morning the orders came through, and we had our gear outside ready for a truck to pick us up. We were ordered to turn over our weapons to the supply sergeant, and I readily admit a sense of loss when I handed over my M1 Garand rifle—it had never failed me during those months of the war I served in.

We were due to board a truck in an hour, and I hoped the CO and the company would show up so I could say farewell properly. I was finding it unbearable to know they were not due back until late in the day. And as our truck pulled away, I was hit with a feeling of desolation mixed with anger—anger at how the army did things such as that.

For more than a year, I served in the Army of Occupation, and I retained some sense of fraternity because I ran into other men who wore the beloved patch of the 94th on their shoulder. I served in a mechanized-cavalry unit with a man from C Company, 302d, who had taken part in storming into Schomerich to help us repel the last SS attack. We became close buddies, Roy Fournier and I, along with a few new buddies from the 90th and other combat outfits.

One by one, we left for Bremerhaven to board ships for the States and our discharge. The train ride north—not "40 and 8's" this time—took us to an airport where we were assigned to huge airplane hangers. Temporary second floors had been built to hold the thousands of cots for men waiting to ship out. After several days, a few hundred of us were put aboard an army ship for a noneventful trip to Hoboken, New Jersey.

When my turn came to descend the gangplank, I saw a small group of older civilians behind a guardrail. Immediately, I saw my parents waving to me, their hair considerably whiter than when I last had seen them. I broke from my assigned place and burst past the MPs to embrace my mother and father. The MPs allowed me some thirty seconds as my father reached over and pinned a ribbon to my ETO jacket under my Combat Infantry Badge, announcing that I was now a member of the VFW (Veterans of Foreign Wars). And as during other enlightening moments in my life, I had a sudden realization; this time I grasped that I would not choose to become a member, nor would I ever again join anything. This would hurt my parents, but the decision held until a half century later when I rejoined the men of the 94th through our division's association.

On the first Fourth of July at home, I awoke to the sound of distant drums and bugles. It was the same sound of celebration I had participated in as a bugler in the Sons of the American Legion marching band of the post in Teaneck, New Jersey. As I lay in bed, I was confronted with irrefutable evidence that I was a stranger in a strange land, however. The evening before I was looking forward to attending the parade, yet the sound of military music at this point filled me with a terrible sadness and a loneliness for the men of my platoon. I pulled on a robe and headed downstairs—not stopping until I reached the cellar where I could no longer hear the martial music. There in the recreation room at the bar stood my father, waiting. He had two glasses on the mahogany surface and was pouring full glasses of wine. He smiled and handed me a glass, and without saying anything, we drank. And I remembered how he had rarely attended parades, except for those I marched in playing the bugle. We were infantrymen of two wars with our memories but no words. I recall having three or four glasses over the next several hours, talking little about this and that. By then, the parades were over and done with. I never have attended a parade since the war.

My memory of the war continues to look like a black-and-white movie—I literally do not see colors when I recall it, just as I did not see colors while I lived through it. Thus, it was appropriate that I used pencil to describe it graphically. In Czechoslovakia, I had a difficult time using oil color over some of the pencil drawings. Attending art school in the late '40s on the GI Bill, everything I painted came out in cold gray blue or black mud. After graduation, I illustrated for Bell Aircraft in Niagara Falls. At night, I hung around the oldest steel mill in the area, sketching and painting. Little by little, I made the emotional transformation from war to peace in this atmosphere of men who resembled warriors poking long lancelike poles at white-hot ingots, causing tracer flashes and small sparkling explosions in the dark caverns of their workplace. While resembling something of the starkness of war, they were engaged in producing steel for building up civilization, rather than tearing it apart.

In time, my eyes saw white-hot ingots and fire transformed into yellows and reds, while the soot-black workplace took on all the marvelous and exciting hues of blue, green, amber, and purple: I was healing.

In 1957, I left behind a commercial illustration career and spent the next twenty years painting rainbow colors in Mexico, where I married and had my children. The walls of my

Dallas apartment are covered with some twenty of these canvases.

I recall my daughter, Irene, phoning me in 1996 after finding the portfolio of lost war art. She was crying, finding it difficult to describe her feelings in seeing the graphic evidence of her father's wartime experiences. She immediately sent the collection to me in Dallas. I knew they should be published, and then I decided to attempt the impossible: with no real experience of writing, to try to describe in words what I meant the art to convey.

For half a century, I was not a joiner. I wondered whether I would have joined the 94th Association years ago if I had known about it. I do not think so. The comradeship that existed in our ranks had to do with faces and personalities under steel helmets and their guts behind cartridge belts. I had no desire to see those men in seersucker suits and ties. Right or wrong, that was how I felt.

Fifty-one years later, I had come full circle as I wholeheartedly joined our 94th Association, attending the following reunion in Albuquerque. I can find no way to describe the healing warmth from the welcome given me by these men— none of whom I recognized and none who recognized me. But we were family.

I had been asked to set up an exhibition of my war artwork for the reunion, and it went over extremely well with the hundreds of men who attended. Four men from G Company were there, one from each platoon; I alone represented our 2d Platoon. I discovered that Sergeant Siegel, Roberts, McKay, and many others had passed away. But someone had the CO's California phone number. With a feeling of anticipation and delight, I headed for the hotel phone, when the distressing news was passed around that Capt. Jim Griffin had, that exact morning, died at the wheel of his car in California.

But even with the news of the passing of so many of us, I discovered a new and unfamiliar lightness in myself while at the reunion. I finally recognized the weight of the emotional baggage I had been carrying all these years. I was so conditioned to its presence that I had not even suspected it was there. The baggage left me at dawn on my second day in Albuquerque. I strolled out of my motel room to stand on the empty road and watched the sun rising over the mountains. Finally, the essence of spirit must have taken over, as I found myself spontaneously raising my arms and shouting, "I feel great, really, really great!" while the tears cleansed away much of what had been hanging over me.